Deer Rifles

& Cartridges

Wayne van Zwoll, Ph.D.

OUTDOORSMAN'S EDGE®

Deer Rifles & Cartridges

Wayne van Zwoll, Ph.D.

Stoeger Publishing
Great Outdoor Books Since 1924

STOEGER PUBLISHING COMPANY
is a division of Benelli U.S.A.

Benelli U.S.A.
Vice President and General Manager:
Stephen Otway
Vice President of Marketing and
Communications:
Stephen McKelvain

Stoeger Publishing Company
President: Jeffrey Reh
Publisher: Jennifer Thomas
Managing Editor: Harris J. Andrews
Creative Director: Cynthia T. Richardson
Graphic Designer: William Graves
Special Accounts Manager: Julie Brownlee
Publishing Assistant: Stacy Logue

Trade paperback edition
first published in 2007 by:
Stoeger Publishing Company
17603 Indian Head Highway, Suite 200
Accokeek, Maryland 20607

BK0706
ISBN-13: 978-0-88317-348-0
ISBN-10: 0-88317-348-4
Library of Congress Control Number:
2007924090

Manufactured in the United States of America.

Distributed to the book trade and
to the sporting goods trade by:
Stoeger Industries
17603 Indian Head Highway, Suite 200
Accokeek, Maryland 20607
301 283-6300 Fax: 301 283-6986
www.stoegerpublishing.com

OTHER PUBLICATIONS:

Shooter's Bible
The World's Standard
Firearms Reference Book
Gun Trader's Guide
Complete Fully Illustrated
Guide to Modern Firearms
with Current Market Values

Hunting & Shooting:
The Bowhunter's Guide
Elk Hunter's Bible
High Performance Muzzleloading
Big Game Rifles
High Power Rifle Accuracy:
Before You Shoot
Hunt Club Management Guide
The Hunter's Journal
Hunting Tough Bucks
Hunting Whitetails East & West
Hunting the Whitetail Rut
Modern Shotgunning
Shotgunning for Deer
Sure-Fire Whitetail Tactics
Taxidermy Guide
Trailing the Hunter's Moon
Whitetail Strategies

Firearms:
Antique Guns:
A Collector's Guide
Beretta Pistols:
The Ultimate Guide
Firearms Disassembly
with Exploded Views
Guns & Ammo:
The Shooter's Guide to
Classic Firearms
Gunsmithing Made Easy
How to Buy & Sell Used Guns
Model 1911: Automatic Pistol
Modern Beretta Firearms
Successful Gun Trading

Reloading:
The Handloader's Manual of
Cartridge Conversions 3rd Ed.

Fishing:
Big Bass Zone
Catfishing: Beyond the Basics
The Crappie Book
Fishing Made Easy
Fishing Online:
1,000 Best Web Sites
Flyfishing for Trout A-Z
Out There Fishing
Practical Bowfishing
Walleye Pro's Notebook

Cooking Game:
The Complete Book of
Dutch Oven Cooking
Dress 'Em Out
Wild About Freshwater Fish
Wild About Game Birds
Wild About Seafood
Wild About Venison
Wild About Waterfowl
World's Best Catfish Cookbook

Nature:
U.S. Guide to Venomous
Snakes and Their Mimics

Pocket Guides:
The Pocket
Deer Hunting Guide
The Pocket
Disaster Survival Guide
The Pocket
First-Aid Field Guide
The Pocket
Fishing Basics Guide
The Pocket
Outdoor Survival Guide

Fiction:
The Hunt
Wounded Moon

Nonfiction:
Escape In Iraq:
The Thomas Hamill Story

PHOTO CREDITS:
Cover photo courtesy of Kimber Mfg., Inc.

TABLE OF CONTENTS

MORE THAN A TOOL

The well-dressed hunter from The City was usually successful. I mean, he killed a deer almost every year. We farm boys liked to see bucks shot, but it did seem The City Hunter had more than his share of shooting. Once, he looked into a patch of low briars in an open woodlot the locals were about to walk by. With his binoculars he saw a shiny black thing. It turned out to be the nose of a nine-point buck. He killed it. Another time, he waited by the pickup while Ron, Bill, and I prowled through a treed swale. Ron broke cover 100 yards shy of the pickup and unloaded. In short grass halfway to the truck, a buck jumped. He'd been right there, hiding! Helpless, Ron watched as The City Hunter killed that buck too.

We had to admit, he was a good shot. And that he was patient and knew where to look for deer.

The City Hunter could have carried a fancy bolt-action rifle. He looked oddly equipped with his iron-sighted Winchester 94. Then again, maybe he knew something we didn't.

Deer rifles are what we take deer hunting. But unlike claw hammers or chain saws, deer rifles are not easily defined. Analogous to muscle cars, they're a subset, but one without clean delineation. You know one when you see one, if you're a deer hunter. And if someone shows you one that looks like something else but is effective from the stump, you accept it, charitably, as a deer gun. After all, muzzle-loaders now include rifles with black synthetic stocks and turn-bolt mechanisms. They wear scopes and digest shotgun primers. Speaking of shotguns, we must now corral traditional smoothbores with those designed for deer hunting. Rifled barrels drill minute-of-angle groups with jacketed bullets from plastic sabots.

It's even harder to define deer hunters. They come from many backgrounds and hie to the woods and mountains for many reasons. They're old and young, male and female, urban and rural. Some are educated, but degrees count for nothing at trailhead. Some are wealthy, but a buck is as apt to appear in front of the penniless. Deer hunters are good marksmen and not, accomplished woodsmen and not, successful and not. Some take deer hunting seriously; for others, deer camp is a refuge, a place to shed tensions. Some deer hunters don't hunt at all. They buy the license and tag and join the group or the family, but they never kill a deer. They find time only to cook, build fires, wash dishes, drive to town for more groceries, fill Coleman lanterns, and, in the West, wrangle the horses. They also shepherd the youngsters. To steer a budding hunter to his or her first deer is a privilege to be guarded jealously.

To some deer hunters, rifles are merely tools, one of the necessary trappings for a week in the woods. During the off-season, they store the rifle in a closet or hang it on pegs or stash it in a case behind the pickup seat.

Many of these hunters have used the same rifle for decades. It looks well used. It may shoot no better than it looks, but it's more lethal than you'd suspect because the hunter has become used to it. He handles it with unstudied ease, as he might the family truck with 150,000 on the odometer. This hunter typically reads more about deer hunting than about deer rifles, though he may read nothing about either. He does not hand-load, and a box of cartridges may last him a half-dozen seasons because he doesn't shoot a lot. When the price of ammunition climbed above $10 a box, he said that was way too much and that it was time for him to give up deer hunting. He hasn't.

Other hunters are riflemen first. Or rifle enthusiasts. There's a difference. Riflemen are marksmen, while enthusiasts may not shoot much more than the hunter with one battered smokepole. Riflemen practice the shot. Enthusiasts read about, collect, and fondle the rifle. When a buck pops out of cover, good shooting matters more than an encyclopedic knowledge of rifle history or mechanics. But neither fellow is guaranteed a sagging meat pole. Deer hunting, after all, is mostly about finding deer. Hunters who study deer get luckier in the woods than do students of the rifle. Practiced marksmen kill more of the deer they see.

This book is about deer rifles and how to use them to become a more successful deer hunter. You'll find rundowns on classic deer guns and the newest models, the best ammunition for deer hunting, with ballistics tables, plus expert advice on hand-loading. Also on tap: shooting advice from the best marksmen in the world, with tips on snap-shooting in thickets, and long shots across fields and mountain basins. How do deer rifles stack up against each other? What can you expect from new slug guns and muzzle-loaders? Can lightweight rifles shoot as accurately as heavier guns at long range? What's the best sight for a deer rifle–and how do you find the perfect scope? You'll find answers here, from shooters and hunters with decades of field experience. If you hunt deer–whitetails, blacktails or muleys–this book is for you. It's an especially good read if you like deer rifles or want to become a better marksman.

Whether you're after big antlers or a haunch of venison, or hunt mainly to get back in touch with the woods, your rifle helps define your mission. The deer rifle is, in fact, part of the American story, an institution passed down in tents and cabins, around the fire and at moonlit trailheads. Rifles fed pioneers and have filled the Boone and Crockett Records books. For thousands of hunters each fall, in those breathless seconds before a shot and during that compressed instant of recoil, a deer rifle becomes more than a tool. That is why some deer rifles will never be sold, and why they're still worth writing about.

–Dr. Wayne van Zwoll

1
GRANDFATHERS OF DEER GUNS

I t was my misfortune that Ferd's deer rifle went to his first son-in-law. It was a Browning Model 81 lever-action–the original all-steel, silk-smooth rack-and-pinion rifle. The trigger stayed with the lever when you cycled the 81, and the stroke was very short. I liked the exposed hammer; with the straight grip and 20-inch barrel, it gave the rifle a saddle-gun look and feel.

The detachable box magazine added nothing esthetically, but it allowed the use of pointed bullets. Ferd's gun was a .308. The 81 came also in .243 and .358, later in other chamberings. All those deer rounds and the 81's mechanism came along well after John Moses Browning had died. But it was a gun I think he would have approved: a reliable, fast-firing, quick-handling rifle, like so many of the firearms John Browning produced for Winchester. The greater reach of high-velocity cartridges and the precision of Ferd's 4x scope would have impressed even John. Someday I'll shoot a deer with an 81, if I have to buy one myself.

SNAPSHOT OF A CENTURY

You could say that we haven't had any new rifles since the 1890s, when Paul Mauser refined his 1888 Commission Rifle and came up with the 1898 turn-bolt design. Among the first rifles designed for smokeless, high-velocity cartridges, it was strong and reliable. In short order it became the first choice of most of the world's armies. Germany used it through World War II. The action is still a favorite of many custom-rifle builders, and you can clearly see Mauser ancestry in every modern bolt rifle.

Lever guns are 50 years older. During the late 1840s, inventor Walter Hunt developed a "volition repeater" that fired caseless "rocket balls" fed from a tube magazine. After much gunsmithing by Lewis Jennings, Horace Smith, and Daniel

The Winchester 1886 (right) and Dakota Longbow span a century of rifle development.

1

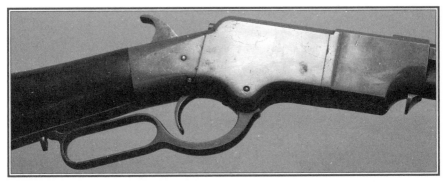

The Henry: "That damned Yankee rifle you loaded on Sunday and fired all week."

Wesson, the rifle became a cartridge repeater, further enhanced by the brilliant B. Tyler Henry. The Henry saw Civil War service as that "damned Yankee rifle you loaded on Sunday and fired all week." It and the subsequent Model 1866 rescued Oliver Winchester's New Haven Arms Company from bankruptcy. John Browning brought the lever mechanism to blossom with designs that gave Winchester its 1886, 1892, 1894, and other classic rifles.

Cartridges have changed a great deal since the Henry. Its 216-grain bullet, pushed by 26 grains of black powder, ambled downrange at only 1,025 fps. Three decades later, Paul Mauser's rifles were sending bullets of the same weight twice as fast, and even the lever-action 1894 Winchester eked 1,900 fps from its first 160-grain soft-points. In 1905, the Germans developed a lighter, pointed (spitzer) bullet for their 8x57 Model 98s. It sped away at 2,880 fps, prompting American ordnance officers to abandon the 220-grain .30-03 bullet in favor of a pointed 150 that clocked 2,700 fps.

The advent of the .30-06 in the 1903 Springfield confirmed a trend the improved 8x57 had started. Spitzer bullets at high velocities dominated battlefields in both world wars and remain a primary offensive tool of modern infantries. They've also come to define contemporary big-game ammunition. While a few hunters hew to the tube-fed lever gun and the blunt bullets mandated by that design, most sportsmen now prefer bolt rifles, with their stouter breeches. You get more velocity out of a bolt rifle because you can load to higher pressures. And the bolt action is inherently more rigid–meaning you can expect better accuracy.

Auto-loading rifles have, of course, taken over the battlefront. But enfilading fire doesn't account for many whitetail deer. Precise placement of the first shot matters most to hunters. At long range, the bolt rifle's precision gives them an edge. Its simplicity and relatively light weight are bonuses.

Remington remains the only

Remington's 760, (with the subsequent 7600 and Model Six), is *the* pump-action deer rifle.

2

player with a slide-action rifle. The Model 7600 has endured several cosmetic changes since it was cataloged as the 760 in my youth. It looked better then, a combination of sleek line and stout lock-up that derived from the well-built but less potent Models 14 and 141.

The Model Four, here in stainless synthetic form, is Remington's current autoloader for deer hunters.

While the popularity of both auto-loading and pump rifles has diminished, the mechanisms remain top sellers in the American shotgun market. And they're runaway best sellers in that part of the market aimed at deer hunters. In some states and portions of states, center-fire rifles may not be used to hunt deer. The danger from errant bullets in populated areas is deemed too great. From the bird guns stuffed with cut shells and buckshot have evolved specialized slug guns with rifled bores. They wear scopes and launch jacketed bullets from sabot sleeves. They shoot as flat and accurately as traditional deer guns, and deliver a more lethal payload.

In the same way, muzzle-loaders are no longer the side-hammer flintlock and percussion guns of 18th-century profile. Save in states hewing literally to the term "primitive weapon" (Pennsylvania currently mandates flintlocks), you'll find a lot of modern technology in front-stuffers. The in-line striker, shotgun-primer ignition, scope and pelleted powder charges behind sabot sleeves clutching jacketed bullets–all give the modern muzzle-loader more reach, accuracy, and reliability than could have been imagined even in the early days of reproductions from Thompson/Center and Lyman. Now you can get dropping-block black-powder rifles as well. Knight's features an easily removable firing mechanism.

Dropping-block center-fire guns remained clinically dead for most of a century after lever-action repeaters put the skids under the John Browning-designed Winchester 1885 High Wall. But Bill Ruger's elegant Number One, the lovely Dakota 10, and Browning's resurrection of the High Wall have gained a following. A single-shot rifle imposes no real handicap; your first shot at deer is almost always your best, and should then be the only one necessary. Dropping-block guns offer the advantage of a short breech that accommodates a long barrel in a compact package. Accuracy varies in dropping-block guns, partly because of their two-piece stocks.

Since the 1960s, when Winchester emasculated its Model 70, Remington announced its 700 and Ruger entered the bidding with its 77, there's been little real innovation in commercial bolt rifles. Belted magnum cartridges have been shouldered aside by rimless magnums, and the crude plastic stocks of yore have blossomed into lightweight carbon-fiber beauties. The best are nigh as fetching as walnut; they're a lot more stable and more durable. In a fit of practicality, manufacturers have also cataloged more stainless-steel rifles, and, to their

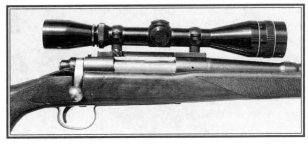

The Model 721 (here a Deluxe) was Remington's flagship bolt rifle from 1948 to 1962.

credit, matte finishes on stainless and chrome-moly metal alike.

Two trends have appeared in the last couple of decades: one toward very lightweight rifles, the other toward rifles of great reach. While you can chamber a long-range cartridge in a handy, short-barreled rifle, the match is not perfect. Jaw-busting recoil and muzzle blast that would trigger rockslides do little to improve your marksmanship. So with the introduction of the .30-378 Weatherby Magnum, Remington's Ultra Mags, and the rocketship cartridges from John Lazzeroni's shop, we've also been sold big game rifles that weigh 6 pounds. Make that 5 1/2 pounds, and dropping. Short magnums offer the closest thing to a compromise: the punch of traditional belted magnums like the 7mm Remington and .300 Winchester, in a case you can squeeze into a mechanism designed for the .308 and kin. Winchester's Super Short cartridges include .243 and .257 rounds that perform like the much longer .240 Weatherby and .25-06.

This fine Colorado mule deer fell to a Titanium Remington 700 in 7mm SUM.

Deer rifle sights have evolved to match the greater reach and accuracy of modern bullets. Before the turn of the last century, almost everyone hunted with iron sights–a bead-front sight paired with either an open, barrel-mounted V-blade or an aperture sight on the receiver or tang. The first rifle scopes of any consequence in the U.S. were long, fragile affairs fitted to sniper rifles during our Civil War. They offered dim sight pictures and questionable precision. But they were a start.

Since the first short, receiver-mounted rifle scopes appeared a century ago (Zeiss offered one in 1904), hunters have fueled improvements. Glass quality, and that of polished-lens surfaces, is uniformly higher than could have been imagined when young Bill Weaver brought out his 330 during the Depression. Lens coatings, discovered by Zeiss engineer Smakula a few years later, boosted light transmission. Multiple coatings now used even in mid-priced scopes ensure still brighter images. The advent of nitrogen-filled tubes to prevent fogging, with variable magnification and constantly centered reticles, made scopes popular during my youth. Then you could buy a Redfield 4X–a carriage-class scope–for $50. An enterprising man named Dave Bushnell kept scope prices low for years by importing Japanese optics that performed almost as well as much more expensive sights.

By the end of the 20th century, when illuminated reticles and turret-mounted parallax dials had became established, the prices of all scopes had risen sharply. Oddly enough, even those with four-figure stickers sold. Well, it seems odd to me because by then techniques for making high-quality scopes were widely known. Machinery controlled by computers kept such tight tolerances on glass and metal parts that even inexpensive scopes delivered the ruggedness, reliability, and high-quality images once associated only with venerable European brand names. You had to look hard to see any optical differences between the pricey and bargain-bin models. And if your horse fell on the rifle (as mine did once), German scopes came out of the mud looking just like the others.

Good optics are still good investments; because you'll carry a scope for many seasons, it's poor strategy to count pennies at purchase. On the other hand, as scopes climb in price, value has become more important to many hunters. You might justify a top-dollar binocular or spotting scope, which might be plastered to your eye for most of a hunt. It makes less sense to spend lavishly for a rifle scope used for just a few seconds.

If you inherited someone else's deer rifle or borrowed one and didn't know any more about it than to load the right ammo and hold it still while you pulled the trigger–you'd get all the utility the rifle had to offer. But what matters, after October's venison is in the freezer and snow marks another year gone, and you think less about what you got from it and more about how many you have left . . . well, what matters is the trip to the woods and the weight of the rifle in your hand, the noisy camp and cold feet and a ring of compatriots around the fire. If you're lucky, you'll recall a sliver of rib against your crosswire. You'll long remember a shot, the frantic run, flag down, and the snap of deadfall under a deer collapsing just out of sight. Rifles don't just kill bucks; they evoke images. They're primitive, too, compared to most of what we take in our hands each day. The rifles we use to hunt deer still show clearly the thinking of people born more than a century ago. And in many ways those people are more interesting than the rifles they designed.

A PIONEER: ELIPHALET REMINGTON II

By the end of the 18th century, adventurous New Englanders were heading toward richer soil "just up the Mohawk." On 50 acres, for which he'd paid $275, Eliphalet Remington built a clapboard house and began raising hay and grain. New York taxes were low: a sixth of one-acre's produce for each 100 acres, 12 cents per 100 acres of forest. Eliphalet prospered. In 1807, he bought an adjoining 195-acre parcel for $585, and a year later added 71 acres more. Starting a new house in 1809, he quarried limestone in winter when he could transport it by sled. His son, Eliphalet II, or "Lite," was schooled at home. Lite courted Abigail Paddock five years before they married and moved into the Remington house. In August 1816, on his father's forge below a home-built dam on Staley Creek, Lite built his first rifle from iron scrap and walnut.

Pumping the bellows, Lite heated the rod he had chosen for his barrel to a glow, hammered it until it was half-an-inch square in cross section, then wound it around an iron mandrel. Next, he heated the barrel until it was white, sprinkled it with Borax and sand, and, holding one end in his tongs, pounded the other vigorously on the stone floor to seat the coils. After the tube cooled, Lite checked it for straightness and hammered out the curves. Then he ground eight flats because most barrels in that day were octagonal. Rifling took special skills and equipment, so

Lite Remington's first rifle was a flintlock. Later, caplocks like this offered more reliable ignition.

Lite traveled to Utica, a growing town of 1,200, where some say that Morgan James cut the grooves. The price of four double reales–a dollar in country currency–was fair for two days' work at a time when mill hands made $200 a year.

At home, Remington bored a touch-hole and forged a breech plug and lock parts, finishing them with a file. He brazed priming pan to lock-plate and treated all metal parts with hazel-brown, a preservative of uric acid and iron oxide. The walnut stock, shaped with drawknife and chisel, was smoothed with sandstone and sealed with beeswax. Lite assembled his rifle with hand-wrought screws and pins, then took it to a local match and placed second. The winner wanted a Remington rifle. How much would it cost and when could he have it?

"Ten dollars," Lite said, "and you'll have it in ten days." So began America's oldest gunmaker.

Lite, Abigail, and their son Philo shared a new home on Staley Creek with customers, many of whom stayed to help build their own rifles and save money. Remington scoured the countryside for scrap iron: pots, plowshares, horseshoes–anything that could be smelted down and hammered into gun parts. His fourth year in business, Lite sold more than 200 barrels and rifles. At that time, plain iron bar-

Remington's Model 8 and later Model 81 (shown) were the company's first autoloading deer guns, cataloged 1906-1950.

rels cost $3 and steel barrels $6. "Stubbs twist" (Damascus) sold for $7.50. But the Staley Creek foundry could not stay abreast of demand, and in October 1825, the Erie Canal opened, cutting the cost of moving a ton of goods from New York to Buffalo from $100 to $12. In January 1828, Lite bought 100 acres on the Mohawk's bank–most of what is now Ilion's business district. Remington Arms still occupies ground purchased by its founder for $28 an acre160 years ago.

But while the firm prospered, tragedy struck Lite's family. On June 22, 1828, his father was thrown from a loaded wagon on a steep grade. Despite the driver's frantic efforts to brake the four-horse dray, a huge iron wheel rolled over Eliphalet's chest and five days later he died.

Lite's son Philo soon became part of the business. Instead of straightening rifle barrels with a plumb line, the accepted method of the time, Philo used the shadow of a window bar in the bore, and he installed steel facings on trip hammers, for closer tolerances. The Remingtons used a scaled-down cannon drill to bore a small-caliber hole through four feet of bar stock, so barrels could be made without seams.

But these innovations proved shallow comfort for Lite when, on August 12, 1841, he suffered another personal loss. Abigail and their daughter Maria had hitched a spirited horse to a carriage and were traveling on the same road that had taken Lite's father when Maria opened her parasol. The sound cracked like a shot and the horse lunged, galloping out of control across a stream. The carriage smashed to splinters against an oak, killing Abigail instantly.

Though Abigail's death profoundly affected Lite Remington, his company continued to grow. Twenty years to the day after he lost his wife, Lite died of internal "inflammation," perhaps appendicitis. It was just one month after the Yankee defeat at Bull Run. By the end of our Civil War, Remington assembly lines would ship almost 1,000 rifles a day. Ammunition production during that conflict totaled 9,759,750 cartridges.

AN INDUSTRIALIST: OLIVER F. WINCHESTER

The Hall rifle was America's first breech-loader in military service. Adopted in 1819, just after Lite Remington got into the gun business, it used paper cartridges. Its flintlock mechanism was heavy and so weak that wrought-iron straps were bolted on to stiffen it. When war with Mexico drained arsenals in 1845, the U.S. scrambled to build not Halls but Harpers Ferry rifled muskets. Alas, a new repeating breech-loader designed by William Jenks for the Navy was languishing in red tape. Seeing promise in the gun and in its buoyant Welsh designer, then working at the N.P. Ames Company, Remington promptly bought the business, including contracts, machinery, and stock, plus the services of William Jenks, for $2,581.

Remington fitted the Jenks flintlocks with Dr. Edward Maynard's percussion lock, which used caps on a strip of paper that advanced for each shot. In 1858, J.H. Merrill would contribute a lock that used tallow-coated cardboard cartridges that still performed after a minute under water. The Jenks was the first successful breech-loader made in the U.S. In its wake, a year later, came the Hunt. Steven Taylor had already patented a hollow-base bullet housing its own powder charge. A perforated end cap admitted sparks from an outside primer. Walter Hunt developed a similar bullet, with a cork base seal–a "rocket ball" that changed history.

Hunt, then 50, had many interests. His inventions ranged from stoves to the safety pin. He came up with (but did not patent!) a lockstitch needle, which would spawn the sewing machine. In 1849, he was awarded a patent for a breech-loading "Volitional" repeating rifle. Fellow New Yorker George Arrowsmith helped with cash and business savvy. The tubular magazine and delicate primer advance had weaknesses, but gun mechanic Lewis Jennings made improvements. He assigned patent rights to Arrowsmith, who sold all rights to the rifle for $100,000 to Courtlandt Palmer, a New York merchant and financier.

Sales of Hunt-Jennings rifles were so slow that Palmer soon decided to halt production. And there the project might have died, had not Horace Smith and Daniel Wesson, joined by B. Tyler Henry, brought their talent to bear. The partnership was then bought by a group of New York financiers, and Henry was hired by its new president, Oliver F. Winchester.

"It may revolutionize the whole science of war. Where is the military genius . . . (to) so modify the science of war as to best develop the capacities of this terrible engine–the exclusive use of which would enable any government . . . to rule the world?" Long ago, this might have been written of the horse. Now we think of the atomic bomb. But this was Oliver Winchester's appeal to the U.S. Government for military adoption of the Henry repeater. Besides the advantages of increased firepower, breech-loading repeaters were proving safer in battle. A Navy report showed how, in the heat of battle, muzzle-loading rifles could become dangerous:

"Of the whole number (27,574 guns collected) . . . we found at least 24,000 of these loaded; about one-half of these contained two loads each, one-fourth from three to ten loads each. . . . In many of these guns, from two to six balls have been found with only one charge of powder. In some, the balls have been found at the bottom of the bore with the charge of powder on top of the ball. In some, as many as six paper regulation-caliber 58 cartridges have been found . . . Twenty-three loads were found in one Springfield rifle-musket."

Oliver Winchester was in the right place at the right time. His family had come early to America, John Winchester sailing from England at the age of 19 to land near Boston in 1635. He settled there, and his descendants stayed mainly in Massachusetts. Oliver's father, Samuel, was probably a farmer and had 10 children by two marriages before his third wife bore Oliver and his twin brother Samuel C., the youngest of her five children.

Samuel Winchester Sr. died a year later.

Oliver went to work on farms at age seven, attending school only in winter, and at 14 he was apprenticed to a carpenter. In 1830, Winchester moved from Boston to Baltimore, where for three years he supervised the construction of homes. In 1834, he married Jane Ellen Hope of Portland, Maine, and that year opened a retail store of men's furnishings in Baltimore. Despite a financial panic in 1837, Oliver expanded his business with a downtown store. Over the next decade, he prospered and fathered three children.

In 1847, Oliver Winchester thought the world could use a better shirt. He was disturbed by the "pull of the neckband" and proposed to "remedy this evil" with a curved seam. He sold his Baltimore business, moving to State Street in New Haven, Connecticut, to make shirts. A patent (U.S. 5421) for his seam was granted in February 1848.

The following year, Oliver Winchester teamed up with John M. Davies, a leading New York importer. Their partnership produced the Winchester & Davies factory. Winchester supervised shirt production while Davies handled marketing. By 1860, Winchester & Davies had used 1.5 million yards of cotton cloth, 25,000 gross of buttons, and 50,000 pounds of starch! There were 500 foot-pedal sewing machines in use then, and the payroll for 40 male and 1,500 female workers approached $17,000 a month. Annual sales of 480,000 shirts: $600,000. By 1855, when Oliver Fisher Winchester invested in Volcanic Repeating Arms, he was living comfortably.

The company didn't last long. In February 1857, it was declared insolvent. Winchester bought all assets for $40,000 and reorganized the firm into the New Haven Arms Company in his home town. He set out to improve Volcanic rifles and ammunition by assigning shop foreman Henry to the task. Henry earned a patent for a lever-action repeating rifle with a tubular magazine and a two-pronged firing pin that struck both sides of the cartridge rim. The 44-caliber 216-grain pointed bullet was driven by 26 grains of black powder to 1,025 fps.

The Henry's main fault was its under-barrel magazine, weakened by a full-length slot. Dents rendered the follower unreliable, and debris got into the slot. But the rifle had two advantages over its rival, the Spencer: It held 15 rounds to the Spencer's seven; and one motion of the lever would reload and cock, while the Spencer required a separate cocking motion. In the Civil War, Northern troops coveted the Henry and Southern soldiers feared it: "Give us anything but your damned Yankee rifle that can be loaded on Sunday and fired all week."

In 1866, after B. Tyler Henry left the firm, successor Nelson King redesigned the rifle's troublesome magazine by engineering a spring-loaded port into the receiver. King was issued a patent for this change that, with the addition of a wooden forend, gave the Winchester Repeating Arms Company a new rifle. The Model 1866 would become the cornerstone of a lever-action dynasty.

Much of Winchester's early growth came from abroad. In 1866, Benito Juarez, the Mexican leader opposing Emperor Maximillian, ordered 1,000 rifles and 500,000 rounds of ammunition. Winchester salesman Thomas Emmett Addis got the goods and waited in Brownsville, Texas–only to hear that Juarez would pay on delivery. Defying company orders not to leave the country, Addis smuggled the arms across the Rio Grande to Monterrey. There he rented an empty store with a cot so he could guard the guns until Juarez's people arrived.

When the buyers showed up and didn't want to pay, Addis threatened to sell the guns to Maximillian. He left town in a hired coach with $57,000 cash, sticking a scarf pin in his thigh periodically during the grueling three-day trip home so he wouldn't fall asleep and be robbed by his guards.

Addis was one of the most colorful of Winchester salesmen. Born Thomas

Winchester's Model 71, in .348, was made from 1935 to 1957. A truly potent deer gun.

O'Connor, he tried to change his name to Thomas Addis Emmett, after a celebrated Irish patriot, but the clerk recorded it as Thomas Emmett Addis. He ran away from home before he was 13 to work as a filer at Remington's Ilion plant. Later, at Winchester, he became the first salesman with unlimited territory and authority to conduct company business without approval, and took coffee, lumber, and other commodities in exchange for rifles. During the 35 years he worked for Winchester, he negotiated with foreign governments and lured top talent to the company.

Oliver Winchester would never see the lever-action rifle mature. In the late 1870s, his hopes were fixed on a bolt-action rifle his company had acquired from inventor B. B. Hotchkiss, an American living in Paris. Ordnance tests in 1878 gave the Hotchkiss cherished government approval. Alas, the first infantry rifles were flawed, and soldiers didn't like the unfamiliar mechanism. Awaiting better reports, Oliver Winchester died December 10, 1880, at age 70. His only son, William Wirt Winchester, succumbed to tuberculosis just a few months later. It was Thomas G. Bennett, Oliver's son-in-law, who would guide the firm through its most rapid growth. ■

2

PRODIGIES OF RIFLE DESIGN

Charlie sent the rifle with a black leather butt sleeve that held four cartridges. I liked that, and the 24-inch barrel. I didn't like the long muzzlebrake, but it would take more than a brake to spoil the looks of that 1895. Lean and muscular, with crisp detail and hairline wood-to-metal fit, it had the clean, trim, classic profile of deer rifles a century in the making. The gaping 45-caliber mouth and beefy 2/3 magazine spoke testosterone.

At the range, I thumbed three Hornady loads into the gate, then settled into the rifle as if it were a fine but willing woman in a public but shadowed place.

The first three rounds cut a neat cloverleaf. "I must hunt with this rifle," I muttered.

Some rifles point themselves. This one did.

Some rifles shoot accurately. This one drilled a cloverleaf at 100 yards, first firing.

Some rifles feel lighter than they are. This one did.

Some rifles leave you thinking you don't have to kill a deer to make a day in the woods better than one that didn't find you hunting.

I had to hunt with that Marlin.

THE GENIUS OF JOHN MOSES BROWNING

It was July 24, 1847. Brigham Young's band of Mormons, thinned by time and hardship to just 143 people, had been over a year on the move. Fleeing persecution in Nauvoo, Illinois, they'd arrived at the Great Salt Lake, and there they would stay. Gunmaker Jonathan Browning, who had stayed behind to produce firearms for the group, arrived with his family five years later. He bought a parcel of land in the Ogden Valley and, with $600 hidden under the floor of one his six wagons, began building a house. Jonathan's family already included 11 children. By a second wife, he would father 11 more. One of them was John Moses.

Young John went to school until he was 15, when the schoolmaster told him matter-of-factly, "No sense coming back. You know as much as I do." John was only 10 when he built his first gun, a flintlock made from a scrapped musket barrel and a board shaped with a hatchet. He fashioned a crude metal pan, screwed it to the board, and wired the board to the barrel. He stuffed the barrel with a heavy charge of powder and rough shot, then heated a batch of coke on the forge. John's gun had no lock. The coke would provide fire, but to keep it burning, he had to keep air pumping into it. That was brother Matt's job. It was Matt who swung the perforated can on a long string to keep the coke lit, and carried a splinter to light and poke through the touch-hole when John aimed and gave the signal.

Near town, the boys crept up on two prairie chickens. Matt lifted the splinter to the touch-hole, and the charge went off with a roar, knocking John to the ground. But he and Matt retrieved a brace of birds.

"Can't you make a better gun than that?" Jonathan Browning seemed less annoyed with the boys for sneaking out to hunt than with John's workmanship. Shamed, the lad broke his gun into pieces on the forge.

John Browning knew early on that he wanted to build guns. Not just fix them to augment the family's income, but to fashion the parts, even design them. He was in a good place for that. The transcontinental railway had just been finished at Promontory Point, only 50 miles from Ogden, and Jonathan had established a solid gun business that was quickly becoming John's responsibility.

In 1878 John turned 23. "You've a good head, John Mose," said his father. "Build your own rifle." In a spartan room, with no drafting tools, he sketched a single-shot rifle action. With no milling machine, he hand-forged parts, shaping them with file and chisel and a foot-lathe Jonathan had brought by oxcart from Missouri.

The rifle functioned perfectly–its massive parts and simple construction suited it to the frontier–and John filed for a patent May 12, 1879. While he was awaiting action, his father died, leaving him the head of two households.

With help from brothers Ed, Sam and George, John and Matt built a small factory and ordered power equipment they didn't know how to install or use. By great good luck, Englishman Frank Rushton was touring the West and stopped in. His knowledge of British gunmaking and machines helped the Brownings immensely.

John Browning priced his rifle at $25. A week after opening a retail counter, Matt sold all the rifles they had finished in three months! And a burglar made off with John's prototype.

Browning's Model 81 is a smooth-shucking lever gun with a rack-and-pinion mechanism.

Even before he'd received a patent for his first rifle, John built another dropping-block action, this one with a fixed trigger guard and forward-mounted lever. By 1882, he'd built a repeating rifle. The following year, Winchester salesman Andrew McAusland picked up a used Browning single-shot rifle and delivered it to Winchester president Thomas Bennett, who lost no time traveling to Ogden, and what was billed as the biggest gun store between Omaha and the Pacific. He found half-a-dozen men barely out of their teens, in a shop smaller than a livery. But Bennett was no fool. He met with John Browning and came straight to the point: "How much will you take for your rifle?"

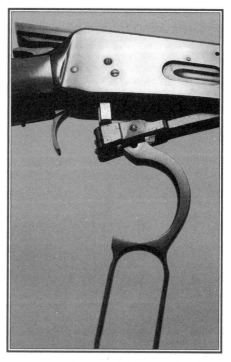

"One rifle?"

"No, the rifle. All rights."

"Ten thousand dollars," said John coolly, as if selling paint. It was an enormous sum in Utah in 1883.

"Eight thousand, plus jobbing grants." Bennett would surely have paid ten, but didn't have to. Less than six hours after he arrived in Ogden, Bennett was on a train for the six-day ride back to New Haven. The rifle came out as Winchester's Model 1885,

In a primitive shop with hand tools, John Browning crafted lever rifles that sold big for Winchester.

and John immediately turned to his next project, a lever-action.

In May 1884, he applied for a patent, and Bennett bought the gun, which became Winchester's Model 1886, a repeater that could handle cartridges previously used only in single-shots. It cost Winchester $50,000, "more money than there was in Ogden," according to Browning. But an astute friend called the rifle Winchester's future.

Bennett would not let John Browning rest. "Could you build a lever-action shotgun?" he asked. John told him of course he could—but that a pump would sell better. Bennett gave him two years to come up with a lever-action; John delivered one in eight months.

In 1887, just after John turned 32 and started a family, he was sent to the mission field by the Mormon Church. One day he spied the first Model 1887 Winchester he had ever seen in a shop window. Reluctantly, the shopkeeper let the dusty lad handle the shiny new gun. Watching, he remarked that John seemed to know a bit about guns, even this one in particular.

"He should!" exclaimed John's companion. "He designed it!"

After returning to Utah in 1889, John Browning worked on mechanisms "so simple, so foolproof that he measures in inches, not thousandths." This according to one of his shop foremen.

Thomas Bennett kept John busy. During their twenty-year association, Winchester bought 44 Browning patents, apparently for asking price but with no royalties. Only 10 were manufactured as Winchesters. Bennett, who was Oliver Winchester's son-in-law, paid for designs he couldn't use, just to keep them from competitors. One of the most successful was the pump shotgun Bennett had at first declined. Introduced as Winchester's Model 1893, it later became the Model 1897, an instant hit and a gun that stayed in production for sixty years. Another success

was the Model 1890 .22 pump rifle, which John proposed by mailing some rough sketches. No one liked the idea, but John built the little gun anyway and then shipped it to New Haven with a note: "You said it wouldn't work, but it seems to shoot pretty fair for me."

Made only between 1924 and 1932, the Winchester 53 was a variation of the popular 1892.

About then, Bennett asked Browning for a lever-action rifle to replace the aging 1873–the gun "that won the West." Bennett offered $10,000 "[I]f you can get a prototype to me in three months. Make it two months and I'll give you $15,000."

John Browning replied, "The price is $20,000 if I can deliver it in 30 days. If I'm late, you get it free."

Incredulous, Bennett agreed. Within two weeks, John and his brothers had built a prototype for what would become the Winchester Model 1892. Bennett cut a check for $20,000.

One of John Browning's greatest achievements was his development of reliable self-loading guns that could be economically produced. He allegedly found inspiration for his first autoloader at a rifle match, where grass in front of prone shooters was flattened by muzzle blast.

At home, he laid a wooden block near the muzzle of a Model 1873 rifle, the block's center drilled to allow passage of the bullet. At the shot, the block flew into the shop wall. The subsequent Browning machine gun in .45-70 chewed through 1,800 rounds in Colt's test lab without a malfunction. It had fewer parts than a Colt revolver, and at 40 pounds, weighed half as much as a Gatling. Improvements gave the U.S. a fearsome battle weapon. At the end of World War II, German aviators would remark that if they'd had Browning .50s, the outcome of the conflict might have been different.

By 1900, three of every four guns used by American sportsmen were of Browning design, and they were all Winchesters. Ironically, the relationship between Thomas

Bennett and John Browning would be ruined by one gun so good that the Winchester president said no: In March 1899, John proposed an auto-loading shotgun.

Bennett balked.

Shotshells of the day swelled and malfunctioned even in pump guns. Sportsmen might not like the mechanism, for which tooling would be expensive. A successful Browning repeater would put the skids under the '97. Besides, John also insisted on royalties. In the end, the men were unable to reach a compromise.

"It was not a dignified parting," John recalled. "I'll bet Bennett would have given $100,000 to have been rid of that gun."

In 1902, their product in hand, John and Matt courted Remington, but as they waited for an audience with company president Marcellus Hartley, he died of a heart attack. Traveling to Belgium, the Brownings found a buyer in Fabrique Nationale de Guerre (FN), and late in 1903, 10,000 shotguns were en route to New York. Even John Browning must have been surprised when the lot sold within one year. Remington soon acquired rights to manufacture the auto-loader as the Model 11. The Belgian Auto 5 lasted into the 1970s; Japanese versions were built for another quarter century.

John Browning's next project was a pistol with an operating slide that served as action housing, sight rib and bolt, mated by rails to a frame that held magazine, trigger and hammer. By 1902 he'd built a 38-caliber prototype. But the Moro uprising in the Phillipines had shown a need for bullets that could not only disable an attacker, but stop him. Browning responded with the Model 1911 pistol in .45 ACP. So fault-free from the start that it weathered two world wars with no substantial design changes, it is still considered by many who carry handguns to be the finest defensive sidearm ever.

In 1926, checking shotgun production on his 61st visit to the FN plant, John said that he wasn't feeling well. Minutes later, lying on an office couch, he observed "I wouldn't be surprised if I am dying." Then he was gone, at age 71. The military ceremonies could hardly do justice to a man whose genius garnered 128 patents for 80 distinct firearms. No gun designer has yet been as prolific, or as adept at converting ideas into steel. No other has been so able to marry complex functions with a handful of rugged parts without blueprints.

JOHN MARLIN'S MARVELOUS LEVER-ACTIONS

John Mahlon Marlin was only 18 years old in 1853, when he became an apprentice machinist in Connecticut. He agreed to work for no wages for six months, after which he'd get shop pay of $1.50. One year later, he qualified for a raise to $2.50. Per week.

Gunmaking followed. During the 1860s, John designed and built derringer-style pistols. Then he manufactured Ballard rifles. Unfortunately, his own under-hammer lever-action repeating rifle gave trouble feeding and didn't sell.

The first successful Marlin lever-action was a side-loading, top-ejecting rifle designed on patents from John Marlin, H.F. Wheeler, Andrew Burgess, and E. A. F. Toepperwein. Named the Model 1881 for its year of introduction (but not until 1888), the rifle featured a 28-inch octagonal barrel chambered either in .45-70 or

.40-60. It held 10 cartridges and was initially priced at $32. You paid extra for a set trigger. Marlin later offered a 24-inch barrel and trimmed the receiver. The lightweight version weighed 8 1/2 pounds, two pounds less than the original. New chamberings were added: .32-40, .38-55, and .45-85 Marlin. The 1881 came with open sights; late models were also drilled for folding tang sights.

According to many historians, the 1881 was the first successful big-bore lever-action repeater–by some accounts, the first modern deer rifle. It had a couple of weaknesses, however. One was top ejection, eliminated on the Marlin 1889 rifle and never to be revisited. The other was a problematic carrier that often produced jams at the rear of the magazine. A wedge and a split carrier appeared in rifles after 1884, and they made feeding more reliable. Most of the 20,000-odd 1881 rifles built were shipped between 1881 and 1891, though some left the plant as late as 1903.

In 1888, Marlin announced a new lever gun, designed by L. L. Hepburn and chambered for short-action cartridges: the .32-20, .38-40, and .44-40. This side-loading, top-ejecting model retailed for $19.50 with a 24-inch octagonal barrel. It weighed only 6 1/2 pounds! A round-barrel model followed shortly, at $18, and for $2 or $4 extra, you could have a 26- or 28-inch barrel. Rifles with the longest barrel held 16 cartridges. Case-hardened lever, hammer, and butt plate were standard. Only about 4,800 Model 1888s were built; the last on record went to the shipping room in 1892.

By this time, L. L. Hepburn had come up with a better rifle, one that would become the patriarch of the Marlin line. His Model 1889 rifle was introduced in September of that year. Like the 1888, it fired the .32-20, .38-40, and .44-40 cartridges, and it locked with a square vertical bolt sliding up rails in the frame. But it had a solid receiver top. Even in the days of iron sights, side ejection made sense. You didn't have cases bounding up through your line of sight. The 1889 was made with barrels as short as 15 inches and as long as 30. Standard rifle barrels were 24, 26, and 28 inches long, round or octagonal. A carbine version had a 20-inch round barrel. Priced at $18 (rifle with 24-inch round barrel) and $17.50 (carbine), the 1889 could be ordered with select walnut stock for $6 more, and hand-checkering added $12 to the cost.

A distinguishing feature of this rifle was its rear lever lock, a catch that kept the lever tight to the grip during carry. It was eliminated on subsequent Marlins. Tang sight holes were standard. The company shipped 55,000 Model 1889s by 1903. Roughly 10,000 were saddle-ring carbines, only 367 with the special-order 15-inch barrel.

In 1891, Marlin built a lever gun around the .22 rimfire cartridge. During its 25-year production run, this rifle became famous as the choice of "Little Miss Sure Shot," Annie Oakley. It was succeeded in 1895 by the Model 1892 Marlin, which was similar but had a superior trigger mechanism without a lever-operated safety. Both rifles could be had in .32 rimfire or .32 Long and Short Colt (centerfire), and both initially retailed for $18. List price of the Model 1892 later dropped to as low as $13.25.

The Model 1897 that followed featured Hepburn's single-screw take-down mechanism that's still used on the Marlin 39, one of the most acclaimed .22 sporting rifles of all time. About 81,000 Model 1897s came off the production lines at Marlin between 1897 and the end of recorded manufacture in 1905.

L.L. Hepburn wasted no time in refining the Model 1889. The result: a rifle that handled longer cartridges than the .44-40. The Model 1893 appeared first in .32-40 and .38-55, was later offered in .25-36, .30-30, and .32 Special. Its lockup and two-piece firing pin differed markedly from the 1889s. When the lever was ajar, the rear piece would fall out of line with the front piece, preventing discharge. The standard 1893 had a 26-inch barrel and full-length magazine, though barrels from 20 to 32 inches could be ordered. A lightweight version wore an 18- or 20-inch barrel, with shorter forend, and magazine. Both round and octagonal barrels appeared on Model 1893s.

In 1905, Marlin offered a Grade-B variation, the barrels marked, "For Black Powder." These were chambered only in .32-40 and .38-55. Other barrels were designated "Special Smokeless Steel." The 1893 weighed 6 1/2 to 8 3/4 pounds, depending on barrel and chambering. Carbines could be ordered with or without a saddle ring.

In 1923, a "Sporting Carbine" joined the 1893 line. This "CS" version had a hard rubber butt plate, ivory bead front sight, and 2/3-length, five-shot magazine. Otherwise it was the same as the "S" or standard Carbine, with a case-hardened receiver and ladder-type folding rear sight.

The Model 1893 became the Model 93 in 1905, though nothing was changed on the rifle. By the 1920s, it had established itself as a favorite among deer hunters, a rival to Winchester's Model 94. In 1932, the 93 listed for $36. The last of recorded production went to J.F. Galef Company in New York four years later. The price by then had dropped to $25. The 93 was a strong, modern rifle–a prototype for the Model 1936, from which came the 336. During its production run, ending in 1906, more than 73,000 Model 1893 Rifles and Carbines left the company docks.

An elegant 19th-century Marlin reposes at a Cowboy Action shoot. The later .336 beguiled deer hunters.

It didn't take Marlin long to realize that the 93 would be successful. A short-action version came along right away, chambered in .32-20, .38-40, and .44-40 (the .25-20 too, though it was not announced at the time of introduction). Like the 1893, the Model 1894 could be ordered as a takedown rifle. And like its long-action counterpart, the 1894 became a hit. Roughly 36,000 rifles were built between 1894 and 1906, plus nearly 11,000 carbines. Prices and barrel lengths were nearly the same as for the Model 93. A favorite among deer hunters, the 1894 remained in Marlin Catalogs until 1917. Marlin Firearms Corporation had planned to reintroduce this model but went bankrupt in 1924. Entrepreneur Frank Kenna bought the real estate for $100, then negotiated the mortgage down to $95,000. The reorganized company brought the 1894 back, but sales sputtered during the

Charlie Sisk tuned, refinished, and equipped this Marlin 1895, a deer gun with .45-70 muscle.

Depression. Marlin revived this rifle (with modifications) in 1969, after failing to get the .44 Magnum round to work in Model 336 rifles. The 1894 has become very popular on the Cowboy Action circuit. It's now chambered in .45 Colt and .357 Magnum, as well as in .44 Magnum.

Marlin's original Model 1895, first cataloged in 1896, was essentially a large-frame Model 1893. It was chambered for the .38-56, .40-65, .40-82, .45-70, and .45-90. The .40-70 was added in 1897. Like the Model 1893, the 1895 wore a case-hardened receiver and blued barrel, round or octagonal. In 1912, Marlin added a lightweight rifle in the potent .33 WCF. It had a 24-inch barrel, half magazine, and shotgun-style hard rubber butt on a straight-grip stock. It held five cartridges and weighed 7 3/4 pounds. Cost: $18.50 for the solid-frame version and $22 for the take-down.

Between 1895 and 1906, Marlin shipped 5300 Model 1895s. Only about 200 were carbines with 22- and 15-inch barrels. Lightweight rifles in .33 and .45-70 closed out original Model 1895 production just before the First World War. Marlin resurrected the 1895 in 1972 (in .45-70) and has produced several variations since, including the wildly popular "Guide Gun" and "Outfitter," in .45-70 and .444 respectively, plus the similar 1895M in .450 Marlin Magnum. These three rifles have four-shot, 2/3-length magazines under 18 1/2-inch barrels. Current versions do not feature the porting standard on the first Guide Guns. The muscular profiles of Marlin's 1895 carbines evoke images of an untamed frontier, of saddles and freighter canoes and a timbered wilderness alive with grizzlies, moose, and other game made to order for big bullets. Shooters have responded with their checkbooks.

This customized Marlin belongs to a hunting guide in the Territories. It's a bear-stopper.

Clawing its way clear of the Depression in the 1930s, Marlin reintroduced its Model 93. Then it changed the sights, stock, and forend–and gave the rifle a new name. The Model 1936 replaced the 93 in company catalogs in 1937. Heralded as "a new gun especially for American big game," the 1936 featured "solid-frame, 20-inch round-tapered special smokeless barrel, proof-tested, crown muzzle, Ballard-type rifling, visible hammer, case-hardened receiver, steel butt plate. New design full pistol grip butt stock of genuine American black walnut . . . New 'Sure-Grip' semi-beavertail forearm, rounded and nicely shaped, Silver-bead front sight dovetailed to the barrel, and flat-top Rocky Mountain rear sight, especially adapted to quick accurate shooting. Length overall: 38 inches. Weight: About six pounds. Full magazine: Seven shots in caliber .30-30 or .32 Special."

That was the carbine model, with barrel bands. The 1936 Sporting Carbine owned a 2/3 magazine and steel forend cap. The rifle version was the same as the SC but with a 24-inch barrel. All variations had pistol-grip stocks. Though a steel butt plate was specified, many if not most 1936 rifles wore hard rubber plates, presumably to cut costs. Curved butt plates came late. Fluted combs on early stocks were eventually abandoned; and the forend, initially beefier than the 93s, was made even larger in subsequent production. All Model 1936s retailed for $32 in 1937.

Three variations of the 1936 have been recognized. The first frame was drilled and tapped for a tang sight but not for a receiver sight. The second variation was drilled and tapped for both. A third type featured a blued receiver, sandblasted on top, instead of the original case-hardened steel. In 1940, a 36ADL was added. It featured a checkered stock, detachable sling swivels, and a leather sling. All were evidently known as both the 1936 and Model 36 Marlins–the number designations are interchangeable, and "Model 36" appeared in the literature from the start. These rifles, carbines, and sporting carbines stayed in Marlin's line to 1947. When discontinued, the 36C and 36SC listed for $61.45, while the rifle cost $72.55 and the ADL version retailed at $87.50.

In 1948, the Model 336 replaced the 36. The most obvious difference between the two actions is the round bolt of the 336. The company promoted it this way: "In this sturdy locking mechanism, the round breech bolt is completely encased in the area of the locking bolt by a solid bridge of steel in the receiver . . . furnishing a strong, safe breech for the .35 caliber cartridge. . . . And, with a newly designed extractor, these high-power repeaters function smoothly with the new bolt."

A solid-top receiver made early Marlins more scope-friendly than the Winchester Model 94.

The bolt was chrome-plated, "easily removed for cleaning and oiling," and featured the two-piece firing pin of the 93. The flat mainspring of the 36 and earlier rifles gave way to a coil mainspring. The "Marlin bullseye," deleted for a time on Model 36 stocks (just ahead of the toe) as a cost-saving measure, was reinstated on the 336.

Some early literature specified Ballard-type rifling for the Model 336, while some told of a "new Micro-Groove barrel." In 1951, Marlin's 336 Carbine was redesignated the 336C. The 336SC and 336A versions followed the Model 36 nomenclature for Sporting Carbine and Rifle. The 336A (and the Deluxe variation) were dropped in 1962. The SC survived one more year, and the original 336C prospered until 1983.

From 1954 to 1962, there was a Deluxe Sporting Carbine, and the straight-grip 336T (for Texan) filled out the line from 1954 to 1983. The original 336C was chambered in .30-30 and .32 Special, but Marlin added the .35 Remington in 1953. For five years, beginning in 1955, hunters could buy the 336SC in a .219 Zipper. These rifles remain among the most desirable 336s among collectors. So, too, the 336TDL (Deluxe Texan), manufactured from 1962 to 1963, and the 336 Marauder (with 16 1/4-inch barrel), built from 1963 to 1964. A year-long listing of the 336 in .44 Magnum ended in 1964, too. That year, Marlin began manufacturing its budget-priced Glenfield line. In 1984, that series was replaced by the Promotion Model 30AS. It survives as a basic 336 carbine in .30-30 only, with hardwood stock. The pressed "checkering" imposed on hunters who owned Glenfield 336s from 1969 to 1982 was abandoned in favor of smooth grip surfaces for a time, but was then replaced by cut checkering.

The .32 Special vanished from the 336 line in 1964. The Model 444 Rifle, a 336 chambered for the powerful .444 Marlin cartridge, appeared in 1965. It was changed in 1971 to the 444S, and in 1983 to the 444SS. From 1983 to 1986, Marlin assembled a handful of "Extra Range" 336s chambered for the .356 Winchester, a new cartridge at that time. The company advertised but never built rifles in .307 Winchester. In 1984, the 336C became the 336CS with the addition of a cross-bolt safety, and the .375 Winchester began a three-year run as a rifle chambering. This cartridge lasted in the 336CS for another three years.

Several special-edition 336s have been made, including a Zane Grey commemorative in 1972 and an octagonal-barreled carbine that appeared only in 1973. Six years later, Marlin reached a milestone in 336 production, with its three-millionth rifle. A highly-engraved carbine, gold-inlaid, and stocked with select walnut, was built to mark the occasion.

Excepting Glenfield and AS variations, Marlin 336s sold for years with white-line spacers under grip cap and butt plate. Recently they've been dropped in deference to shooters who prefer a conservative look. Again excluding the economy models, the company has stayed with plain-grained American walnut, and the latest versions are cut-checkered. Early on, only the 336A Deluxe Rifle stock was checkered. It also had a Monte Carlo comb. In 1957, Bishop supplied a 336ADL stock with a cheekpiece. For all 336s, the fit of wood to metal has remained remarkably tight over the years, while rifles from other makers show greater attention to production costs than to fit. Marlin's method of induction-heating the stock, and pressing it into the receiver to achieve close fit, came about in 1974.

While many small changes have been made in the production of internal parts for the 336 since the model's inception, it is essentially the same rifle. It remains, in this era of the bolt gun, a popular choice of deer hunters in the East. Marlin is proud to note that its receivers are forged and machined, that their steel innards give you the same smooth, solid feel of rifles that were built before alloy castings, and music wire invaded parts rooms. In fact, Marlin's current stable looks, at a glance, much as it did decades ago when the 336 arrived. The reason: The 336CS (.30-30 and .35 Remington) and 336W (.30-30) have the profile of the 36 and original 336. There's also a straight-grip 336 Cowboy in .30-30 and .38-55. It's designed expressly for long-range cowboy events and features deep-cut Ballard rifling. Actually, the only 336 with strikingly modern cosmetics is the new "M" model, built from stainless steel. Even most action parts are stainless (a few are nickeled). The 336M, like the 336CS, 336W, and 336AS, has a pistol-grip stock and full-length six-shot magazine.

Marlin still chambers rifles for the .444–but in the 1895 line, not the 336. The .444, essentially a rimmed .30-06 case necked to take a .44 Magnum pistol bullet, came from Marlin's shop. Tom Robinson and Art Burns brought the cartridge to production. Remington's Earl Larson improved it in 1980 by adding a 265-grain load to the original 240-grain offering. The Model 444 had a 24-inch barrel and 2/3 magazine that held four rounds. A straight-grip stock with Monte Carlo comb was replaced in 1971 with a pistol-grip stock that had a straight comb. Recoil pads were standard; so was a sling in QD swivels, until 1988, when rifles came packaged only with swivel studs. The first 444s retailed for $124.95. By 1988 they'd climbed to $385.95–three times their original price! The 1895 Marlins currently cataloged cost more still.

Marlin's brief fling with a varmint cartridge in lever rifles probably won't be repeated. The .219 Zipper was (is!) a fine cartridge, but shooters got relatively poor accuracy and short barrel life from Micro-Groove bores. Conventional rifling might have yielded tighter groups, but the hard fact is that the stringent demands of dedicated varmint shooters are best met by bolt guns and single-shots. Marlin's 336 is a superb deer rifle–one of the most accurate of its type with traditional big-game cartridges. It wasn't designed for small bullets or to compete with heavy bolt rifles built for long-range sniping. In 1955, a Model 336SC in .219 Zipper listed for $73.70. When it was discontinued, 3,230 rifles later, it sold for $80.79.

Current 336s, like the short-action 1894s and heavy-duty 1895s, show the practical design that's kept Marlin products popular

There's no better woods rifle than a Marlin lever-action, here an 1895.

with shooters for more than a century. Beyond that, these rifles show the fit and finish and traditional elegance of their forebears. Marlin has managed to apply modern manufacturing methods without sacrificing the "gunny" looks and handling qualities of these guns–without losing solid feel and slick, smooth lever movement. Pick up a 336, and you can't help but marvel that the mechanism is older than the automobile! Carved from the American frontier, it has gotten better, incrementally, with age. Throw that rifle to your cheek, and you'll see a whitetail buck streaking through the trees. Flick the lever, and you get an eager response. Snick, snick. This rifle wants to be in the woods. It's the quintessential deer rifle, the best of what rifles used to be when people depended on rifles for more than fun.

THE LIFE AND GUNS OF ARTHUR SAVAGE

The last half of the 18th century brought a flood of new gun designs from American inventors. Beginning in 1849, with Christian Sharps' dropping-block rifle and the Hunt Volitional Repeater, men found ways to marry mass production with powerful cartridges and to build rapid-fire guns that worked every time. Horace Smith and Daniel Wesson, rifle mechanics turned pistol-smiths, followed Sam Colt in a bid for multiple-shot pistols and wound up refining rimfire cartridges. By the turn of the century, metallic centerfire rounds with smokeless powder and jacketed bullets were chambered in pump-, lever-, and bolt-action magazine rifles. The Sharps was history and the Volitional Repeater a relic.

Among the few rifles that bridged the black-powder era with that of smokeless rounds and long-range rifles is one so far advanced when it debuted that it survived for nearly a century with no major changes. The Savage 99 hasn't needed improvement.

Like many of his predecessors, Arthur William Savage used one successful gun design to found a company that would later manufacture a variety of firearms. As remarkable as the longevity of that original design was Mr. Savage's dedication to the growth of his business. He seemed at first more likely to make his mark as an explorer–or wind up an itinerant inventor.

Born June 13, 1857, in Kingston, Jamaica, Arthur Savage went to school in England and the United States. His father was England's Special Commissioner to the British West Indies, where he developed an educational program for newly-freed slaves, and he made sure Arthur was properly schooled.

But young Savage had an adventurous streak and, immediately after college, sailed for Australia, where he found work on a cattle ranch. Arthur also found a wife, Annie Bryant, and started a family. One of his sons was born in a wagon on a wilderness trek. Eventually the Savages would have four sons and four daughters. An astute businessman, Arthur quickly built himself a stake in cattle. At the end of his 11-year stay in Australia, he was said to own the biggest ranch on the continent.

The Outback had given him fortune and thrills (Aborigines once captured and held him for several months), but Savage itched for new frontiers. He sold his ranch, moved back to Jamaica and bought a coffee plantation. There he tinkered with machinery and pursued an interest in firearms and explosives. With another inventor, he developed the Savage-Halpine torpedo. It got good reviews from the U.S. Navy, but no contract was offered, and this torpedo was later sold to the Brazilian government.

Savage also worked on recoilless military rifles. Then, in 1892, when he was just 35 years old, he finished blueprints for a new infantry arm. The competition was fierce, as post-Civil War gun designs had come on like a catapult attack. Remington, Winchester, and Marlin offered sound, marketable rifles, but the demise of the Sharps Rifle Company demonstrated that not all sound firearms would survive in the coming century. New products had to be different, better by a big margin and marketed aggressively. Arthur Savage was undaunted.

His gun was a hammerless lever-action, a daring design in the wake of analyses blaming the failure of the Model 1878 Sharps-Borchardt on its lack of a visible hammer. The operating lever was part of the guard bow but admitted only one (rear) finger. Between this loop and the trigger, a guard extension lay flat against the belly of the grip. The magazine, housed in the receiver, held eight rounds. The full-length stock was fastened to the 29-inch barrel musket-style, with two bands. By this time, Savage was living in the U.S. He submitted his rifle for testing at the 1892 ordnance trials on New York's Governor's Island, but it was beaten by the Krag-Jorgensen, which became the official U.S. infantry rifle.

Turning next to sportsmen, Arthur Savage redesigned his gun, paring magazine capacity to five for a trimmer profile and altering the lever to accept three fingers. He also developed a new cartridge for the rifle and in 1894 formed the Savage Arms Company in Utica, New York. Factory operations began within a year.

Savage's first commercial rifle was called the Model 1895. Its rear-locking bolt abutted a thick steel web machined into the tail of a streamlined receiver milled from a solid forging. There were no channels or openings rearward to allow the escape of gas from a ruptured case. Side ejection kept cases out of the line of sight and would later prove a requisite for scope use. Savage's action was less vulnerable to dust, water, and debris than were contemporary Winchester lever guns.

Quick to point, short-barreled Savage 99s were notably popular with small-framed shooters.

The 1895 also featured a coil mainspring–the first of its kind on a commercial lever-action–and a through-bolt to join the butt stock and receiver. The through-bolt was much stronger than the wood screws commonly applied through a tang extension.

But the most exciting part of this gun was its magazine, a spring-loaded brass spool neatly housed in the receiver. A cartridge counter in a window in the left receiver wall showed how many rounds remained. No magazine was simpler, smoother in operation or better protected from the elements or rough handling.

Savage's spool boasted other advantages over barrel-mounted tubular magazines of its day. First, it didn't affect rifle balance, because the weight was always between your hands. Long-barreled Winchesters became muzzle-heavy with full tubes. Secondly, the Savage magazine didn't affect barrel vibrations as tubular magazines did. Accuracy was thus enhanced by the barrel's independence. Most importantly, pointed bullets were safe to use in the Model 95 because the cartridges did not rest primer-to-bullet tip. You could use bullets of higher ballistic potential and, thus, greater range.

Arthur Savage's new cartridge, designed for this rifle, drove a 190-grain bullet at around 1,900 fps. It was christened the .303 Savage, though bullet diameter was .308, not .311, as for the .303 Lee-Enfield. Case dimensions were about the same as those of the .30-30 Winchester, but the longer, heavier bullet gave Savage's .303 an edge in the woods. Shortly after its introduction, testimonials from hunters told of its great power.

"I have just returned from my hunting trip with one bull moose and two bull caribou, all killed stone dead in their tracks with one of your incomparable .303 rifles. I shot the moose at a distance of 350 yards."

"In November [my guide] killed a very fine large mountain sheep [with] the first shot 237 yards off and in a very strong wind. He says he likes the Savage to shoot in the wind as the barrel is small and [has] no long magazine to catch the wind and blow your rifle to one side."

E.E. Jones of Townsend, Montana, bet all comers $50 that he could "shoot through a grizzly endwise" with his Model 1895. E.T. Ezekiel of Wood Island, Alaska, claimed to have killed a whale with his .303. A frugal marksman in British Columbia used his first box of 20 cartridges to take 18 big-game animals, including grizzlies. Other compliments came from W.T. Hornady ("Campfires in the Canadian Rockies"). Government hunters and forest rangers also used and liked Savage lever-action rifles.

The Model 1895 was offered only in .303, with a straight grip, crescent butt, schnable forend, and a barrel 22, 26, or 30 inches long. About 6,000 rifles were made between 1895 and 1899, when Savage changed the gun slightly and renamed it the Model 1899. A year later it became available in .30-30; in 1903 the .25-35, .32-40, and .38-55 were added.

Early Model 99s looked much like their predecessor in profile. Barrels came in lengths of 20 to 28 inches and were designated by letter according to shape: "A" for round, "B" for octagonal, "C" for half-octagonal. The .303 Model 99-D with its full-length military stock died in 1905. In 1903, Savage offered its Model 99-A "Short Rifle" with a 22-inch barrel. It came to be called the saddle gun–not to be confused with the original 99-F (saddle-ring) Carbine.

Some of the original Savage chamberings had a short life. The .303 and .30-30

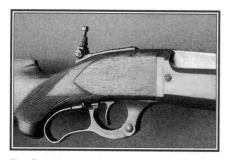

The Savage Model 99 offered a hammerless action. This one wears a tang-mounted peep sight.

would survive until World War II; the .25-35, .32-40, and .38-55 were dropped by 1920. In 1913, a brilliant ballistician named Charles Newton designed for Savage a cartridge to replace the .25-35. Image ch 2-18 It had the same head dimensions as a .30-06 but was much shorter. Newton recommended a 100-grain bullet for his new .25, but Savage chose an 87-grain because it could be driven 3,000 fps, an attention-getting speed in those days. Called the .250-3000 when it debuted in 1913, this round became an immediate hit with deer hunters and it is still loaded commercially. Newton also designed the Savage .22 High-Power, or "Imp," with a 70-grain .228 bullet at 2,700 fps.

By 1920, Savage was offering its Model 99 in five styles, with both take-down and solid frames. That year the company introduced its .300 Savage cartridge, intending to duplicate .30-06 performance in short actions. Falling well short of this lofty standard, the new round nonetheless proved popular. When, in the early 1950s, ordnance officers were looking for a cartridge to replace the .30-06 in battle rifles, they turned to the .300 Savage. Finding its neck too short for reliable functioning in machine guns, they lengthened it, and reduced shoulder angle 10 degrees. The resulting T-65 experimental round became, in 1953, the .308 Winchester. Three years later, the U.S. Army adopted it as the 7.62 Nato.

An early Savage 99 with a new XS aperture sight. Note the lever safety and hand-checkered walnut.

The first Savage catalog listed Model 99s for $20. Stock checkering cost extra: $2 and up. The least expensive engraving added $5 to the price, a sling and swivels $1.50. You could get a Lyman tang peep sight or globe front sight for $3.50. Stocks shaped to your specifications were available, too, though a caveat in the 1905 catalog warned, "Any deviation from [standard dimensions] requires the stock to be cut from the solid block by hand. This is expensive work and there is an extra charge of $10 for altering the length or drop of a stock."

The 99 gained popularity as it gained the favor of famous outdoorsmen. "It is the handsomest and best turned-out rifle I have ever had," wrote Teddy Roosevelt in 1901.

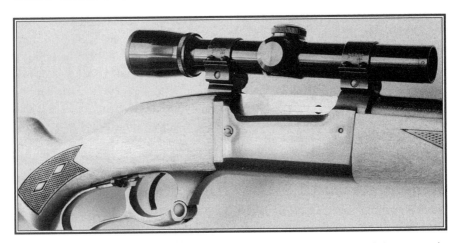

This late-model 99 features a birch stock with pressed "checkering" but an early safety and magazine.

Roy Chapman Andrews called the .250-3000 "the most wonderful cartridge ever developed," and routinely carried Savage rifles on his Asian treks. Frank Buck "brought 'em back alive" with the help of his Savage, shooting the branches out from under treed animals so they'd fall in his nets.

In nine decades as one of North America's premier deer rifles, the Savage Model 99 was listed in 31 versions and 14 chamberings–not including a take-down model that came with a .410 shotgun barrel. The action stayed essentially the same, though its safety jumped from the lever to the tang hump in 1961, and four years later the lovely spool magazine was replaced by a cheaper detachable box. Chamberings have included some still-popular modern rounds: the .284, .358, and .375 Winchester, and the .22-250 Remington. Savage last offered its legendary 99 only in .243 and .308 Winchester.

Arthur Savage no doubt relished the early success of this gun, but he was too much a pioneer to put his feet up. And he knew that his company would grow only if it diversified. In 1903, Savage announced a slide-action .22 called, predictably, the Model 1903. Short runs of slightly modified 1903s followed–the Models 1909 and 1914. A take-down .22 pump came in 1925, to be replaced four years later by the Model 29. Savage entered the bolt-action rifle market with the Models 1904 and 1905 single-shot .22s. In 1912, an auto-loading .22 joined the line, a box-fed take-down rifle that lasted only four years. The Model 19 NRA, a box-fed bolt-action, did better, remaining in catalogs until 1937. Of the 50,000 Model 19s produced, some 6,000 were used to train U.S. military forces.

Savage started making pistols in 1907, with single-action auto-loaders in .32 ACP and .380 ACP. Improved versions, the Models 1915 and 1917, came just before war gave U.S. arms-makers other priorities. Savage discontinued its auto-loading pistols in 1928.

When Archduke Ferdinand collapsed to an assassin's bullet in Sarajevo, political dominoes began to fall as well. Treaty-bound statesmen with better sense had almost no room to maneuver. War came with the murderous inertia of a toppling tree, each nation dutifully removing its share of the kerf. Savage Arms joined other

American firearms companies gearing up for war-time production, and merged with the Driggs-Seabury Ordnance Company of Pennsylvania to build Lewis machine guns. Designed for aircraft, the Lewis' firing cycle could be synchronized with a bi-plane's engine so as to fire between spinning propeller blades.

Government military contracts kept Savage and its compatriots fat during the war, but all could see the precipice ahead. Peace would bring an end to lucrative contracts. Debts incurred by the arms companies for war-time expansion would have to be paid from diminishing peace-time receipts. Tooling for machine guns was not readily adapted to the manufacture of sporting rifles; and most companies had no new models to offer because design departments had been busy with military assignments. Company payrolls would have to be cut, people laid off because a civilian market could not absorb all the guns and ammunition possible to produce.

To smooth its post-war landing and strengthen its competitive position, Savage introduced a new rifle, the Model 1920. This centerfire featured a Mauser-type action and a checkered stock with schnable forend. Available in .250-3000 and the new .300 Savage, it did not prove as popular with deer hunters as the Model 99 and was discontinued in 1926. Two years later, its successor, the Model 40, was cataloged in .30-30 and .30-06 as well as in the two Savage chamberings. It and a deluxe Model 45 lasted until 1940.

Savage was forever looking for new opportunities to further diversify and expand its product line. In 1920, it bought the J. Stevens Arms and Tool Company of Chicopee Falls, Massachusetts. This venerable firm was founded by Joshua Stevens, who had started his business by the time Arthur Savage was beginning grade school.

Born in Chelsea, Massachusetts, in 1814, Stevens grew up working in machine shops. But his interest in guns eventually led him to Cyrus B. Allen, a Springfield gunsmith of some acclaim. Under Allen's eye, Joshua Stevens learned how to repair firearms, then build them. Samuel Colt was impressed by the young man and one day invited him on a tour of possible sites for an arms factory he was planning. The two men parted friends, but soon they were in court. Stevens had invented (apparently on his own) a revolver that incorporated ideas already patented by the Colt team, and the judge told Joshua he could no longer make the gun.

But the tiny shop Stevens had built beside a Chicopee Falls sawmill in 1864 was soon swarming with customers wanting him to repair sporting guns of all types. By 1875, that shop had doubled in size, and in 1886 Joshua Stevens became the J. Stevens Arms and Tool Company. By 1896, he was manufacturing guns in a factory that covered eight acres.

Stevens shrewdly trod a path no one else had taken. Winchester, Marlin, and Remington had already established a formidable block of competition in the repeating-rifle market. Smith & Wesson had boldly challenged Colt for a share of revolver sales. Parker and Lefever had earned reputations for building fine shotguns. Avoiding the crowd, Joshua Stevens developed inexpensive guns for farm and frontier, and target rifles for the serious marksman. His single-shot "tip-up" pistols and single-barrel shotgun met with great success, as did his match rifles. He was the first American to forge a hinged-breech shotgun barrel and lug in one piece, and before World War I he claimed to be the biggest manufacturer of sporting arms in the world.

To make his guns more marketable, Stevens hired famous barrel-maker Harry Pope. Pope checked the quality of Stevens barrels, and his name gave the company credibility among target shooters. Like Arthur Savage, Joshua Stevens saw in diversity a hedge against market fluctuations. His company developed several useful cartridges, the best-known of which came about in 1887. We know it as the .22 Long Rifle. The .25 Stevens rimfire was introduced in a single-shot falling-block rifle called the Ideal. A successor, the Favorite, came in .22, .25, and .32 rimfire. These affordable guns comprised a plinking and small game-hunting line. The Walnut Hill was a target-style .22 rifle claimed by many in that day to be the finest of its kind. By the time Joshua Stevens died in 1907 at the age of 92, his gun company had become familiar to sportsmen. Two years after his death, the firm started making a 12-gauge repeating shotgun under a Browning patent. In 1913, it trotted out the first American-built .410 shotgun. Savage's purchase of the J. Stevens Arms and Tool Company seven years later gave a marketing advantage for both plants and a diversity that would keep the marriage stable in hard times.

Though Stevens had cataloged some shotguns, the Savage people apparently thought more would be better. In 1929, Savage bought the A.H. Fox Gun Company of Philadelphia. The next year, he broadened its market further by purchasing the Davis-Warner Arms Company. A year after that it got the Crescent Firearms Company. Despite the Depression, Savage designed and marketed many new guns during the '30s: the Models 19L and 19M, built between 1933 and 1942, added barrel and sight options to the Model 19 NRA. A Model 19H was available in .22 Hornet. The Model 3 single-shot .22 and magazine-equipped variations came along in the mid 1930s, as did the Model 10 .22 target rifle. Models 6 and 7 auto-loading .22s followed in 1938 and 1939.

Savage introduced its Model 220 single-shot hinged-breech shotgun in 1938, and a Model 420 box-lock over/under. By then the company had been marketing for eight years its Model 720, an autoloading shotgun on a Browning patent. This long-recoil workhorse survived for 19 years, to be succeeded by the similar Model 755, made from 1949 through 1958. Each gun had an alloy-frame counterpart: Models 745 and 775. The final product in this series, the Model 750, survived until 1967. It was Savage's last auto-loading shotgun.

In 1939, Nazi activities in Europe prompted war preparations in the U.S. During the ensuing conflict, Savage manufactured 2.5 million submachine guns, aircraft machine guns, and infantry rifles. Between 1941 and 1943 production, its lines operated around the clock every day, and the payroll jumped ten-fold, to 13,000. There were no strikes, no missed deadlines.

But as in 1919, peace brought new challenges. Savage anticipated the slowdown and in March 1944 bought the capital stock of the Worcester Lawnmower Company. The assets of this 50-year-old firm were moved to Chicopee Falls, where the Worcester corporate structure was dismantled in January 1945. The following year,

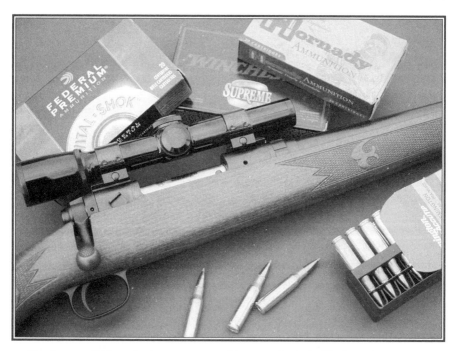

The Savage 111 is a sturdy, accurate, and inexpensive bolt rifle, here in 7mm-08.

the Savage Arms Company closed its Utica operation, consolidating gun production at Chicopee Falls. By 1950, Savage was marketing several new guns, including the Model 340 centerfire bolt-action rifle. Image 2-16 Designed to offer utility at little expense, the 340 came in .22 Hornet, .222 Remington, and .30-30. The .223 Remington was added later, a homely but serviceable gun that stayed in the Savage line for 35 years, popular among deer hunters who wanted a bolt rifle on the cheap.

In 1950, Savage announced its Model 24, an over/under combination gun in .22/.410. The popular 24 was followed in 1958 by the Savage Model 110, a bolt-action rifle developed for big-game hunters and priced to compete with Remington's 721 and 722. The 110 has spun off variations designated 111, 112, 114, and 116. With the demise of the 99, its success became crucial to Savage's bottom line. The 110 and its offspring are offered in many chamberings, for a variety of game.

A variety of rimfire rifles and pistols followed, with a handful of shotguns. In 1960, Savage moved to its present site, a modern facility in Westfield, Massachusetts, where, in 1963, it was bought by the American Hardware Corporation. Savage Arms Company then became Savage Industries, a subsidiary of the Emhart Corporation, a conglomerate that relinquished ownership in 1980. Operated by private investors for several years, Savage Industries was purchased in 1989 by Challenger International, a Bermuda-based firm, and under Challenger it continued to produce the Models 24, 99, and 110.

Arthur Savage could not have foreseen the results of his work on a curious lever rifle with no hammer. But he didn't take a seat to observe them. Besides organizing

Bolt rifles have replaced lever-actions as hunters demand more reach.

his gun company and managing its early growth, Savage continued to indulge his own curiosity. He invested in a citrus plantation and a tire enterprise, and even went prospecting for oil. He became the Superintendent of the Street Railway in Utica, New York, before he died in 1941, at age 84. That curious rifle has outlived him by more than 50 years, demonstrating the mechanical wizardry of a man who spent his first years punching cattle. ▪

3

BIG NAMES IN BOLT GUNS

The stillness of a snowy woods holds promise for whitetail hunters. But my plans to slip quietly through this Washington thicket had been dashed by a hard frost. It had struck before the snow, and the leaves crackled underfoot. Alice was not so frustrated. She had grown up in northern Wisconsin, where stump-sitting was a local tradition.

"Let's stop for a snack," she whispered.

Grudgingly, I complied, shedding my pack to dig out her chocolate. I was wolfing raisins when she tugged at my arm. "There!" she hissed.

I turned. A buck was slipping through the oaks behind us. Slowly, I eased the Remington to my shoulder. Too many branches! I whistled softly. The deer stopped, and in the 6X Lyman, I found a small alley. At the blast of my .280 Improved, the buck vanished. Again the snowy woods were still.

Deer live and die silently.

PAUL MAUSER'S POPULAR DOOR LATCH

Mauser is to rifles as Mercedes is to automobiles–in Germany. Worldwide, Mauser may have a bigger following. The huge factory in Oberndorf that supplied German troops with rifles in two World Wars, and exported military arms to countless other republics, covers more acres than the market warrants these days. And though it remains one of the most popular high-power magazine rifles across generations of hunters in Africa, it has given way to the competition Stateside. Ironically, the competition is co-opting the design that made Mauser rifles famous a century ago.

While the Mauser label has been applied to a variety of firearms (some with the Mauser banner stamped in the receiver, others simply because they are bolt rifles), most shooters associate the name with the Model 1898. This was not the first Mauser rifle; in fact, it came about when Paul Mauser was 50 years old. Like John Browning, Peter Paul Mauser was a gifted designer who could think mechanisms onto paper and fashion parts that did just what he wanted them to do. His products, like those of Browning, showed an attention to detail that ensured reliable function. His work married inventiveness with artistry, a mastery of mechanics with a drive to achieve what had not been attempted before.

Oddly enough, many riflemen think of Mauser only as a machinist who developed a breech bolt that worked like a door latch. Almost anybody could have done that, and some probably did it before Peter Paul Mauser. In fact, one of his first experimental rifles derived from the turn-bolt action of the Dreyse needle gun, German's primary shoulder arm in the Franco-Prussian War. That work brought no contracts from the Wuerttemberg, Prussian or Austrian War Ministries. But it intrigued Samuel Norris, an American traveling in Europe as an agent for E. Remington & Sons. Norris offered Paul and older brother Wilhelm financial incentive to convert the French Chassepot needle gun to a metallic-cartridge rifle. In 1867, they moved to Liege, Belgium, to begin work. When Norris failed to interest the French government in a new rifle, he bailed out of the agreement. Paul and Wilhelm returned to Oberndorf, where Paul had been born 29 years earlier. There they opened shop. Wilhelm's business savvy complemented Paul's mechanical talent.

As the brothers struggled to establish a firearms business, the Royal Prussian Military Shooting School was testing a Mauser rifle Norris had furnished earlier. It so impressed ordnance people that they asked the Mausers to make specific improvements. The young men followed up and resubmitted the rifle, a single-shot breech-loader firing an 11mm black-powder cartridge. Early in 1872, the Mauser Model 1871 became the official Prussian shoulder arm.

Elated, Paul and Wilhelm were quickly informed that the Prussian army would pay them only 15 percent of what they'd been led to expect for design rights. Also, the rifles were to be built in government arsenals, not by the Mausers. The brothers still needed work. They wound up with a contract to produce 3,000 sights for the Model 1871. A Bavarian order for 100,000 sights eventually led them to build a Mauser factory in Oberndorf. Not long thereafter, the Wuerttemberg War Ministry awarded Paul and Wilhelm a contract to build 100,000 rifles. To do this, they immediately formed a partnership with the Wuerttemberg Vereinsbank of Stuttgart to buy the Wuerttemberg Royal Armory.

On February 5, 1874, it became Mauser Bros. and Co. The sprawling Armory, which had begun life as an Augustinian Cloister, shipped the last of the Model 71s in 1878, six months ahead of schedule. Production of sights and an order of 26,000 rifles for China then kept the brothers busy. Paul invented a single-shot pistol and a revolver, but neither of these succeeded at market. Wilhelm died very early, in 1882, and Mauser became a stock company. Controlling shares were bought by Ludwig Loewe & Co. of Berlin.

In 1889, In Liege, Belgium, Fabrique Nationale d'Armes de Guerre (FN) came about to produce Mauser rifles for the Belgian government. The FN project resulted from development of the Model 1889, Paul's first successful smokeless powder rifle. The 1889 incorporated elements that established Mauser as the dominant gun designer on the Continent. During the next six years, he overhauled the rifle to make it even better. One of the most important changes, a staggered-column, fixed-box magazine, came along in 1893. By 1895 Paul had developed an action that would be perfected as the famous Model 1898. Shortly after its acceptance by the German Army on April 5, 1898, the Mauser 98 became the most popular military arm to that point in history. Exported to many countries, it would be built in many

Each Mauser magazine was fashioned for a particular cartridge, here the 10.75x73, or .404 Jeffery.

more. France, Great Britain, Russia, and the U.S. designed and produced their own battle rifles; but none surpassed the Mauser 98 in function or reliability.

Among the 98's chief attributes was its stout extractor, a beefy length of spring-steel fastened to the right-hand side of the bolt by a forward C-shaped collar with lips on the ends that grabbed a slot on the extractor's belly when you slid the extractor rearward into place. When the bolt pushed a cartridge forward in the magazine, it popped free of the rails, up against the bolt face, and into the massive extractor claw that shadowed the upper right-hand quadrant of the face. The bottom of the bolt face was milled flush with its center to permit smooth travel for the cartridge head into the extractor.

The claw shepherded the cartridge from magazine to chamber, engendering the term, "controlled round feed." It was an asset in the heat of battle because it prevented short-stroking and a jam–or worse, detonation of the primer of a chambered round by the bullet tip of another cartridge rammed forward from the magazine. With Mauser's extractor, if a soldier "double-clutched," chambering a cartridge but not firing it and then withdrawing the bolt to load a second, the first cartridge was pulled out on the bolt's rearward stroke because the claw already had the rim in its grip. One round would have to be ejected before another could be chambered.

In Africa, professional hunters came to favor the Mauser for the same reason. If multiple shots were needed to stop a dangerous animal, the 98's action was forgiving of imperfect bolt manipulation. And in the event of a misfire, the shooter could leave prognostications for later. He knew that as long as there were rounds to strip from the magazine, the rifle would keep firing. While controlled-round feed is less important to deer hunters taking deliberate shots or one quick poke at a bounding whitetail, the feature has legions of advocates. Winchester dropped the expensive Mauser-style extractor from its Model 70 in an ill-advised cost-cutting rampage in 1964, and riflemen howled. The Mauser claw was later reinstated and remains an emblem of quality–not only on the 70 but also on other rifles. Several makers have adopted it; few magazine rifles for dangerous game are made without it.

But the extractor itself is not the only component of controlled round feed. Bracketing the ejector groove on a 98 bolt face are two cartridge support lugs. The lower of these is angled to guide the rim of the cartridge case as the magazine spring pushes it up. Because a staggered cartridge stack is not constricted at the top into a single column that pops the uppermost round into the middle of the action, this lower lug is important. It must herd cartridges from both sides of the magazine toward the center of bolt travel and, as the bolt slides forward, coax the case rim into the extractor claw. Once there, the case head is held tight against the claw by both lugs. The angle, bearing surface and thickness of the lower lug affect how readily the case will step across the bolt face, yield to the extractor, and stay centered as the bolt slides into battery.

D'Arcy Echols, an accomplished contemporary riflesmith who openly marvels at Paul Mauser's engineering, says that the cartridge should spring the extractor claw about .004 for a tight fit. "Trouble is, there's that much variation among various brands of the same cartridge. Weatherby cases manufactured by Norma have extractor grooves that average .010 deeper than the grooves in Weatherby cases turned out

Mausers have been chambered for almost every conceivable deer cartridge. This buck fell to a .280.

by Remington and Winchester." Result: A Mauser-style extractor that properly fits the Weatherby case will be too tight for others, and may prevent the case head from climbing all the way up the bolt face until chamber contact with the case body forces it. An extractor fitted to the Remington or Winchester rim will not hold a Norma cartridge because there's no tension on the claw. In neither instance do you get controlled-round feed–no matter what shape the extractor!

Incidentally, Mauser purposefully did not design his extractor to jump over the rim of a round loaded directly into the chamber by hand. But there's roughly .030 extra clearance broached in the right lug raceway of the receiver ring, should single loading become necessary. You just pinch the extractor spring toward the bolt body as you seat the bolt. The extractor claw, which subtends about 20 percent of the rim's arc, makes the jump. To prevent sticky cases from slipping from the extractor's grasp, Mauser undercut the extractor tongue and its groove in the bolt body so that an extra tug during extraction puts the claw deep into the extractor groove.

After World War II, the Mauser firm was renamed, "Werke" (works) replacing "Waffenfabrik" (arms factory), and Mauser's business shifted toward the sporting trade. The U.S. agent, A.F. Stoeger, Inc., of New York, assigned numbers to the various Mauser actions. By the end of the Depression, there were 20 configurations in four lengths: magnum, standard, intermediate, and short. The short, or "Kurz" version, featured a small receiver ring and was factory-barreled for only three cartridges: the 6.5x50, 8x51, and .250 Savage. Magnum and Kurz actions were made strictly for sporting use. Mauser did not adopt the Stoeger numbers, 1 through 20; however, collectors still use these designations.

While surplus military Mausers have been sold at ridiculously low prices, commercial versions came dear, even before the second World War. In 1939, a new Model 70 Winchester cost $61.25, while a Mauser sporting rifle listed at $110 to $250. Square-bridge actions cost more. For an additional $200 you could have a left-hand Mauser!

Though few shooters these days pay it much attention, Paul Mauser's magazines may top the 98 extractor as his star achievement. He figured out that a staggered column would enable him to fit the most cartridges in the belly of a rifle action. But how to shape the box? Each cartridge needed support–from the box on one side, from the next cartridge or the follower underneath, and on the other side. He decided the stacking angle should be 30 degrees, so viewed from the end, the primers of three cartridges touching each other would form the points of an equilateral triangle. D'Arcy Echols explains that the magazines were made for specific cartridges.

This elegant Mauser was crafted by the late Maurice Ottmar, a custom maker from Coulee City, Washington.

"Mauser didn't fashion one box for many hulls, like the gun companies do today to save money. When you think about what makes Mausers so reliable, you conclude that it's mainly the cartridge-specific magazine. And you have to admire the guy who came up with the formula."

The numbers are easy to crunch once you know the formula: Multiply the cosine of 30 degrees (.866) by the case head (or belt) diameter, then add head diameter to that product. For example, a .300 H&H Magnum case is .532 across the belt. So .866 x .532 = .460 + .532 = .992. Theoretically, that's the correct rear box width for any cartridge deriving from the .300 case. But cartridges are not straight. They taper. To provide adequate support, a magazine must taper too. At the point of shoulder contact or, on a case without a neck, just behind the crimp, you use the same formula to get front box width at that point.

A .458 Lott, for instance, has a front measure of .480; .866 x .480 = .415 + .480 = .895, proper inside width of the box at the case mouth. A box designed for one cartridge will work for others only if they share front and rear diameters and have the same span between them. Overall cartridge length should be close to the same as well. So if you subscribe to Mauser's reasoning, magazine interchangeability is limited. A 7.65 rifle rebarreled to .270 needs a longer magazine, of course–but also one slightly wider up front. A 7.65 box is .801 wide at the shoulder of a .270 round. A properly engineered .270 magazine is .822 wide at that point. With a .270 in a 7.65 box, the triangles between cartridge centerlines get steep up front, and the rounds tend to cross-

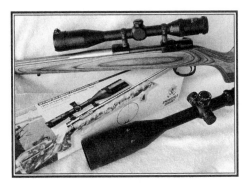

This modern Mauser from Legacy wears a Boyd's stock and a Springfield scope.

stack. The bullet emerges from the box craning its neck. A jam may result.

Paul Mauser knew that not all cartridges have straight sides and that some rimless cases might contact the box between base and shoulder. So he relieved the box sides from just ahead of the cartridge base to just behind the shoulder. He paid equal attention to magazine followers, tapering each to fit the box and shaping the top surface "just so." The width of the follower's lower shelf is matched to the case, with a 61-degree step between the upper and lower shelf. To make the next-to-last cartridge feed, the top shelf is high enough to support that round without lifting it off the last cartridge in the stack. The follower slopes like a ramp to accommodate cartridge taper and keep the rounds level in the box.

Paul engineered considerable side clearance into his followers. Says protégé D'Arcy Echols, "It's common to see floorplates machined to hold the Mauser magazine spring tightly. At first I made a couple that way myself—I figured Mauser's machinists were just sloppy in cutting spring slots .180 too wide at the rear of the floorplate. Was I ever wrong! Those springs are supposed to wiggle back and forth on the plate as cartridges are stripped off the top. If you don't let the spring shuffle, it twists; and the follower tips or gets cocked sideways."

D'Arcy Echols makes his followers .060 narrower than their boxes so they can shimmy a bit. A follower allowed too much play, however, will bang into the front of the box during recoil. While length is perhaps the least critical follower dimension, a short follower will dive in front, and a long one may bind.

Paul Mauser obviously didn't engineer his Model 1898 bolt rifle on a weekend. His ingenuity and insight as well as the time required on this project become evident to any hunter who investigates closely the rifle's design. Cartridge feeding is just one function of any magazine rifle, but it is crucial to reliability. Mauser's brilliant work in this area was largely responsible for the ready acceptance of the 98 by so many armies—and for the enduring popularity of Mausers among hunters and the makers of fine custom rifles.

When I was young, I ogled double-page spreads of Browning's High Power Rifles in catalogs that set the standard of their day for seductive photos. The High Power was assembled by Browning, but unlike the current A-Bolt, of Browning design and manufacture, it featured more than one action type. For long rounds, the mechanism was commercial Mauser. It was impeccably finished and married to impeccably polished barrels. The bluing was deep and lustrous, a perfect match for the hand-checkered, figured walnut in the stock—which also had a mirror gloss. Alas, the High Power is no more.

The latest rendition of the 98 for hunters is an action imported by Global

Trading, an Italian firm that came along in 1995. The mechanism now appears in the lineup of Legacy Sports International, which also offers Howa bolt rifles, Puma lever rifles and Silma and Escort shotguns. Legacy's Mauser shows its military heritage. Two massive locking lugs, plus a safety lug, are pure 98. So are the full-length extractor, sturdy fixed ejector, and gas-deflecting shroud. Refinements include a three-position Model 70-style safety and hardened single-stage trigger adjustable for weight of pull, sear engagement, and overtravel. The bolt handle has an M70 look but is not to my eye as attractive. A square-shouldered bridge and front ring are reminiscent of double-square-bridge actions owned mostly by people who drive Jaguars. Both top flats are drilled and tapped and machined with dovetails for your choice of scope mounts. Steel rings specifically for this rifle come in two heights.

The Legacy's is a heavy action: 3.17 pounds of 32CRM04 steel. Like the bolt, the receiver is investment-cast. Its 8.66 inches includes an extra-long receiver ring for additional barrel support. It has a M70-style gas vent. The 3.11-inch ejection port promises plenty of clearance for long magnum cartridges. An Oberndorf-style latch in the front of the trigger guard secures a hinged floorplate. Magazines hold three magnum cartridges or five standard rounds. You can order deep-well, five-round magazines for magnums. While it's not cataloged at this writing, I'm told Legacy will offer an alloy trigger guard with a detachable steel box magazine. Many hunters apparently think detachable boxes offer a handy alternative to loading from the top and releasing loose cartridges or running them through the chamber. My jaundiced opinion: box magazines are an abomination, no more appealing on a classy rifle than snooze stickers on your Jaguar. But then, you didn't ask me.

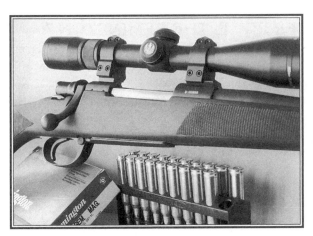

Charles Daly manufactures this Mark X-style Mauser, synthetic-stocked to hold down the cost.

A professional-grade polish graced the steel of Legacy Mausers I've examined. High-gloss blue and Teflon finishes are optional. So is a "Big Five" action for dangerous-game cartridges. A forged, super-size 98 with all the refinements of the standard action, it is 9.37 inches long with a 3.60-inch ejection port. So it can accommodate truly husky rounds like the .505 Gibbs. The traditional straight bolt handle is a nice touch, as is the drop-box magazine and lower tang extension. Unlike the standard version, which Legacy offers in the white, finished or in a completed rifle chambered to .300 Winchester Magnum, the Big Five comes only as an in-the-white action. It weighs 3.77 pounds.

A British Columbia guide carries this Mauser in .30-06. There's no more durable, reliable bolt action!

Next time you have a few moments at a used-gun rack, pick up a Mauser. Commercial beauty or battle-worn service rifle, it deserves a look. Beneath the scars, you'll see genius. Cycle that action and consider the components–their shape, dimensions, and, the fact that for more than a century, Mauser rifles have been the most dependable repeaters around. In the trenches and now in the field, there's never been a more reliable mechanism. Our Springfield and the Winchester 70 borrowed heavily from the Mauser 98. Browning used it in raw form until it became too costly to market. Now Legacy keeps the name and distinctive profile of commercial Mausers alive.

EVERYMAN'S DEER RIFLE: THE REMINGTON 700

Cloud shadows raced across ahead of the wind over black sage and red Wyoming earth. I bellied to the crest and peeked. The buck was alone. Slowly I slid the rifle ahead of my face and snicked off the safety. In the 4x Lyman Challenger, he looked awfully small. I held a foot into the wind and high and fired. The pronghorn streaked away as I rolled over to cycle the Remington 722. In the scope once again, he slowed and stopped. Smaller now. I held farther into the wind, decided I'd shot high and kept the wire on his back. At the report, he sprinted off, but this time I heard the "thwuck" of a 90-grain .244 bullet in the slats. The buck wobbled a bit, staggered, and fell.

Remington's Model 700 made big news in 1963. This first-year-production .30-06 carries a Weaver K4 scope, very popular then.

Remington rifles, like Chevrolet automobiles, date to the beginnings of their industry here in the U.S. And because they're both of common cloth, you'll find lots of Remingtons in the window racks of Chevy pickups. Where I hunt big game, the Model 700 bolt gun is more popular than even the Winchester Model 70, which predated it by 25 years and has long been hailed as "the rifleman's rifle." Among custom 'smiths, the 700's is the action of choice for hunting rigs when accuracy is a chief concern.

For more than 40 years at this writing, the 700 has been the flagship of a long line of Remington rifles beginning in 1816, when Eliphalet Remington II fashioned a rifle in his father's forge in upstate New York. A gunmaking dynasty emerged. By the late 1840s, E. Remington & Sons was supplying government arsenals and had acquired the services of ace designers William Jenks and Fordyce Beals. Manufacturing contracts for the Jenks breech-loading Navy carbine, initiated in 1841, eventually went to Remington–and with them, high-precision gunmaking tools. War with Mexico kept government agents shopping for rifles, while Eli Whitney pioneered the use of mass-produced interchangeable parts. In 1846, Lite Remington adapted Whitney's ideas and tooling to make Model 1841 military rifles. During our Civil War, the North's mass production of weapons was decisive. By 1865, this machinery had also helped Remington become the biggest arms-maker in the country.

Before that war, Remington designer Joseph Rider had worked with Beals and William Elliot on percussion revolvers. His split-breech carbine, patented late in 1863, contributed much more to the firm. It was refined to become the Rolling Block, a huge success for Remington. Military and commercial orders came from all over the world. But when Winchester's Model 1873 lever gun appeared, Remington shifted its focus to repeaters. John Keene, a New Jersey inventor, had what Remington wanted, in a bolt-action magazine rifle bored to .45-70. But this tube-fed rifle was costly to build, and when the Army rejected it in 1881 trials, the rifle's prospects tumbled. Remington made relatively few of this, its first bolt gun, before falling into receivership in 1886.

The company's financial woes during this era were only partly due to the Keene's flagging sales. Remington had diversified beyond reason, and despite the success of its sewing machines, suffered losses to high overhead and poor invest-ments. Heavy reliance on military contracts left tooling idle in peacetime. Hartley and Graham, a New York firm that also owned giant Union Metallic Cartridge Company, bought E. Remington & Sons. The first military contract after its acqui-sition was for the bolt-action Remington-Lee Model 1885 Navy Box Magazine Rifle, invented by James Lee. The first sporting version, a Model 1899, didn't reach market until Winchester's controlling interest in Remington (1888 to 1896) ended. Possibly the New Haven company had sought to nix any repeater that would threaten its lever-actions. Remington-Lee sporters were offered in 7x57, 7.35 Belgium Mauser, .236 Remington, .30-30 Winchester, and .30-40 Krag.

Twelve years after these rifles were dropped, in 1909, Remington announced a new bolt-action for hunters. The 30S derived from the 1917 Enfield, which Remington had produced on government contract during the Great War. Heavy and expensive, the 30S sold poorly. In 1926, it was replaced by the Model 30 Express, offered not only in .30-06 but in .25, .30, .32, and .35 Remington–all developed for pump guns. The 30 Express cocked on opening, had a shorter (22-inch) barrel than its predecessor and a lighter trigger pull. A slim stock helped reduce overall weight to seven-and-a-quarter pounds. Priced at $45.75, the 30 Express became reasonably popular; deluxe and carbine versions followed. In 1931, the 7x57 made the list of chamberings; five years later, the .257 Remington-Roberts. Beginning in 1933, service rifles with 1917 and 30S receivers were produced for Latin America. The last 30 Express came off the line in 1940.

The Model 720 High Power Rifle, developed by Oliver Loomis and A.H. Lowe to replace the 30 Express, had a short life. Its 1941 debut, in .30-06, .270, and .257 Roberts, amounted to only 4,000 units before Remington's production shifted to military hardware. In fact, the Navy acquired many of the first 720s. Those not issued during the second World War were presented, beginning in 1964, as marksmanship trophies by the Navy and Marines. Remington manufactured many thousands of 1903 and (beginning in 1942) 1903A3 Springfields in a wartime effort that all but cancelled manufacture of sporting guns at the Ilion, New York, plant. Just before adoption of the M1C Garand Sniper rifle, Remington delivered 28,365 Model 1903A4s–the first mass-produced run of sniper rifles in the U.S.

Clean-looking, with a functional grace, Remington 700s support the cartridge with three rings of steel.

Instead of resuming manufacture of the 720 bolt-action rifle at war's end, Remington adopted a new design by engineers Merle "Mike" Walker and Homer Young. One goal was to reduce costs. Walker, a bench-rest competitor, insisted on an accurate rifle. The Model 721 and short-action 722 were announced early in 1948, with receivers cut from cylindrical tubing. A clip-ring extractor, washer-type recoil lug, self-contained trigger assembly, and stamped bottom metal helped pare costs. But there was no compromise in function.

The stiff receiver helped accuracy. A bolt head shroud added support to the case and security in the event of case rupture. The 721 in .270 and .30-06 originally sold for $79.95. The 722 in .257 Roberts and .300 Savage cost $5 less. All had 24-inch barrels. In 1949, the .300 H&H was added to the 721 list. At eight-and-a-half pounds (with 26-inch barrel) it weighed considerably more than the standard 721 (seven-and-a-quarter) and 722 (seven) and retailed for $89.95. In 1960, the .280 Remington was offered in the 721; a year later, the .264 Winchester Magnum. The 722 would be barreled in .222 Remington (1950), .244 Remington and .308 Winchester (1956), .222 Remington Magnum (1958) and .243 Winchester (1959). High-grade AC and B versions of both rifles were replaced in 1955 with the ADL and BDL designations familiar to Model 700 owners.

The only flaw in the 721/722 design was with appearance. The rifles had stampings where hunters were used to machined parts. Plain, uncheckered stocks shouted "economy!"–though they performed on par with costlier models. A better-looking option from two Remington designers, Wayne Leek and Charlie Campbell, was the Model 725, introduced in 1958. It featured 721/722 receivers but with hinged floorplate, checkered walnut, hooded front, and adjustable open rear sights. A 22-inch barrel came standard on initial offerings in .270, .280, and .30-06, also in .244 (1959) and .243 (1960). A 24-inch tube bored to .222 came along in 1959. During 1961 and 1962, a Kodiak Model 725 was produced in Remington's Custom Shop. Chambered in .375 and .458 Magnum, it wore a 26-inch barrel with built-in muzzle brake. Just 52 of these nine-pound rifles left the factory. They listed for $310, about the same price as Winchester's M70 African.

Gunsmiths find M700 actions easy to customize. This one has been lightened by fluting.

Three years before the 725 appeared, Remington had introduced the 40X. Designed to replace the costly Model 37 .22 target rifle, the 40X was of single-shot design but included features from the 721/722. The centerfire version arrived in 1959, barreled to .308. In 1960, Remington added the .222, .222 Magnum, .30-06, and .300 H&H Magnum. Free Rifle variations followed, with two-ounce and half-ounce triggers.

In 1962, Remington fielded its most successful bolt-action rifle to date, one that immediately drew accolades from hunters. The Model 700 borrowed heavily from the 721/722. In fact, the basic mechanism is the same. Remington hung much of its early advertising on the 700's strength, "three rings of steel" (the bolt shroud, chamber wall, and receiver ring) supporting the cartridge head. But the trimmer tang, swept bolt with checkered knob, cast (not stamped) bottom metal, and more appealing stock pulled shooters to the cash registers in droves. A big assist came from Remington's brand-new 7mm Magnum cartridge, which offered the reach of a .300 H&H Magnum with less recoil. It was one of two magnum rounds listed for the M700's initial run. The other: Winchester's similar but less ably promoted .264. Both these rifles came with 24-inch barrels, as did the .222 and .222 Magnum. A 20-inch barrel was standard for the .243, .270, .280, .308, and .30-06 (all at $114.95). Two action lengths accommodated this wide range of cartridges, which has since expanded to include almost every modern cartridge made in the U.S. for bolt-action rifles. Indeed, the list of discontinued M700 chamberings is longer than the list of current offerings in many rifles!

Initially cataloged in ADL (blind magazine) and BDL (hinged floorplate) versions, the 700 got its first face-lift in 1969, when Remington jeweled the unblued portion of the bolt and installed a longer rear bolt shroud. A restyled stock featured a buttplate of black plastic instead of anodized alloy. Checkering–pressed into early stocks–got its first overhaul in '69. Now M700 wood stocks have attractive, functional machine-cut checkering. Over the years, changes in manufacturing methods have shown up in the finished product (compare trigger guards now with those of the early 1960s), and the quality of walnut has slipped a bit because figured wood is now hard to come by. Many refinements and economies have been imposed on 700s. Still, a standard version is much the same now as it was before Viet Nam made the six o'clock news.

Myriad variations in the Model 700 have appeared over the last four decades. The most notable:

1965–M700C, a special-order high-grade rifle with fancy wood.

1967–Varmint Special, with 24-inch barrel in .222, .223, .22-250, .243, 6mm.

1973–Left-hand stock and bolt, in .270, .30-06, and 7mm Remington Magnum.

1978–Classic, with satin-finished straight-comb stock, hinged floorplate, in .22-250, .243, 6mm, .270, .30-06, 7mm Magnum. Starting in 1981, limited-edition Classics came in one chambering per year. The 6mm was dropped in 1983; all other original chamberings in 1986.

1982–Safety alteration that locks the bolt down when the safety is "on" to prevent opening of the bolt during carry. This change would later be blamed (not justly) for accidental discharges when hunters unloaded their rifles. Remington would respond by reverting to the original safeties.

1984–Sportsman 78 rifle, a Spartan version of the M700, with uncheckered wood and metal and a blind magazine, in .270, .30-06 (the .243 and .308 were added in 1985, the .223 just a year later). The Sportsman 78 was dropped in 1989.

1986–Mountain Rifle, a six-and-three-quarter-pound, walnut-stocked rifle with slim 22-inch barrel tapered to .560. Initially chambered in .270, .280, and .30-06, it came out in short-action form two years later: .243, .308, and 7mm-08. The .257 Roberts was added in 1991, the .25-06 in 1992.

1987–Kit Guns, finished barreled actions with rough-shaped, inletted wood for do-it-yourselfers. Available in .243, .270, .308, .30-06, and 7mm Magnum, Kit Guns were discontinued in 1989.

1987–Rynite stocks (RS) and fiberglass stocks (FS). They survived just two years, to be replaced by synthetic stocks of lighter materials.

1987–Left-hand stock and bolt in short-action rifles chambered for the .243 and .308.

1988–Laminated stock on the ADL/LS, first in .30-06. A year later: .243, .270, 7mm Magnum.

1992–Stainless Synthetic (SS) version of the BDL, with a 426 stainless barrel, receiver, and bolt, black synthetic stock and blind magazine. It came in .25-06, .270, .280, and .30-06, four magnum chamberings: 7mm, .300 Win., .338, and .375.

1993–European 700 with oil-finished stock in .243, .270, 7-08, .280, .30-06, 7mm Magnum.

1994–Varmint Synthetic Stainless Fluted (VS SF) with aluminum bedding block per the earlier VS model (1992) but with six grooves on a heavy 26-inch barrel and a new spherical, concave crown. Chamberings: .223, .22-250, .220 Swift, .308.

1994–Sendero Special with graphite composite stock, bedding block, heavy blued barrel (initially 24 inches, then 26). This nine-pound rifle started out in .25-06, .270, 7mm, and .300 Win. Magnums.

1994–African Plains Rifle, with laminated straight-comb stock and 26-inch "magnum contour" barrel. It was assembled in Remington's Custom Shop in five magnum calibers: 7mm, .300 Win., .300 Wby., .338, .375.

1994–Alaska Wilderness Rifle, with Kevlar-reinforced stock. Receiver, bolt, and 24-inch barrel were of stainless steel. This six-and-three-quarter-pound Custom Shop rifle was initially offered in five magnum chamberings: 7mm, .300 Win., .300 Wby., .338, and .375. The 7mm STW was added in 1998.

1995–DM or Detachable Magazine versions of the BDL and Mountain rifle.

1996–Sendero SF, or stainless fluted, in .25-06, 7mm, and .300 Win. Magnums (later 7mm STW and .300 Wby. Magnum).

1996–MLS black-powder rifles on the 700 action, with a breech plug and nipple at the rear of the 45- or 50-caliber bore. A cylindrical striker replaced the firing pin. The rifle had a synthetic stock and stainless or chrome-moly barrel, iron sights.

1998–VS SF-P, with two ports on the muzzle to reduce jump and deliver an uninterrupted sight picture during recoil of this rifle in .22-250, .220 Swift, .308.

1998–Youth model with synthetic stock, 13-inch pull, in .243, .308.

Remington has since added significantly to the line, including a five-and-a-half-pound 700 with titanium receiver, and–now discontinued–a 700 Etronx that fired specially-primed cartridges with an electronic impulse provided by a battery in the stock. New cartridge listings include the Remington Ultra Mag series: 7mm, .300, .338, and .375, and the 7mm and .300 Remington Short Ultra Mags.

Remington has built M700s for both military and police forces, beginning in 1966. Paul Gogol, a Remington design engineer and Custom Shop foreman, came up with a sniper rifle based on a 40X action. It won a contract from the Marine Corps. Substituting the Model 700 mechanism, Remington built 995 of these M-40 Sniper rifles for the Corps over the next six years. Many wore Redfield 3-9x scopes; many saw service in Viet Nam. All were chambered for the 7.62 NATO (.308 Winchester). In 1986, the U.S. Army approved for its troops a Model 700 SWS (Sniper Weapon System), with long-action receiver, synthetic Kevlar-reinforced stock, and free-floating 24-inch stainless barrel. These rifles (2,510 for U.S. forces and another 1,000 for Egypt) were shipped with a bipod and a range-finding Leupold M3A 10x scope.

More recently, Remington has supplied domestic law-enforcement agencies with a heavy-barreled Model 700 Police Rifle in .223. An alternative version, in .308, features a detachable box magazine. The sight: Leupold's Vari-X III 3.5-10x. A Harris bipod comes standard; so too a Michael's shooting sling and Pelican case.

Remington has fielded other bolt rifles since the Model 700's debut. The 788 was an inexpensive but serviceable rear-locking gun that remained in the line from

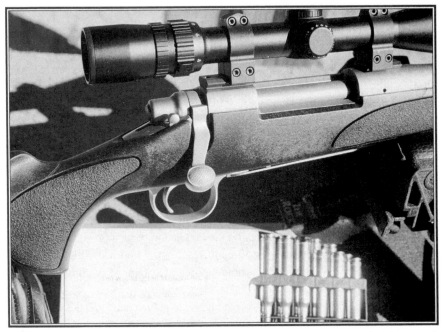

The most recent Remington 700s wear synthetic stocks with grip panels. Stainless steel is popular.

1967 to 1983. The 600 and 660 carbines, with dog-leg bolts that were more distinctive than marketable, had a shorter run—from '64 to '71. They've become sought-after in the used-gun market because now short, lightweight, accurate guns are chic. And because the profile that put everyone off in the '60s has retro appeal.

Remington's handsome Model Seven, introduced in 1983, has been a resounding success and now comes in many guises, including one dressed like the old 600 Magnum. The 710, radically different in its mechanism from traditional bolt rifles, delivers durability and good hunting accuracy at a Wal-Mart price. But no rifle ever boxed up at Ilion comes close to matching the Model 700 in sales. Current Remington catalogs list 20 variations, including four Custom Shop entries (but not black-powder guns). Take your pick of 29 chamberings, from .17 Remington to .416 Remington Magnum.

Not long ago, still-hunting in a Montana thicket, I spied the nose of a mule deer buck through a slender alley in the lodgepoles. The rifle came up as if it had been part of me for 40 years. Well, that was almost true. The Model 78, rebarreled now to .280 Improved, handled just like countless other Remington bolt guns that have snugged to my cheek and nudged my shoulder on crisp autumn mornings. It homed in on the target like a .244 did long ago, when a pronghorn buck stood briefly behind a dancing crosswire.

You can kill big game with just about any rifle. But tradition counts for a lot among hunters. And you get a fistful of tradition whenever you pick up a Remington 700.

BILL RUGER: AN EYE FOR WHAT WORKS

William Batterman Ruger, founder and Chairman Emeritus of Sturm, Ruger & Company, died at his home July 6, 2002, at age 86. He was a rarity, a 20th-century pioneer.

Born June 21, 1916, in Brooklyn, New York, Bill Ruger found his passion for guns when his father, attorney Adolph Ruger, gave him a rifle. Bill was just 12 but had often accompanied his father on duck shoots to eastern Long Island. One day afield, he met a man with a .30-06. The blast of that rifle was intoxicating, and soon he and a pal, Bill Lett, had anteed up $9.75 for a surplus .30-40 Krag. Later, Ruger practiced riflery on a high school shooting team–then designed a light machine gun and built a prototype!

At prep school in Salisbury, Connecticut, Bill had to keep his guns off campus. He spent weekends and holidays in Brooklyn machine shops, learning how to fabricate things from metal. Later, as a student at the University of North Carolina, Chapel Hill, he converted an empty room into a machine shop. There he built an auto-loading rifle from a Savage Model 99 lever-action. In 1938, he came up with an idea for what eventually became a machine gun. He finished the technical drawings on his in-laws' dining room table. Army Ordnance officers liked the result, and Ruger was ready to charge ahead full-time as a gun designer.

Bill Ruger wedded Mary Thompson in 1939. Shortly thereafter, he approached Army Ordnance with plans for another machine gun. The Army turned him down. With money running short, Bill accepted a job at Springfield Armory. The $130 monthly check held him there for a year. Eventually, though, claustrophobia set in. The Rugers moved to North Carolina, where Bill renewed his efforts to develop a better machine gun. His work brought no orders from Winchester, Remington or Smith & Wesson–but several job tenders followed. Ruger accepted a position with Auto Ordnance, which made Thompson submachine guns. The firm thought Ruger's prototypes had promise, but the end of World War II killed government interest in new ordnance.

Bill Ruger stayed with Auto Ordnance for three happy years, earning $100 a week at the design table. There he met Doug Hammond, who broached the idea of building guns from sheet metal to trim production costs. Ruger concluded that modern factory machinery could hold acceptable tolerances, that parts could be made to fit easily and interchangeably, yet closely enough for a solid feel, positive functioning and acceptable accuracy. Short years later, the first Ruger auto-loading pistol would prove him right.

William Batterman Ruger's first dive into the waters of free enterprise had him gasping for air in no time. The product–carpenters' tools–cost too much to make. Lesson: No matter how good the item, it must also be a bargain. Hard on the heels of World War II, the Ruger Corporation expired quicker than had Italy.

But in 1948, Bill Ruger got a boost. Alex Sturm, a graduate of the Yale Art School, had no interest in carpenters' tools. He did have $50,000 to invest, however. And he collected guns. Ever the opportunist, Bill was all too willing to take the small grubstake offered him for the manufacture of the .22 pistol he'd designed to

A more comely deer rifle than the Ruger Number One A is hard to find. This is a 7x57.

be manufactured from sheet steel. This gun must have generated some snickers from the cognoscenti, but at $37.50, it was substantially less expensive than its competition. Bill Ruger had managed to make his gun look good and shoot reliably, too. A 1949 review by NRA's technical staff (including Major Julian Hatcher, Ruger's mentor) helped promote the pistol. An avalanche of orders followed.

The quick rooting of Bill Ruger's new gun company was marred by the death of Alex Sturm. He was not yet 30. To commemorate his partner, Bill had the Ruger "red eagle" emblem (in fact, the likeness of a griffin) changed to black, although red emblems remained in some company literature.

Bill was not just a shooter; he studied guns. Their history and function, changes in metallurgy and marketing–all were interesting. Ruger had started collecting in his teens. Those first Luger and Colt pistols, Sharps and Springfield rifles whetted an appetite that remained. But knowing what came before did not satisfy Bill Ruger.

In 1952, he discarded plans for a tip-up revolver in favor of a solid-frame.22 patterned after Colt's famous Single Action Army revolver. Announced in 1953, this gun gathered a huge following. Like Ruger's auto-loader, it was affordable; but instead of sheet steel, it featured an investment-cast frame–a solid casting held to fine tolerances, and smooth finish by what is commonly called the "lost wax" process. This technique uses wax templates as cores for parts molds. Each part (the frame, in this case) is cast in a mold formed around a template, which has been melted out. The mold's interior is thus wax-smooth. Final machining is either eliminated or reduced, cutting production time, and expense.

The Ruger Single Six sustained a few early modifications, one of the most brilliant being the addition of an auxiliary cylinder in .22 Winchester Magnum Rimfire. More than 250,000 of these guns have been sold.

Bill Ruger was always quick to build on success, and in 1955 he brought to market a centerfire version of the Single Six. The Blackhawk revolver, initially chambered in .357 Magnum, would eventually be offered in .41 and .44 Magnum, .30 Carbine and .45 Long Colt. In 1959, the .44 Magnum Super Blackhawk appeared, with an unfluted cylinder and a square-backed trigger guard. These guns appealed to deer hunters keen to try a handgun on whitetails. That year, a trim single-action .22 revolver called the Bearcat also made headlines. It had a brass frame, fixed sights, and lightweight four-inch barrel. Eventually it was discontinued, along with the single-shot Hawkeye, which looked like a single-action revolver. The Hawkeye was chambered in .256 Winchester, a marginal round for big game and not as popular with varminters as Remington's .221 Fireball in the XP-100 pistol. Ruger later announced the Fireball as a Hawkeye chambering, but no guns were produced for that round.

In 1961, Ruger started building rifles, first with a .44 Magnum Carbine designed for the deer woods. The five-and-three-quarter-pound gas-operated auto-loader with an 18 1/2-inch barrel and factory-fitted peep sight certainly made sense for close-cover whitetail hunting, but in 1986 the company dropped it. As I recall, the first retail sticker on this delightful little gun was only $108.

But the Carbine's design didn't die. In 1964, Ruger announced a look-alike, the 10/22 rimfire rifle, with a clever 10-round rotary magazine that fit flush in the action

Long shots come often on the Texas gulf plains. Here a shooter steadies his Ruger Number One.

This left-handed shooter likes the straight, plain comb of his Ruger 77—and the tang safety!

well of the stock. This gun has now become one of the most popular .22 rifles ever. A cottage industry in custom accessories and services has grown up around the 10/22.

By 1968 Bill Ruger had become well known for his innovative thinking. All of his guns were truly fresh designs, with internal features that made each model better than its competition. In some cases there was no competition, because Bill Ruger wasn't afraid to try something nobody else would–like build a single-shot hunting rifle. The last centerfire of this type had been designed by John Browning when Teddy Roosevelt was in his twenties! The Ruger Number One, introduced in 1968 at a list price of $265, got a lukewarm reception.

Fashioned after the British Farquharson action, but trimmer, it had strength, good looks, a crisp trigger, and an ingenious quarter-rib that accepted Ruger's scope rings–no other mount base needed! But it lacked a bolt handle and a magazine, defining features of contemporary hunting rifles.

The Number One has since gained a loyal if limited following among hunters serious enough to make their first shot count. Available in six styles, in chamberings from .218 Bee to .458 Winchester, it has even generated competition, the true mark of success.

While some combinations of stock style and chambering have been discontinued, the Number One retains its most pleasing and useful forms. The "B" with 26-inch medium-weight barrel (no sights) and a forend of clean, conservative line offers

Ruger 77s come in myriad configurations. This deer hunter likes his rifles short and light.

the widest choice of cartridges. This eight-pound rifle remains a good choice for deer hunters who want to shoot long with powerful cartridges. The "S" version is similar but wears open sights and a barrel-band front swivel stud in front of an abbreviated "Alex Henry" forend. That forend style carries over to the "A," whose trimmer 22-inch barrel (also with sights and stud) makes it easier to carry and quicker to the shoulder. The most recent Number One of interest to deer hunters is the "International," a full-stocked rifle with sights on a 20-inch barrel. Varmint and Tropical (heavy-caliber) versions complete the line.

Bill Ruger introduced another single-shot rifle several years later. The Number Three carbine offered a more utilitarian look, with an action reminiscent of the Winchester 1885 High Wall. A straight grip and the curved steel butt and barrel band of the .44 Magnum Carbine complemented an uncheckered stock. There was no quarter-rib on the 22-inch barrel. Open sights included a leaf rear and a bead front. Chambered initially in .22 Hornet, .30-40 Krag, and .45-70, the six-pound Number Three was later offered in .223, plus .357 and .44 Magnum. A full-stock version appeared briefly. The rifle was retired in 1987, 15 years after its introduction.

Ruger brought out its bolt-action Model 77 in 1969, just a year after announcing the Number One. If a single-shot seemed a lonely venture, this bolt gun faced even greater risk in a field dominated by Winchester's Model 70 and Remington's 700. Sending a new rifle into the ring with these heavyweights, Bill

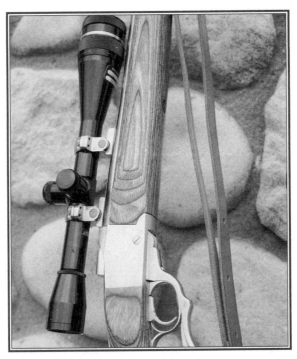

This Ruger Number One is equipped with a powerful Leupold AO scope designed for long shooting.

Ruger showed not only confidence in his product, but a willingness to gamble and a fine sense of timing.

The 77's investment-cast receiver kept costs down. Its conservative-style stock appeared at the height of a revolution against garish angular stock designs. Its great range of chamberings and sensible barrel choices gave it wide appeal. Integral Ruger bases and machined-steel rings provided with each rifle made scope-mounting a snap. A Mauser claw extractor helped both reliability and appearance–though it did not provide controlled-round feeding. In short order, Ruger's 77 muscled aside the giants for a slice of market share. An understudy rifle, the 77/22 rimfire, followed in 1983.

Ruger changed the Model 77 in 1989, replacing the sliding tang safety with a three-position side-swing tab. It also introduced controlled-round feeding and a fixed ejector. The trigger guard was reconfigured, and new versions with stainless steel and synthetic stocks began to appear. The 77 Mark II eventually fathered All-Weather, International, Magnum, Compact, and Ultra Light rifles in a variety of chamberings and with barrels of 16 1/2 to 26 inches in length. The Compact weighs just five-and-three-quarter pounds; the Ultra Light, six. You can get the standard 77 Mark II with open sights or a "clean" barrel. Receivers are forged with the integral base that accommodates Ruger scope rings. Recently, Ruger added to the 77 line with the 77/44, a bolt-action rendition of the original auto-loading Deerstalker. It weighs six pounds, with an 18 1/2-inch barrel, and feeds from a rotary magazine. Announced in 1997, it followed, by a year, a lever-action .44, the Model 96. It too features the spool that made the Deerstalker the talk of deer camps in the early 1960s.

Consistent with his pioneering bent, Bill Ruger followed up his original Model 77 with a cap-and-ball revolver. That was in 1983. Next came a 15-shot double-action autoloading pistol and an over-under shotgun with no visible action pins. His Mini-l4 carbine in .223 and 7.62x39 has become a popular self-loader, not only on the farm and ranch, but in police cars. The firm's double-action revolvers, which come in various frame sizes, have also been selected by law enforcement officers. And the DA .44 Magnum Redhawk is among the best-selling hunting handguns. The subsequent Super Redhawk, with extended frame and integral scope mounts, is even better. Since then (1987), Sturm-Ruger has expanded its line of firearms mainly by cataloging multiple variations of proven models..

"There's really only one gun company in America," Bill Ruger told me once during my visit to his New Hampshire facility years ago. He said it as if he were recommending chowder over sandwiches at a local cafe. No swagger: you want the straight scoop, don't you? Making guns, like making chowder, is something anybody can try, but it's easier to go broke making guns. Bill Ruger was not broke. During 53 years designing guns, he had helped invent and patent dozens of sporting rifles, pistols and shotguns.

Debt-free and with assets of over $100 million, Sturm, Ruger & Company remained for years in Southport, Connecticut, where Bill Ruger's first manufacturing enterprise struggled in 1946 and where the first guns were built. Now the corporate offices are in Prescott, Arizona. The Newport, New Hampshire, factory, currently the biggest Ruger plant, evolved from an investment casting operation called Pine Tree Casting. Most pistol frames and rifle receivers originate here, as do all but the longest revolver barrels, which come from the outside source that supplies Ruger rifle barrels. Shotgun barrels are forged in-house. Ruger button-rifles its long barrels, but short pistol barrels are broached.

The company operates its own wood shop next to the Pine Tree Casting plant, where it fashions rifle and shotgun stocks from American walnut. European walnut is standard on some guns. Ruger lists synthetic stocks for most models. These are supplied by outside vendors, as are revolver grips. Assembly is done in-house. Afterward, the guns are proofed on a range that also serves the company's armorer program, offered to police agencies. Four million bullets fly down Ruger's test tunnels each year!

When not involved in firearms design, Bill Ruger collected antique firearms, early Western American art and automobiles. His garages held more than 30 antique and modern vehicles, including Bentleys, Rolls-Royces, Bugattis, Stutzes, and a lovely 1913 Mercer Raceabout. In 1970, Ruger commissioned the design and construction of a sports tourer he dubbed the Ruger Special. It was based on a 1929 Bentley four-and-a-half-liter model.

Bill Ruger's philanthropy supported several charities and the Buffalo Bill Historical Center in Cody, Wyoming, where he served as a Trustee for 15 years. His son, William B. Ruger, runs the firearms business now (son James Thompson "Tom" Ruger and wife Mary Thompson Ruger died before Bill). The company has, to date, produced well over 20 million firearms for hunting, target shooting, self-defense, and tactical use. Deer hunters know it best for the practical, affordable rifles that began rolling off Ruger lines in the 1960s. Rifles that look and feel good enough to compete with the biggest names in deer guns. ■

4

MORE BOLT RIFLES
OF CONSEQUENCE

We gulped lukewarm oatmeal by flashlight, cinched our packs tight and marched silently up over a rocky plateau. The black rim of the basin cut clearly into the night sky. Dawn was yet two hours off.

On top, wind cut through the sweat and we huddled in the lee of a spruce while the eastern sky turned to steel, then rose. Then we split, Vern easing downslope into this untrafficked basin, while I still-hunted slowly enough to break even with him at the first rockslide.

Just beyond, with the sun now a strong promise, we began the still-hunt we'd shared for years. A rifleshot from ridgeline, I picked my way slowly, throttling my step. Vern, probing thickets of whitebark pine, would be on the deer first.

But he didn't see the pair of bucks that ghosted out in front of him. They stopped on talus to look back. In the 2 1/2x All American, they looked very far.

Sitting, with the sling taut, I nudged the quivering dot up on the big deer's scapula and crushed the trigger. The Model 70 jumped, and its crack echoed from the basin's headwall as the buck collapsed. Vern got busy with his .30-06 then, and the other deer died.

My .270 has been with me for decades now, in places like this basin that I want to show it again. It was my idea of a rifleman's rifle before Winchester came up with that name.

SAKO, SCANDINAVIA'S BRIGHTEST STAR

It's not "Sayko." Nor is it "Sacko." It's "Socko." At least, if you want to sound like you know what you're talking about when in Finland. It was there that Suojeluskuntain yliesikunnan asepaja was established the first day of April, 1919. Sako may be a big firm by local standards, but the factory is small compared to the competition's plants in the U.S. This is a rural area, where in the dark of cold mornings I jog a few easy miles along deserted streets. No skyscrapers in Riihimaki–though the Finns make good use of space and heating dollars with multi-story apartments. They're not high-rise; the tallest structure in town, it appears, is still a church steeple. Birches swing lazily with the wind in pools of yellow light cast by the street lamps. As the sky behind them turns from black to steel, old men and women sift onto the sidewalks. They are bundled in sweaters and greatcoats but obviously used to the weather and just as clearly bound for distant places. Some carry ski poles and walk with the long, pendulous stride of people who spend much of each year coursing snow.

It had been the same in Helsinki, the capital and as metropolitan a city as you'll find here. In the pre-dawn chill of its docks, I passed many people walking to work. Some slowed as the boats backed to the main thoroughfares, their owners setting out smoked fish. An elderly woman sat under a canvas awning, a cup of coffee between her hands. Raw, cold wind raked the awning and teased the woman's black shawl. I jogged toward a park. With a population of just over half a million, Helsinki would hardly qualify for big-city status in the U.S. Roughly 10 percent of the Finnish people live here, hard against the Gulf of Finland. Facing the dock, across the boardwalk, brick street and rails, loom federal buildings built—well, not that long ago. Finland didn't become an independent republic until 1919, two years after breaking with Russia.

Explored by Swedish missionaries as early as 1155, Finland remained a Swedish protectorate until 1809, when it was surrendered to Russia. The Czar proclaimed it a Grand Duchy. Many Swedes remained in-country, and Swedish is still taught in some schools. Of the roughly 91,000 foreigners now in Finland, many are Swedes. Oddly enough, the Finnish language (of the Finno-Ugric linguistic family) is closer to Hungarian than to Swedish. Sami, the tongue of Lapland, is also an official language. Lapland comprises the northern part of Finland and extends well above the Arctic Circle, where the sun doesn't set for 73 days each summer—and doesn't rise for 51 days each winter.

Nearly 80 percent of Finland is forested; forest products account for about 30 percent of exports. But as I was to find out shortly, there are lots of openings in the rolling woodlands—small farms that bring to mind the upper Midwest where so many Scandinavians have settled in the U.S. It's perfect whitetail habitat, but I didn't know that Finns shoot 17,500 of these animals annually. Where'd the deer come from? The U.S.! In 1934, six whitetails were imported from Minnesota. They escaped from an enclosure in 1938. A decade later, six more fawns arrived from the States; four survived and were released. By 1960, Finland had nearly 1,000 deer—enough for a hunting season. Their subsequent increase is due partly to the lack of predators. Wolves, which raided farms in the closing years of the 19th century and took dozens of children, were trapped and shot aggressively. They remain only in the wildest areas. You'll see foxes here, but no big cats. Bears are an occasional hazard to fawns. Feral dogs don't get much sympathy from Finnish hunt clubs that manage the game—though they use dogs to drive moose and often to move or trail deer on hunts.

Sako rifles evolved to serve an active hunting industry. Compared to that in the U.S., it is highly regulated, but no less tradition-bound. I was told that all big game is managed by 300 state-sanctioned hunting associations that currently comprise 2,370 clubs and 140,000 members. The country is divided into 15 game conservation districts administered by a Central Association of Hunters. You needn't be a club member or landowner to hunt, though membership has advantages. About 300,000 riflemen take to the woods each fall, more per capita than in any other

European country. Moose (or, traditionally in Finland, elk) are by far the most important economically. Moose hunters spend the most, and moose meat sold at market adds to the coffers. Of 10 million kilograms of game (roughly 22 million pounds) sold in the year 2000, a whopping 84 percent came from moose. Some places in Finland, moose trails snake through the woods like deer highways in our high-density whitetail coverts.

Given the local importance of big game, it might seem strange that the first rifle from Finland's best-known firearms manufacturer was built for small-game hunting. In fact, it was named after a fox.

By the end of the second world war, Sako had developed its "Vixen," a now-legendary bolt rifle scaled for small centerfire cartridges like the .22 Hornet and .218 Bee, which had appeared in the 1930s. It was subsequently offered in .222 (circa 1950) and the .222 Magnum and .223 (developed beginning in the late

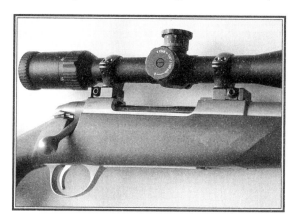

1950s). Stoeger brought the Vixen Sporter to the States in 1946. A heavy-barrel version and a full-stocked carbine with 20-inch barrel came along the next year. Production of these rifles followed a tough time in Finnish history. During the winter of 1939-1940, the Soviet Union attacked Finland. Brutal fighting ensued, in what has come to be known as the Winter War.

Sako's reputation for clean lines and fine workmanship shows in this Zeiss-scoped .300 Weatherby.

As Europe fell to the Nazis, Finland renewed its struggle against the Russian Bear in the Continuation War, which cost the smaller country some territory. But when the smoke cleared in 1944, Finland was still independent.

In 1955, Finland joined the United Nations, a year later the Nordic Council. By this time, Sako had committed to expanding its rifle line, and two years later announced the L-57 Forester. This action, built on the Mauser design but with refinements, was sized to accommodate the then-new .308 Winchester and its derivative, the .243. L-57s were also chambered in .22-250. Like the Vixen, the Forester came in Sporter, Carbine, and Heavy Barrel configurations. They became available to U.S. shooters in 1958.

Three years later, Sako came up with another, longer action. It looked like the Forester, but the L-61 Finnbear chambered the popular .30-06. You could also specify .25-06 or .270, the .264 Winchester or 7mm Remington Magnum, the .300 or .338 Winchester Magnum, even the .375 H&H. Catalogs listed no Heavy Barrel option, but did include a full-stocked carbine (20-inch barrel), as well as a standard version with 24-inch tube.

In 1961, Sako also came up with the Finnwolf, a hammerless lever-action rifle with a one-piece stock. Available in .243 and .308 with a four-shot detachable magazine, it looked a little like Winchester's 88 and lasted for about a decade. You'll search hard to find one now. A Model 73 followed the Finnwolf. Identical save for its flush three-round magazine and lack of a cheekpiece, this rifle sold only until 1975.

By this time Sako was eight years into new ownership and had designed a new rifle to replace the Vixen, Forester, and Finnbear. The Model 74 maintained separate action lengths for three main classes of cartridges. Produced from 1974 until 1978, it was succeeded by the A1 series (the A11 and A111 were the medium- and long-action models). In the mid-1980s, Sako replaced it with the Hunter, again in three action lengths. A left-hand version appeared in 1987. By the time the company's current TRG rifle came along in 1993, only Sako collectors could tell you all the minor differences that distinguished the various series of rifles that had evolved from the lovely Vixen. Along the way, Sako built a Model 78 rimfire, a classy box-fed bolt-action sporter cataloged from 1977 to 1987. You could also buy this model in .22 Hornet.

Early Sakos were characterized by hand-checkered walnut stocks that, from the late 1950s, wore a glossy finish. It seems to me a few early stocks came from Finnish birch, common on other, less expensive rifles. Metal finish was uniformly excellent, the resulting blue gleaming but not glittery. Wood-to-metal fit as well showed great care. Never inexpensive, Sako rifles earned a reputation for fine accuracy and caught the fancy of riflemen who wanted something a cut above ordinary Remington and Winchester rifles. Crisp, adjustable triggers, and buttery bolt operation helped sell the Sakos. Dovetail receiver rails that required the purchase of costly Sako rings worked fine but may not have added market share. The extractor, an external claw much smaller than the 98 Mauser's, apparently matched its reliability if not its strength.

Smooth cycling makes Sako the choice of this Scout-rifle shooter, here reloading at a speed-shooting event at Arizona's Gunsite Academy.

In 1997, Sako's current flagship, the Model 75, appeared in four action lengths, to accommodate a broad spectrum of cartridges from the .17 Remington to the .416 Remington. Its three locking lugs are a departure from the early sporters, offering a 70-degree bolt lift. The right-side two-position safety has the traditional look, so, too, the steel bottom metal, and the barrels are still hammer-forged–though by a new, more fully automated process. Sako's catalog points out that there's .02 inch-clearance between the barrel and forend channel. Perhaps the most striking feature of the 75 is its bolt shroud. It incorporates a lock you can manipulate with a supplied key to render the rifle inoperable. I don't like this, but then, neither do I like heavy triggers, crossbolt safeties on lever guns or any other device that diminishes the utility of a rifle in the name of safety. Rifles difficult to cycle quickly or shoot accurately are like dull axes.

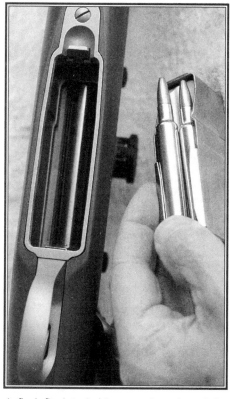

A flush-fit detachable magazine gives Sako rifles a clean profile; and unloading is a snap.

Enough said on that.

The Sako 75 comes in several versions: The Hunter, Hunter Stainless, and Deluxe feature walnut stocks and 22-, 24-, and 26-inch barrels. The Finnlight, with 20- or 22-inch fluted barrel, and the Synthetic Stainless are both stainless, synthetic-stocked models. There's a walnut-stocked Battue, with quarter-rib and 19-inch barrel. And Varmint and Varmint Stainless configurations with 24- and 26-inch barrels. The 75 comes in 18 chamberings, including the .17 Remington and .22 and 6mm PPC. You can order it in .340 Weatherby and .338 Lapua, and if your tastes run Continental, in 6.5x55, 7x64, and 9.3x62.

Sako's other centerfire is the TRG. Most renditions are for target and tactical shooters, but there's a TRG-S in .338 Lapua or .30-378 Weatherby. The three-lug action differs from the 75's and includes a detachable box magazine, straight stack. Like the 75, the TRGs feature integral top rails on the receiver. These dovetail cuts, angled 3.7 degrees, secure Sako's Optilock mounts under the force of recoil. There's a center cut in the rear bridge, a stop that accepts a pin in the mount base. The Optilock base clamps to the receiver with a right-hand clamp. Scope rings feature rotating polymer inserts to guarantee perfect ring alignment with the scope's axis. Available in three heights and two diameters (one inch and 30mm), the rings are also supplied with quick-detach bases and thumb levers.

Though Sako's line of shooting irons is limited by U.S. standards, the company is more diversified than it appears. The Sako Finnfire, cataloged in Hunter, Varmint, and Sporter versions, is Finland's premier .22 rimfire, stocked in walnut. In 1983, Sako conspired with another Finnish firm, Tikka, in a joint effort to produce the Model 555 rifle, seldom talked about now. At that time, Tikka was older than Sako, having manufactured gun parts for 80 years. During the second World War, it had built sewing machines and sub-machine guns. By 1970, it had abandoned its own brand of sewing machines to concentrate on the Tikka Models 55 and 65 rifles and 17 shotgun. The 77 shotgun followed.

During the 1980s, Sako acquired Tikka, along with the shotgun manufacturer, Valmet, established in 1925. Valmet had auto-loading mechanisms in its past, but the strength of the union came from its over/under smoothbores. By 1989, all Tikka production at its Tikkakoski Works had been moved to Sako's Riihimaki plant. Tikka's Whitetail rifle was well built but poorly publicized in the U.S. Its successor, the T3 has received much more attention here. It is built in the Sako plant, using components of the same quality as are used in Sako rifles. Tikka barrels come from the same bin and must meet identical specs. Yet the T3's list price is much lower.

Finland's premier rifle-maker, Sako at the Riihimaki facility also produces Tikka rifles.

I shot this Austrian roebuck with a Sako short-action rifle in .308 Winchester.

Since I was old enough to keep my fingers off their finely polished steel, I've held and coveted quite a few Sakos. I've shot a few but owned only one. It's a little embarrassing to admit that, because these rifles are commonly acknowledged as the best bolt rifles east of Cape Cod. But while they've been imported steadily through Stoeger, they've not been as common in the U.S. as our own domestic rifles. Some Sakos, in fact, have stayed pretty much within commuting distance of the Riihimaki plant. Take those in 9.3x66, a proprietary cartridge I saw for the first time on a visit to Sako's plant. It's a powerful number, on the order of the .338 Winchester Magnum, a 9.3-bore cartridge a tad longer than the 9.3x64 but with a .30-06-size case rim. It won't come Stateside.

"We're marketing Sako rifles more aggressively to U.S. hunters now," said Paavo Tammisto, who handles press relations for Sako. "Since Beretta bought the company in 2000, we've benefited from their selling style and muscle. But the rifles will continue to be made the same way, right here in Riihimaki, to our highest standards."

ROY WEATHERBY: MAGNUM MAN

During the late 1940s and 1950s, post-war prosperity plowed returning GIs back into civilian life. Many popped up again soon as entrepreneurs, new industries fertilizing their ambitions. California called some away from more pedestrian places. Whatever you had to sell, there was a market in the Golden State. Roy Weatherby no doubt considered that when he began selling rifles and ammunition. But he went a step further. He packaged an image, and his ability to peddle that image to people with disgusting amounts of money brought success to a fledgling company. It would become, in time, the sequined gun company, one that courted favor with Hollywood and flourished in a period that redefined American culture and big game hunting.

Roy Weatherby belonged in the California that produced Tinseltown. The quintessential promoter, he placed himself in photos with actors like Roy Rogers, world-traveled hunters like Elgin Gates, even foreign dignitaries like the Shah of Iran. He shared the lens with Elmer Keith and Jack O'Connor, with Jimmy Doolittle, Joe Foss, and Robert L. Scott. He parlayed his associations into business because he believed what he preached: Weatherby rifles can bring you extraordinary hunting success. He reminded customers that owning a Weatherby is joining elite company. The subliminal message: Weatherby helps you become more than you are.

Roy certainly became more than his boyhood promised. Born in 1910 to a sharecropper in central Kansas, Roy knew poverty. He and his nine brothers and sisters moved a lot. There was no automobile, no electrical service or indoor plumbing at the George Weatherby house. Roy recalled walking behind an old plow-horse, watching a neighbor pull five bottoms three times as fast with a Fordson tractor.

In 1923, George opened a one-pump filling station in Salinas. Then there was the move to Florida, "nine of us in a four-passenger Dodge, camping in a tent along the way." George laid bricks while Roy hauled mortar. Growing up, Roy would clerk in a music store, sell washing machines, and drive a bread truck. He later enrolled at the University of Wichita, where he met Camilla Jackson. They married in 1936, and Roy got work at Southwestern Bell Telephone. Not long thereafter the couple headed west, winding up in San Diego. Employed by a local utility, then the Automobile Club of Southern California, Roy was soon making very good money: $200 a month.

Since his boyhood days trapping possums, Roy had indulged an interest in the outdoors. He liked to hunt, and he liked to experiment with guns. Working in his home shop with rudimentary equipment, he reshaped the .300 Holland and Holland case to increase its capacity. He reduced body taper and gave it a "double-radius" shoulder. The full-length version became the .300 Weatherby, but his first magnums were necked to .257, .277, and .284 and shortened for .30-06-length magazines. In 1946, he pledged "everything I owned" to get a $5,000 business loan from the Bank of America. It was a start. But for the first couple of decades, Roy Weatherby's custom-rifle enterprise teetered. With bankruptcy a constant threat, Roy pushed ahead.

One day, behind the counter at his small retail store, he watched Gary Cooper walk in the door. It was a pivotal moment. Soon Roy was meeting other Hollywood stars. He wrote an article, "Overgunned and Undergunned" for a magazine; Sheldon Coleman saw it and became a customer.

By 1949, Roy's hard work had produced a larger shop and store, but he needed more capital to put the company on the next rung. Business partner Bill Wittman agreed to incorporation, and in May the two men offered $70,000 in stock. One of the company officers was Herb Klein, a wealthy Texas oilman who owned a .270 Weatherby Magnum rifle. Herb bought $10,000 of that stock. He would later become a key source of business acumen and additional capital. (The early growth of Weatherby's company is chronicled in a book, *Weatherby: The Man. The Gun. The Legend,* by Grits and Tom Gresham,

Beginning in the 1940s, Roy Weatherby promoted his rifles and cartridges by stressing their reach.

Cane River Publishing.) The company would remain true to Roy's vision. Now, under the leadership of Roy's only son, Ed, it has also shown itself nimble, adapting to market changes and bringing a stream of new products to shooters.

Roy built his first rifles on Mauser actions. In 1957, he and company engineer

Fred Jennie came up with an action of their own: the Mark V. They engaged Germany's J.P. Sauer & Sohn to produce it. Since then, this mechanism with its low-lift, inter-rupted-tread, lug-diameter bolt has remained essentially as Roy and Fred fashioned it. In 1971, rifle manufac-ture moved to Japan, then came Stateside in the 1990s. Now all Weatherby rifles are built in the U.S.

During the 1990s, a six-lug Mark V appeared. This scaled-down action weighs 26 ounces–10 ounces or 28 percent less than the Mark V Magnum. Teamed with slim, fluted barrels, this receiver better fitted .30-06-size cartridges and enabled Weatherby to build rifles as light as five-and-three-quarter pounds. It became the nucleus of several hunt-ing models, and heavy-barreled

Weatherby's Mark V (left) and the Remington 700 both accommodate long cartridges.

varminters for traditional short-action rounds. In developing the Ultra Light rifle, Weatherby did not chop the barrel to pare ounces. That ploy would have reduced bullet velocity and impaired rifle balance. Barrels for Weatherby Magnum rounds have remained at 26 inches, but those for standard cartridges and the 7mm Remington and .300 Winchester Magnum measure 24. A deer hunter who doesn't want the power of a full-length .300 Weatherby Magnum cartridge certainly won't want to carry the heavy original rifle up a mountain or prowl the woods with some-thing so cumbersome. The six-lug Mark V with a lightweight barrel makes more sense.

One of my all-time favorite rifles is the .338-06 Ultra Lightweight. It weighs an even six pounds with 24-inch barrel, a few ounces more than its Ultra Lightweight siblings. That's because the Kreiger barrel is of slightly greater diam-eter to leave enough metal at the base of the flutes around a .33 bore. To me, this rifle seems ideally balanced. The efficiency and versatility of the .338-06 has appealed to me since I first read of its forebear: the .333 OKH, developed in the early 1940s for Jeffery bullets. My friend Larry Barnett at Superior Ammunition in Sturgis, South Dakota, provided the first .338-06 A-Square ammo fired in this Weatherby, with 210-grain Nosler Partition and 225-grain Swift A-Frame bullets. Norma, which manufactured cartridge cases for Weatherby beginning in 1953, now loads .338-06 ammo with the rest of Weatherby's line.

Larry's Noslers clock 2,765 fps. That's only 65 fps shy of chart values for these bullets in the .338 Winchester Magnum as factory loaded! With nearly 3,600 foot-pounds of thrust at the muzzle, the .338-06 Superior loads hit harder than any 180-grain bullet from the .300 Winchester Magnum! A 200-yard zero puts the Partitions eight inches low at 300, 24 inches low at 400. Deer hunters who might also hunt elk and moose with the same rifle owe themselves a few shots with a Weatherby in .338-06. The 225-grain Swift bullets leave the muzzle of my .338-06 at 2,685 fps. For tough game, this bullet excels.

Like other Weatherbys, the Ultra Light wears a high-backed comb that reduces cheek slap. Even with heavy loads, it is not unpleasant. The Weatherby one-and-a-half-inch guarantee means less to me than a rifle's "pointability" and its field accuracy from hunting positions. Still, barrels that deliver tight groups inspire confidence. Button-rifled Criterion barrels from John Krieger's shop are cryogenically treated in-house. That is, barrel temperature is lowered to -300 degrees F to relieve stresses bound in the steel by manufacturing operations. At the Brainerd MN Acrometal plant that assembles Weatherby's rifles, I once examined targets from then-new Super VarmintMaster rifles. The hand-lapped barrels kept some clusters to less than .six inch.

Not long ago as this is written, Weatherby introduced a Special Varmint Rifle. The plain-vanilla seven-and-a-quarter-pound rifle wore a 22-inch barrel in .223 and .22-250. Initially priced at $999, it cost considerably less than the Super VarmintMaster. The SVM was followed by the Super PredatorMaster, a six-and-a-quarter-pound rifle for the "walking" varmint hunter. PredatorMasters sold better than expected in .243, 7mm-08, and .308. Weatherby's Marketing VP, Brad Ruddell, decided that the buyers weren't all shooting 'chucks and coyotes. "Hunters thought it was an ideal deer gun."

Weatherby quickly developed a lightweight big-game rifle patterned on the PredatorMaster. A year later, it announced the Super Big GameMaster. Built on both the six- and nine-lug actions, this rifle weighs five-and-three-quarter to six-and-three-quarter pounds. Barrels are stainless and hand-lapped, with six flutes and an 11-degree crown. The adjustable trigger is factory-set at four pounds, with .012 to .015 sear engagement. Like its predecessor, the SBGM wears a "laid" stock of Aramid, graphite and fiberglass. Its aluminum bedding block ensures precise recoil lug seating and stiffens the magazine mortise.

Super-accurate Weatherby rifles are now so designated. Deer hunters who shoot long take note!

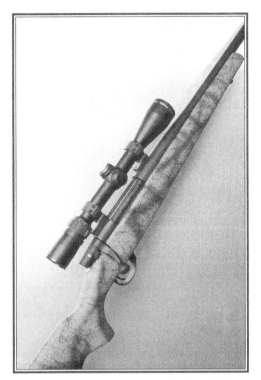

The Weatherby Vanguard, a mid-priced rifle on the Howa action, is also chambered for short magnums.

Magazine capacity for the SBGM: five in .240 Wby., .25-06, .270 Win., .280, .30-06, .338-06. Capacity is three for magnums: .257 Wby., .270 Wby., 7mm Wby., 7mm Rem., .300 Win., and .300 Wby. In many ways, the SBGM is the modern version of Weatherby's original Mark V rifle, stocked in figured Claro walnut and listing, in 1964, for $285. The SBGM retails for $1,561 (standard calibers) and $1,623 (magnums).

Weatherby's Custom Shop has become more flexible, offering not only "California style" stocks, but also more conservative handles. Despite the steep pitch of the Mark V tang, Weatherby gunmakers have managed to make the grip long and attractive. They also build guns for dangerous game, chambered for the likes of the .458 Lott, as well as for Weatherby's own hard-hitting .378, .416, and .460.

The Vanguard, once the "entry level" Weatherby, reappeared in the line late in 2003. Built on the Japanese Howa action, it is an affordable alternative to the Mark V. A Butler Creek injection-molded stock helps keep retail of the least expensive rendition at $476 ($595 for the stainless version). The Vanguard is offered in 11 chamberings, from .223 to .338 Winchester Magnum. The Howa action has been used for a number of U.S.-produced sporting rifles. It's a bit heavy (though not in comparison with the magnum Mark V!). The trigger is a good one. I've used this stout, smooth-cycling mechanism on both deer and elk hunts.

Weatherby has been in the shotgun business for years. Best-known are its boxlock over/unders. The Athena and Orion come in 12, 20, and 28 gauges. A modified Greener crossbolt with automatic ejectors and single selective trigger complement back-bored barrels with long forcing cones and interchangeable chokes. A Prince-of-Wales grip and trim lines bring these guns quickly on target.

Deer hunters in slug country have more truck with the Weatherby SAS, a revamped SKB. Its self-compensating gas system lets you interchange target and hunting loads. Field guns with walnut stocks, and specialty guns wearing camo, are a step up from the $649 SAS with black synthetic stock. At seven-and-a-quarter pounds, these auto-loaders are not lightweights, but they seem nimble in the hand, and they point where I look. The weight and gas system soak up recoil from heavy

Weatherby rifles are popular among deer hunters in the West, where flat-shooting bullets rule.

loads–a real blessing on the SAS slug gun. Its 22-inch rifled barrel wears a cantilever scope mount. While earlier SAS shotguns came from Japan, the new models come from Italy and include shims that let you change stock dimensions that most affect fit: cast and drop.

WINCHESTER AND THE RIFLEMAN'S RIFLE

By 1890, gun design in the United States had eclipsed the development of cartridges. Black powder was essentially the same mixture the Chinese had used in the 14th century. Developments in Europe, however, would soon make it obsolete. Following the work of the Swiss chemist Schoenbein and the Italian Sobero, who discovered nitrocellulose and nitroglycerin, Vielle, a Frenchman, found in 1885 that dissolving nitrocellulose in ether produced a stable colloid that could be dried and used as propellant. The compound became single-base smokeless powder. Alfred Nobel and Frederick Able later added nitroglycerine to get double-base smokeless.

Winchester didn't catalog smokeless ammunition until 1893, when it advertised shotshells with new "nitro" propellant. Within a year, the company was offering 17 smokeless centerfire cartridges. Ammunition fueled much of Winchester's growth in the early days of the automobile. By 1914, the company was loading 175 smokeless cartridges. Though it marketed to hand-loaders, Winchester called the hand-loading of smokeless cartridges "impractical."

Between the advent of smokeless powder and the start of World War I, Winchester developed some of its most famous guns: the Model 1890 .22 rimfire pump rifle and Model 1897 pump shotgun, its models 1892 and 1894 lever-action rifles. The Model 1903 auto-loading .22 was the first successful self-loader produced in quantity in the United States. The Model 12 pump shotgun became one of the most popular smoothbores ever.

Winchester pioneered the use of nickel steel barrels in the Model 94, perhaps the most popular whitetail rifle in the past century. The 92, chambered for shorter, less potent rounds like the .44-40, was advertised it as "the rifle that helped Peary reach the North Pole."

The 20th century brought new men to Winchester. Thomas Bennett's split with John Browning was a blow, but in Thomas Crossly Johnson the company found another gifted gun designer. Johnson specialized in auto-loading mechanisms, developing the recoil-operated Winchester Self-Loading Rifles, Models 03, 05, 07, and 10. Johnson engineered Winchester's first auto-loading shotgun, a recoil operated, hammerless, five-shot repeater designated the Model 11. He had to work around the Browning patents–which he had helped write!

During the first World War, Winchester supplied more than 50,000 Browning Automatic Rifles, plus thousands of short-barreled Model 97 shotguns for trench fighting. Each shell had six 34-caliber pellets. They proved so devastating that the German government protested, warning that any American carrying a shotgun when captured would be shot. Other contracts called for 44 million .303 British cartridges and 400,000 Enfield rifles for the British government, plus nine million .44 WCF rounds for the British Home Guard's Winchester 92 rifles and 50 million .22

Long Rifle cartridges, also for England. Winchester's plant had doubled in size, to three-and-one-quarter-million square feet. During hostilities, 17,549 people worked there. But long-term military contracts didn't cover steeply-rising labor costs. At war's end, with demand on a slide, these oversights crippled Winchester.

In 1920, Thomas Bennett and other patriarchs reorganized the firm. The Winchester Repeating Arms Company made guns and ammunition, while its sister firm, the Winchester Company, manufactured cutlery, gas refrigerators, skates, flashlights, fishing gear, hand tools, washing machines, baseball bats, skis, batteries, paints, and household brushes. This diversification failed to reduce debt; ironically, the gun division prospered.

For some time after armistice, Winchester gun designers had almost no budget. Still, they came up with two fine rifles: the Model 52 bolt-action rimfire in 1919 and the Model 54 centerfire in 1924. The 54 was Winchester's first successful bolt-action centerfire rifle, though the company had tried to enter that field for 30 years. The .45-70 Hotchkiss was discontinued in 1900; the Lee Straight Pull, lasted from 1897 to 1903. Engineers working on the Model 54 borrowed the 1903 Springfield's coned breech. The ejector was of Newton design. The Mauser-style bolt cocked on opening and wore a beefy extractor and safety. The stock was patterned after the popular Sedgely sporters of that period. A nickel-steel barrel on a cyanide-hardened receiver bottled pressures from the new .270 WCF cartridge, whose 130-grain bullet at 3,000 fps awed hunters used to .30-30s. The 54 cost more than a surplus military rifle, but much less than a Sedgley or Griffin & Howe sporter. Though it never earned the accolades given the earlier Model 94 or the Model 70, Winchester's M54 appeared at a pivotal time. The

This three-position side-swing safety is a Model 70 hallmark. Several makers have adopted it. This rifle is a Kimber.

Springfield had introduced shooters to the potential of bolt rifles and powerful cartridges. The 54 was delightfully nimble, and the .270 shot flatter than anything most deer hunters had ever seen.

When the Depression hit, Winchester was too weak to stand. In February 1929, the old organization was dissolved and The Winchester Repeating Arms Company of Delaware took its place. The company went bankrupt January 22, 1931, the year the Model 21 shotgun would come to market. In December, Winchester was acquired by the Western Cartridge Company. Western assumed the Winchester Company for $3 million cash and $4.8 million (par value) of Western stock. The company entered the Depression under Franklin Olin's son, John, who had a keen interest in firearms. In the next decade, 23 new Winchester guns would appear.

The decision to replace the Model 54 with another rifle was prompted largely by a desire for a better centerfire target rifle. Since its introduction in 1919, the Model 52 rimfire had steadily built an unassailable record on small-bore ranges, and Winchester wanted centerfire laurels to

A "stainless synthetic," this rifle in 7mm WSM is unmistakably a Model 70.

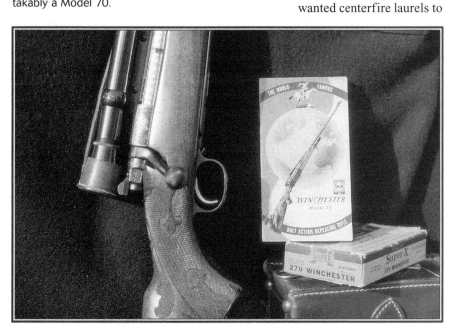

This early Model 70 is one of the most ornate ever produced by the Winchester Custom Shop.

match. Western had kept the 54 alive, allowing T. C. Johnson and his staff to refine the rifle they had engineered. Ten configurations came about, with 10 chamberings. Prices (in 1936) ranged from $59.75 for the basic Model 54 to $111.00 for a Sniper's Match.

The Model 54's main weakness was its trigger. Fashioned after military triggers of the day, it also served as a bolt stop. Competitive shooters grumbled. Hunters content to fight a mushy trigger balked at the high-swing safety, which precluded low scope mounting. Bill Weaver's affordable Model 330 scope had shown shooters what optical sights could do, and rifles that wouldn't accommodate them had a dim future.

The Model 54 was cataloged and available through 1941, but production became a trickle during the last five years. Beginning December 29, 1934, Winchester started work on a stronger, better-looking rifle–the Model 70. It came to market slowly. The 54 was still viable, and changes were given close scrutiny. Also, lots of men were still eating in soup kitchens; there was no screaming demand for a new hunting rifle. On January 20, 1936, the first M70 receivers got serial numbers. On the official release date (January 1, 1937), 2,238 rifles were awaiting shipment.

The 70's barrel and receiver looked a lot like the Model 54's. But the trigger was much better, a separate sear allowing for adjustment in take-up, weight, and overtravel. The bolt stop was also separate. To eliminate misfires–too common with the 54's speed lock–striker travel on the Model 70 was increased 1/16 inch. The first Model 70 safety was a tab on top of the bolt shroud. It swung horizontally; four years later it would be redesigned as a side-swing tab, a middle detent blocking the striker while permitting bolt manipulation. Like the Model 54, the Model 70 had three guard screws, but instead of a stamped, fixed magazine cover and guard, the 70 wore a hinged floorplate secured by a spring-loaded plunger in the separate trigger guard. A low bolt handle acted as a safety lug. The square bolt shoulder precluded low scope mounting and was later eliminated.

Model 70 barrels (with the same contours and threads as Model 54 barrels) were drop-forged, straightened by hand with a 15-pound hammer, then turned true on a lathe. They were deep-hole-drilled, then straightened again. Next, each bore was reamed to proper diameter and hook-rifled by a cutter slicing progressively deeper on several passes, one groove at a time. Rifling took roughly 11 minutes per barrel. After lapping, barrels were threaded and slotted for rear sights and front sight hoods. Forged, hand-stippled ramps appeared on the first 70s; later ramps were soldered on and machine-matted. Just before chambering, each barrel was inspected, then stamped underneath with caliber designation, and the last two digits of the year of manufacture. The last of four chambering reamers left the chamber undersize for headspacing. The barrel then was roll-marked, given a caliber stamping, polished, and blued. Barrel material had evolved by several stages in 1936. In 1925, stainless steel had appeared; in 1932, chrome-molybdenum.

Model 70 receivers were machined from solid bar stock, each beginning as a seven-and-a-half-pound chrome-moly billet. After 75 machinings, a finished receiver weighed 19.3 ounces. It was 8.77 inches long, 1.357 inches through the receiver ring. Spot-hardening the extraction cam behind the bridge preceded a full heat treatment. Next, each was immersed in a 1,200-degree salt bath for 24 hours. Hardness after cooling: 47C. The test left a dimple in the tang. Most small parts were drop-forged, then machined. The extractor was fashioned from 1095 spring steel.

The Model 70's stock was more substantial than the 54's, though similar in appearance to the late Model 54 version. Standard stocks were roughed by bandsaw from 2x36-inch American black walnut. After center-punching, they went eight at a time to the duplicator for contouring. Final inletting was done by hand. After buttplate fitting, the stock was drum-sanded, then hand-sanded. Minor flaws were repaired with stick shellac, glue or a matching wood match. The first stocks got a clear nitrocellulose lacquer finish over an alcohol-based stain. Because these lacquers contained carnauba wax, they produced a soft, oil-like finish. After the war, when carnauba wax became scarce, harder lacquers appeared. Hand checkering with carbide-tipped cutters followed.

Headspacing came first in assembly, then the matching of bolt parts, trigger, and sear honing and a function check. The Winchester Proof (WP) stamp signified firing of one "blue pill" cartridge (70,000 psi). After its serial number was etched on the bolt, each rifle was zeroed at 50 yards. List price in 1937: $61.25. Early Model 70s were offered in .22 Hornet, .220 Swift, .250-3000 Savage, .257 Roberts, .270 WCF, 7mm Mauser, and .30-06–plus .300 and .375 H&H Magnums. Between 1941 and 1963 nine more chamberings were added; however,

A deer hunter shoulders his Featherweight, a Model 70 variation that first appeared in 1952.

the .300 Savage was never cataloged. The rest of the stable of Model 70 cartridges (all from Winchester) appeared in the 1950s and early 1960s: the .243, .264 Magnum, .308, .300 Magnum, .338 Magnum, .358, and .458 Magnum. Eventually, "pre-64" Model 70s would come in 29 basic styles and 48 sub-configurations–not including special orders. Deer hunters kept sales of standard-weight .30-06 and .270 rifles at the top of the charts. The first rifles retailed for $61.25.

So successful it earned the title of "the rifleman's rifle," Winchester's Model 70 became less and less profitable as labor costs escalated. In 1960, company accountants urged reducing production costs. Two years later, engineers had identified 50 changes; these were implemented in 1963. The most visible drew public outrage. The stock wore crude, pressed checkering and a barrel that "floated" in its channel between gaps wide enough to swallow Tootsie Rolls. The recessed bolt face had a tiny hook extractor instead of the beefy Mauser claw. Machined-steel bottom metal was supplanted by aluminum, solid-action pins by roll-pins, and the bolt stop's coil spring by music-wire. A red-painted cocking indicator stuck out like a tongue from under the bolt shroud, arrogance on insult. The overall effect was depressing. Prices of pre-64 Model 70s shot through the ceiling; new rifles languished on dealer racks.

Winchester improved the "new Model 70" with an antibind device for the bolt in 1966, a classier stock in 1972, a Featherweight rifle that looked and handled much better in 1980. A short-action Model 70 arrived in 1984. Three years later, Winchester reintroduced the Mauser claw extractor on custom-shop 70s, and three years after that, a "Classic" version with controlled-round feed entered the catalog line. Current Model 70s, while lacking the handwork of the originals, are accurate, attractive, and thoroughly dependable.

Winchester's accountants still ponder profits, but they've apparently learned that no matter how much money you save in manufacture, you don't make any if rifles don't sell. New Haven's 1964 changes gave Remington, with its new Model 700 rifle and 7mm Magnum cartridge, a big break.

In 1936, the M1 Garand rifle became the main infantry weapon for U.S. armed forces. The first Winchester-built Garands were delivered a year before Pearl Harbor. In 1940, Winchester also developed a lightweight carbine. In preliminary work, company designer David "Carbine" Williams used a new short-stroke piston to operate the action, later scaled down to accept the .30 Carbine cartridge.

The second World War fueled huge production jumps at Winchester-Western. Total wartime output: 1.45 million guns and more than 15 billion rounds of ammunition. After the war, John Olin's ammunition firm concentrated on the development of sporting ammunition. Ball powders came in 1946, Baby Magnum shotshells in 1954, the .22 Winchester Magnum Rimfire round in 1959, a compression-formed shotshell in 1964.

In August 1954, Olin was swallowed by the huge Mattheson Chemical

I shot this Washington whitetail with an early Winchester 70 in .270.

Corporation. Ten years later, Winchester guns were redesigned to take advantage of cheaper materials and manufacturing processes. Sound on paper, the change triggered a colossal revolt in the marketplace. Pre-64 Winchesters suddenly commanded premiums on the used-gun market. The company scrambled to correct its blunder. In relatively short order it was offering guns with the traditional features shooters wanted, but without the hand finishing that had become prohibitively expensive. When Olin-Mattheson sold the Winchester Sporting Arms business in July 1981, the new company, U.S. Repeating Arms, continued improving its products, contracting some shotguns from Japan.

In 1984, USRAC filed for Chapter 11 bankruptcy. In 1987, five investors bought the company. Among them was Fabrique Nationale (FN), a Belgian firm that also owned Browning. FN is itself owned by Societe Generale, which controls 70 percent of Belgium's GNP. Early in 1991, a French conglomerate bought FN and, with it, USRAC. These days, you'll likely hear "Use-rack" in talk about guns of New Haven lineage. They're still Winchesters to shooters who value history. ∎

5

LIGHTWEIGHT DEER RIFLES

The buck had been nibbling forbs on the rockslide we called The Glacier. North exposure at 8,000 feet kept snow on the little bowls above the slide all summer. The melt sent trickles of water between the rocks, irrigating small alpine plants that stayed tender and nutritious when mid-elevation shrubs and grasses were dry. You couldn't see the green, but deer did. And we'd shot several bucks off The Glacier.

This deer had finished eating and struck off on a trail that snaked around a steep bowl beyond the slide. I wouldn't catch him, so I slinged up, sat, and leveled the Ruger Number 1A at the buck, now quartering away. The reticle hung well above his hip when I fired, but the bullet struck low. I fumbled for another cartridge and shoved it home. The "thwuck" of a hit came back as the deer scrambled, favoring a hindquarter. He was out of range quickly–maybe had been all along. I watched him crest the next ridge and vanish. Then I followed, quickly.

The basin beyond was rocky and steep, rimmed by a cliff laced at its base by deer trails. I played a hunch and walked briskly across the top of a talus apron above a boulder field, within rifle-shot of the cliff.

Suddenly, the crippled buck squirted from a fissure in the headwall, darting between boulders. The little 7x57 came up like a shotgun, swung itself to the only visible gap in the rocks and fired. My bullet met the buck's rib as he scooted through the opening. He somersaulted down the face, dead.

Such is the magic of a carbine. Quick as a glance and lethal in the clutch.

THE CHARISMATIC CARBINE

If mobility is a signal aspect of life, a carbine is indeed lively. The name itself derives from the French "carabin" for "mounted rifleman." Carbines are to rifles what race cars are to sedans: a responsive, quick-wheeling departure from ordinary. With carbines, hunters travel faster. Easy on the carry, lightning-fast to point, and eager on follow-ups, carbines take years off my age. I'm quick, confident, even dashing, like hard-riding cavalrymen of legend. At least, that's what I like to think.

A carbine has the same allure as a sports car to those of us reluctantly plodding through middle age. We've lost reflexes and the taut profiles of youth. In the sleek, fast, powerful roadster, we show other people what we'd like them to think about us. Ditto for the carbine. Would you rather ride in memory at the wheel of a Porsche or on a Massey-Ferguson? Fancy yourself a soldier now: Are you the

Taut and muscular, this Marlin looks the part of the quintessential carbine.

horseman at full gallop, deftly levering bullets from a carbine, or an artilleryman holding his ears while a sedentary gun heaves projectiles the size of oil drums? You may collect your venison from the far edges of crop fields with a heavy-barreled 7mm magnum, but if you never think about taking a whitetail's track through the alders with an iron-sighted carbine in hand, you've missed some of hunting's romance–and roots!

Image has a lot to do with what we buy, and I'll confess to falling in love, again, with carbines. The first time, nearly 40 years ago, carbines fascinated me because they were what real hunters used in the woods. The Winchester 94, of course. And the Marlin .336 and Savage 99H. The short-barreled versions of Remington's 742 auto-loader and 760 pump. We talked of rifles, but we envisioned carbines. On black-and-white television westerns, cowboys didn't yank long-barreled bolt rifles from their saddle boots. They drew carbines–and almost as quickly as they flicked single-action Colts from their bullet-studded belts. In the northern Michigan woods, carbines made more sense than rifles. "Quick enough to catch a whitetail buck," nodded one plaid-clad veteran, cradling his Savage on a stump one gray November noon. I couldn't tell if he was talking about himself or the short-barreled .303; I'm sure now he'd meant to blur any distinction.

Winchester's 94 was beefed up at the rear to handle the .307 and .356 Winchester rounds.

The hunter's quest for more bullet speed and power, and the use of scope sights to extend reach, began after World War II. Roy Weatherby marked the starting line, with his new magnum cartridges in the early 1940s. Winchester and Remington followed with their magnums in the 1950s and 1960s. Since then, companies designing rifles and ammunition have tripped over each other in a race to add foot-pounds and straighten trajectories. They've used bolt actions, and barrels of at least 22 inches. Built light, these rifles remind us that potent cartridges kick hard, and that muzzle brakes can deafen.

Carbines chambered for sensible deer-hunting rounds are coming back, though. Marlin's masterful rendition of its short, muscular Guide Gun a few years ago has led to other carbines from Marlin and the lever-action competition. Bolt guns with abbreviated barrels have also cropped up. But not all short rifles are carbines–at least, not all deliver that tangible but hard-to-articulate feel of a saddle-worthy smokepole, or a woods-wand that instantly targets the blink of a white flag

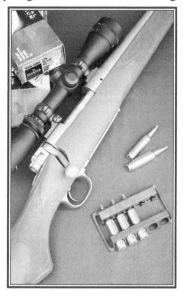

A carbine properly designed isn't just an abbreviated rifle–though many carbines derived from long-barreled rifles. The Krag Carbine, with a 22-inch barrel, was a stubbed-off version of the infantry arm with 30-inch barrel. So, too, early lever-action carbines had longer siblings. Many shooters soon found the short tubes more to their liking and realized that full-length barrels were largely holdovers from the black-powder era. These had no more business on smokeless lever guns than has the long bonnet of a vintage Cord on a new BMW coupe. While the first carbines for metallic cartridges appeared as shortened rifles, it's more accurate to say the first cartridge rifles were carbines that hadn't yet shed over-length barrels. By the time the 1903 Springfield came along, military rifles had been equipped with barrels long enough to service the cartridge but not so long as to impair handling. Carbine versions of the 98

This .270 WSM was built on a Model 70 action by Hill Country Rifles of New Braunfels, Texas.

Mauser and British SMLE later proved that a battle rifle didn't have to be over 40 inches long to be effective.

As a lad, I badly wanted an SMLE Jungle Carbine. But at nearly $50, it cost twice as much as a WWI infantry version. I restocked a standard-issue .303, then installed Williams open sights. In a stand of mustard poplars that fall, two deer dashed into view. I had no time to aim, so I swung as if the rifle were a shotgun. The lead deer somersaulted. Other fast-moving deer would later flip at the report of that SMLE. I recall, too, a fox that jetted from underfoot, and like the first deer, piled up before I heard the rifle fire. This was a rifle that handled as if it were shorter and lighter because I handled it so much. Still, I should have bought the Jungle Carbine. What a great name. It had a flash-hider, too.

In a perfect world, every carbine would start out as a carbine. You grow a carbine from seed stock; you don't plant a rifle, then graft a carbine onto the shoot. But bean counters will tell you that if you're going to build both, it's cheaper to engineer a rifle, then change parts or dimensions to get the carbine. No doubt they're right. They were also right in the early 1960s when they told Winchester the Model 70 could be built for a lot less money.

You can kill game with a dubbed-off rifle, just as you can kill birds with a double shotgun built to sell for $300. But when you loft a real carbine–or a best-grade British grouse gun–you'll feel differences all out of proportion to obvious disparities in form. Balance, line, fit. They all count for more in a rifle (or a shotgun) to be fired quickly. Chopping a well-balanced rifle to fit a carbine scabbard leaves you with a muzzle-light hybrid that feels awkward. Don't expect it to fly to your shoulder; you'll have to muscle the rear end yourself, without help from the front. It won't track smoothly on a swing, or give you a natural follow-through. Its stock will have been proportioned to match the metal or pare production costs. So it'll have too much bulk, too much weight. Instead of swiveling and pivoting inside the cup of your hand like the slender wrist of a fine upland gun or even a Depression-era woods rifle, it occupies your palm, front and rear. It fills your hands as might a thick section of banister, and it's about as responsive. That may be one of the reasons Winchester's Model 70 carbine, produced briefly in mid-century, didn't fare well. The 20-inch barrel looked out of place in a stock that was designed for barrels 24 and 26 inches long. Lopping the barrel saved a few ounces, but on a rifle as heavy as the early 70s, the percentage loss was insignificant.

Winchester might have built a salable bolt-action carbine if it had reviewed the endearing qualities of its short 92 and 94 lever-actions, the deer rifles of choice for more than a generation at that time. It might also have returned to the trim profile of the Model 54 carbine. Winchester could even have turned its eye to Europe.

The first bolt-action carbines with the wand-like handling of saddle rifles came from Mannlicher-Schoenauer. The short version of its Model 1905 set a very high bar for the competition. Successive M-S carbines changed little in form but offered new chamberings. The Model 1924 gave shooters the chance to carry a truly lightweight .30-06. Mannlicher-Schoenauers of the early 1950s are nothing shy of lovely: still slim and stocked for iron sights but chambered for high-performance rounds.

This early Mannlicher-Schoenauer has the slim lines and great balance that make for fast aim.

The Model 1961 featured a high-comb stock and white stock spacers for fittings, hardly in keeping with a carbine's defining elements: Spartan dimensions, elegant lines, essential components.

Mannlicher carbines had barrels of 18 to 20 inches in muzzle-length stocks. Full-stocked rifles of other brands were subsequently said to have Mannlicher stocks, though the company did not supply stocks for other rifles. Standard Mannlicher-Schoenauers had ordinary half-length forends, and the 24-inch barrels common on high-power bolt rifles from the turn of the century to the 1960s. Until Ruger's 77 and Number One RSIs (with 18- and 20-inch barrels), full-length forends got little attention from rifle-makers Stateside. In 1968, Winchester put a long stock on a Model 70 with a 19-inch barrel. It did not sell and was dropped three years later. On the other hand, short barrels remained as options on other bolt rifles.

In 1962, Remington announced its Model 700 with a 20-inch barrel. By then Winchester had been building Model 70 Featherweights with 22-inch barrels for a decade. Savage 110s, introduced in 1958, also came with 22-inch barrels. Soon Remington would adopt that length for standard chamberings. In 1968, Ruger's Model 77 debuted with a 22-inch barrel. Carbines, it seemed, were all but dead–largely because the standard length of rifle barrels had been shrinking. Aside from the Mannlicher-Schoenauer, about to vanish, the only high-quality bolt rifle with a 20-inch barrel was Sako's short-action Forester, offered from 1958 to 1971. The last year of that run, Sako fielded the long-action Finnbear with a 20-inch barrel. Both rifles were full-stocked. I should have bought a Forester.

In 1964, the Ford Mustang emerged, peace symbols proliferated and Winchester Model 70s got a new look, Remington engineers came up with its Model 600 carbine. This short-action bolt gun wore an 18 1/2-inch barrel with a ventilated polymer rib. The bolt handle had more kinks than an airport check-in line. Still, this six-pound rifle handled better than it looked and shot well. The 600 came in .222, .223, 243, 6mm, .308, and .35 Remington. A laminated stock appeared on carbines chambered for two short belted rounds: the new 6.5 and .350 Remington Magnums. In 1968, Remington replaced the 600 and 600 Magnum with a ribless sequel, the 660. Both standard and magnum versions had 20-inch barrels. But shooters didn't like the 660s any more than they had the 600s. By the end of 1971, all had been dumped from Big Green's line.

As I remember it, about a decade later, hunters quietly began buying up Remington 600 and 660 carbines in .350. It had occurred to experienced woodsmen that a short six-and-a-half-pound rifle wielding a ton-and-a-half of muzzle energy made sense where big bull elk spent most of the season. Even 600-series guns in standard chamberings were in demand. Deer hunters suddenly saw them for what they were: bolt-action reincarnations of the lever-action carbines that had once dominated gun racks in deer camps. They carried easily, jumped on target quickly and cycled reliably. In addition, they offered more power and low, topside scope mounting.

The main advantage of carbines–quick handling–may be oversold. Well-balanced, lightweight rifles with 22-inch or even 24-inch barrels can point as deftly. If short

Remington's 600 carbine (top) got a tepid reception. A brawnier 673 reflects the style 40 years later.

barrels were sure to turn a sprinting whitetail into venison, English grouse guns would feature 20-inch barrels too. Even in thick cover, fast shots come from fast shooters, not fast rifles. Maneuvering, though, is easier with a carbine. It moves with you instead of tagging along behind. Its snout is more often where you want it, less often captive in vines or branches. If you're making time through the woods with the rifle on your shoulder, the carbine's muzzle stays even with your clavicle (or should). It's not sticking up like a periscope.

Carbines are lighter in weight than rifles of the same design with longer barrels, but they're not so much lighter as to make much difference on the trail. These days, rifles with 22-inch barrels can be made as light as you'll want a rifle: around five-and-a-half pounds, unless you're willing to put up with skeletonized metal and bizarre abbreviations in the stock. Actually, I prefer rifles that scale no less than six-and-a-half pounds, so when I'm breathing hard or the wind is blowing, I still have a chance for an aimed shot. Hard-kicking cartridges also call for heft to soak up recoil. A six-and-a-half-pound rifle will weigh seven-and-a-half to eight pounds with its

scope, sling, and ammo. That's less than what most of us carry all year long as extra belly.

If you're hunting on horseback, a carbine certainly gives you an edge. No matter how you hang the scabbard (mine goes on the left side, muzzle forward, butt angled up and to the rear), a short barrel means easier movement for the horse. You reduce contact with brush and leverage on the saddle. When you're in a hurry to shoot, the carbine clears the scabbard faster than a rifle.

Long hikes in mule deer country call for lightweight rifles. Many hunters also prefer short barrels.

Some hunters dismiss carbines because their short barrels don't match up well with cartridges that generate high velocities with slow powders. While you do sacrifice some bullet speed as you reduce barrel length, that loss may not be as great as you think (see chart). Then too, the least efficient cartridges in short barrels hardly give you top efficiency in long ones. They're also the cartridges that deliver the most blast and recoil, and they eat throats. Cartridges suitable for carbines include the most popular deer rounds and those magnums you might want for elk.

Accuracy? The notion that longer barrels shoot tighter groups should be as dead as witch trials. A short barrel of the same diameters is stiffer and vibrates less at the shot. Result: greater consistency. Bolt-action pistols with match-grade barrels often out-shoot rifles of similar build. "Urban tactical" rifles offered these days for black-gun enthusiasts and law enforcement wear short, thick barrels, not long ones.

Whether you choose a bolt-action carbine or a traditional lever gun–or a Remington auto-loader or pump–you're smart to preserve its fine handling with a lightweight sight mounted low. A receiver sight and a front blade from XS Sight Systems make sense on lever-actions. Some bolt rifles have stocks with combs too high for irons, and even where irons fit, you may want the optical advantages of a scope. My choice is a 2 1/2x fixed-power: Leupold's compact, or the Weaver K2.5. Burris and Sightron offer good ones too. If you need a variable, consider the 1.5-4.5x Nikon. Alloy rings like those from the Talley shop appeal to me. Keeping the carbine's weight between your hands

A takedown rifle like the 4-pound Kifaru also allows you to switch barrels.

is crucial. High or heavy scopes destroy balance and impair handling.

A few years ago in New Mexico's mountains, I sneaked over the rocks and through the oaks and into the teeth of a snowstorm. Flakes the size of cheeseballs sped by like bullets. The wind roared through the peaks and tore into the thin pines where I'd seen the elk. My visibility cut to inches, I hunkered in the lee of a rock, carbine clutched close.

As suddenly as it had barreled in, the storm lifted. I eased forward, glassing at every step. The elk could have slipped away, could have turned the long shot I'd declined earlier into my only chance. Careful not to let the oakbrush slap, I moved, finger alongside the trigger, muzzle at eye level, heart in my throat . . .

He came up fast, but stopped. The crosswire in the Weaver K2.5 found his fifth rib and the little rifle fired itself. He stumbled, recovered, and vanished as the reticle again found his chest. I waited for a long time, listening. Then, cradling the carbine, I eased up the ridge at right angles and came down behind the pines, slowly.

He was dead, shot perfectly but tenacious like all six-point bulls. I slipped the .350 round out of the chamber and ran my fingers over an antler tine. Yes, it would have been easier with a long poke from the rocks above. But you don't carry a carbine for that. You bring a carbine to hunt.

Here's an overview of current rifles that meet a loose definition of carbine: barrels shorter than 21 inches.

Rifle Make/Model	Action	Barrel Length	Stock Type
Browning BAR Lightweight (short action)	auto-loading	20	walnut, synth.
Browning Lightweight '81 (short action)	lever	20	walnut
Browning A-Bolt Micro Hunter (short action)	bolt	20	walnut
CZ 527 FS	bolt	20	walnut (full length)
CZ 527 Carbine	bolt	18 1/2	walnut
CZ 550 FS	bolt	20	walnut (full length)
Henry Big Boy 44	lever	20	walnut
Howa 1500 Ultralight	bolt	20	synthetic
Marlin 1894 (all)	lever	20	walnut
Marlin 336 (all)	lever	16 1/2, 20	walnut
Marlin 1895M. G. GS	lever	18 1/2	walnut

(Note: Some special Cowboy versions of these rifles have longer barrels)

Rifle Make/Model	Action	Barrel Length	Stock Type
Puma 92 Carbine	lever	20	hardwood
Remington Model Seven LS, SS, Youth	bolt	20	laminated, synthetic, hardwood
Remington Model Seven MS (Custom)	bolt	20	laminated (full length)
Remington 7600 Carbine	pump	18 1/2	walnut
Remington 7400 Carbine	auto-loading	18 1/2	walnut
Ruger Number One RSI	dropping block	20	walnut (full length)
Ruger 96/44M	lever	18 1/2	walnut
Ruger Ranch Rifle, Mini-14, -30	auto-loading	18 1/2	walnut, synthetic
Ruger Deerfield Carbine	auto-loading	18 1/2	walnut
Ruger 77RL Mk II	bolt	20	walnut, synthetic
Ruger 77RSI Mk II	bolt	20	walnut (full length)
Sako Finnlight	bolt	20	synthetic
Savage 10 FM, FCM	bolt	20	synthetic
Savage 10 FP-LE1, FP-LE1A	bolt	20	synthetic
Springfield Armory M1A Scout Squad	auto-loading	18	synthetic
Thompson/Center Encore Katahdin	hinged-breech	18	synthetic
Winchester M70 Classic Compact	bolt	20	synthetic
Winchester M94 Trad'l, Trails End, Ranger	lever	20	walnut
Winchester M94 Trapper, Ranger Compact	lever	16	walnut

FEATHERLIGHT AND LIGHTNING-QUICK

The longer I hunt, the more I appreciate lightweight rifles–and not just because they're easier to carry. They're more responsive. A properly balanced bantam-weight rifle can help you shoot faster and hit more often. Of course, lightweight rifles can punch you silly when they detonate cartridges the size of hot sauce bottles. But deer these days don't take any more killing than deer did 100 years ago, when a .30-30 shooting a 160-grain bullet at 1,970 fps was considered potent. That's the other thing I like about lightweight rifles: they steer me to mild cartridges.

The world is full of gentle but flat-shooting rounds. The .250 Savage was among the first to take hold in commercial form. Since its inception in 1913, we've welcomed a host of other sub-.30s and a few rounds like the .300 Savage that qualify for game bigger than deer. In the Model 99 Featherweight, the .300 Savage is still a delightful deer round. A few seasons back, I carried such a rifle into the snowy Washington woods on a November still-hunt. From a trail skirting an old cut, I spied a buck as it sun-fished away from me. With time for only one quick shot, the little .300 hurried to snatch the opportunity. A 150-grain Power Point minced the deer's lungs. Most of my hunting now is for mule deer in more open places, and I seldom carry lever-action carbines. But even on the prairie or in the Rockes, I find cartridges like the .300 Savage adequate. It's a puzzle to me that some deer hunters choose magnum power and rifles as burdensome as bazookas. Lightweight rifles help you hunt longer, farther, and more effectively. And they help you shoot quicker. Savvy shooters knew that before female suffrage.

Settling the American West, pioneers toted ponderous black-powder muzzleloaders. Even those built by the Hawken brothers for men on horseback weighed around 10 pounds. Civil War muskets had all the pointing qualities of a five-foot length of sewer pipe. Trap-door Springfield carbines gave pony soldiers a welcome reprieve, but it wasn't until the advent of smokeless powder and stronger barrel alloys that rifles really began to shed weight.

Winchester trotted out a truly lightweight lever-action in 1924. The Model 53 was a half-magazine rifle derived from the Model 92, itself a nimble package. Its most potent chambering was .44-40, hardly fearsome by today's standards, but a match for the buckhorn sight on the 22-inch nickel-steel barrel. At just under six pounds, the 53 was lightning-quick to aim and, given its mild recoil and fine balance, fast on the follow-up.

By the time Winchester introduced its Model 70 in 1937, bolt-action rifles had been whittled down to eight pounds or so. The Savage Model 1920, hardly ever mentioned now, had the feel of more costly rifles and scaled only seven pounds, about the heft of a Winchester 54 before the M70 replaced it. As optical sights and wildcat cartridges gave bolt guns a boost in popularity, shooters focused more on ballistic performance. Riflemen pined for greater reach; rifle weight mattered less.

Remington offered its serviceable, affordable Models 721 and 722 (long and short actions) beginning in 1948. They weighed nearly a pound less than the 720,

The Remington Titanium Model 700 features a spiral-fluted bolt body.

an earlier rifle on the 1917 Enfield action. But they were no match for the Model 70 Featherweight that appeared in the early 1950s at seven pounds. In 1962, Remington used alloy bottom metal to drop additional weight from its new Model 700. By this time, Savage had its 110–but no lightweight version. Weatherby, meanwhile, was sticking with eight-and-a-half-pound rifles. The Mark V action Roy Weatherby designed with Fred Jennie in 1957 had 36 ounces of steel! Roy's magnum cartridges needed long barrels to deliver top bullet speeds. At that time, Browning was importing rifles on FN and Sako actions; only the small-action Sakos could be called light. In 1968, Bill Ruger announced his Model 77, at about seven pounds. Some versions wore trim 22-inch barrels. Len Brownell stocks made these 77s especially responsive.

Four years earlier, Remington had introduced the strange-looking Model 600. At six-and-a-half pounds, this bolt-action carbine was a nimble deer rifle (chamberings: .222, .223, .243, 6mm, .308. It was followed in 1968 by 660-series rifles without the original ventilated rib. But cosmetically, neither rendition appealed to hunters, and the series was dropped in 1971.

During the 1980s, lightweight rifles again began attracting hunters. Morgantown, West Virginia entrepreneur Melvin Forbes designed his Ultra Light action in 1984. It looked like a Remington 700, but bolt and receiver diameters were smaller. Says Melvin: "While the receiver has standard wall thickness, a smaller bolt body means less steel than in actions built to accept magnums." Melvin designed the Model 20 around the 7x57 Mauser cartridge. "Its case is longer than that of the .308 Winchester," he points out. "So is the 6mm Remington,

Melvin Forbes of New Ultralight Arms built this 6.5/284 for Wayne.

.257 Roberts, and .284 Winchester. In a short-action magazine, their bullets must be seated deep. You forfeit case capacity. Our magazine box is three inches long, not 2.85 inches as in most short-action rifles."

Melvin didn't skeletonize the metal or cut barrels shorter than 22 inches. His

Model 20 owes its feathery heft to a stock that weighs just 16 ounces. "Most synthetic stocks exhibit what I call boat-hull technology: they're fiberglass," says Melvin. "I came up with a stock comprising carbon fiber and Kevlar. It's actually stiffer than the barrel."

The M20 stock has no pillars; an aluminum sleeve over the front guard screw prevents over-tightening. The classic lines of this stock, and tight fit to the metal, hardly seem right for the striped camouflage pattern Melvin prefers. But color and pattern remain customer options. There's no checkering; a roughened Dupont Imron finish gives you a grip. Melvin now offers a longer (three-and-three-eighths-inch) action for the .30-06. A Model 28 for magnum cartridges is larger in diameter. A three-inch M28 handles the 6.5mm and .350 Remington Magnums, plus the newer Winchester and Remington Short Magnums. The three-and-three-eighths-inch version accommodates the likes of the 7mm Remington. M40 Ultra Lights swallow cartridges as big as the .416 Rigby. A midget version takes .223-size rounds.

On long days, light rifles are a boon to hunters enabling them to cover more country.

In March 1999, Melvin Forbes sold Ultra Light Arms to Colt, which had just bought Saco, a heavy weapons factory in Maine. Colt intended to build M28 rifles there while Melvin and his crew, working for Colt, produced stocks in Morgantown. But then Colt got into financial trouble. Municipal lawsuits directed at the gun industry sapped money committed to debt service. Absurd though the lawsuits proved, Colt was compelled to scrap the Ultra Light project and sold Saco to General Dynamics. Melvin bought Ultra Light back. Due to litigation involving Colt, Melvin's firm is now New Ultra Light Arms.

New Ultra Light rifles mirror the originals, with a 4140 chrome-moly receiver, Douglas Premium barrel, Timney trigger, Sako-style extractor, and thumb safety that can be pushed down to allow bolt cycling with the firing mechanism locked. Melvin makes one-and-a-half-ounce scope rings that fit directly to the receiver.

In 1986, two years after the Ultra Light M20 debuted, Remington re-entered the lightweight rifle business with its classy six-and-a-half-pound Mountain Rifle. Of mass-produced rifles, this is still the archetype, but similar models have followed. Remington's own Model 7, with its 20-inch barrel, is more a carbine than a lightweight rifle, but it weighs the same. Winchester offers a Compact Model 70 with 22-inch barrel and slightly stubbed stock. Ruger's Ultra Light has a 20-inch barrel, as does Browning's A-Bolt Micro-Hunter and Savage's Model 10 FM Sierra. The Ruger 77UL weighs six-and-a-half pounds, the Savage and Browning six-and-a-quarter.

Beginning with the introduction of a six-lug Mark V rifle for standard cartridges during the late 1990s, Weatherby has developed several lightweight rifles. The first, chambered for standard cartridges, weighed six-and-a-half pounds. Its 24-inch barrel delivered better balance and higher chronograph readings than the shorter tubes on the competition's rifles. In 1999, Weatherby followed the Lightweight with a five-and-three-quarter-pound Ultra Lightweight, also sporting a 24-inch barrel. Additional fluting and some alloy parts pared ounces. In 2001, this rifle became the first from a commercial firm to chamber the .338-06 round. Weatherby's Super PredatorMaster, initially fashioned as a rifle for the walking coyote hunter, sold so well in .243, 7mm-08, and .308 chamberings that Weatherby followed right away with a Super Big GameMaster, a mouthful of title for a rifle of elegant simplicity. Like the Super PredatorMaster, it features a hand-laminated stock of aramid, graphite, and fiberglass. The 24-inch blackened, fluted stainless barrel is from John Krieger's shop. It is button rifled, contoured to keep the weight of standard SBGM rifles down to five-and-three-quarter pounds. Magnums (with the nine-lug action and a 26-inch hammer-forged tube) weigh nearly a pound more.

Another recent lightweight rifle hails from Kimber. The Clackamas, Oregon, company got its start in the 1980s with a Model 82 .22 rimfire. Almost as petite, the Model 84 was chambered for the .17s, .222, and .223. The Kimber 89 looked like a Winchester M70 and chambered standard big game rounds like the .30-06. All these rifles were discontinued when Kimber crumbled under Chapter 7 in 1989. Les Edelman became majority

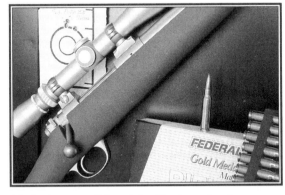

Kimber's super-lightweight Montana is also super-accurate. My Kimber is in .308.

stakeholder in a new firearms company. Strong demand for handguns gave Les the idea of producing a high-quality pistol after the 1911 Colt design. He bought a factory in Yonkers, New York, projecting a run of 5,000 pistols. Now Kimber makes 44,000 M1911-style pistols every year.

In 1998, Kimber fielded a new rimfire designed by Nehemiah Sirkis: the

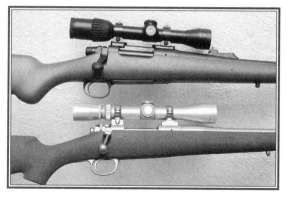

Remington's Model Seven (top) is nimble–but the Kimber Montana weighs a pound less!

Kimber 22. The firm's next rifle, a pet project for sales chiefs Dwight Van Brunt and Ryan Busse, was the 84M. Chambered in .243, .260, 7mm-08, and .308 (also .22-250), it weighs five-and-three-quarter pounds with a 22-inch barrel. Stockmaker Darwin Hensley shaped the trim Claro walnut stock. Checkered 20 lines to the inch, it is glassed and pillar-bedded to the action; the barrel floats. The 84M has a clean-breaking trigger, a claw extractor, steel bottom metal, and an M70-style safety. The newer 8400 is similar but chambered for Winchester Short Magnum (WSM) cartridges. The latest Kimber is the synthetic-stocked Montana, available in standard chamberings at less than five-and-a-half pounds. The first group I fired from the first Montana in my hands measured just under an inch. The rifle balances very well–and makes standard-weight bolt guns seem ponderous indeed!

The trend toward lighter rifles has been fueled partly by custom shops–and by a cottage industry in semi-custom rifles. Besides those offered by Melvin Forbes, you can get reasonably priced super-light rifles from Charlie Sisk and Lex Webernick in Texas, Mark Bansner in Pennsylvania, and a number of other makers. Most hang lightweight aramid-fiber stocks and svelte barrels on standard actions from Winchester and Remington.

Lex Webernick built the Model 70 in 6.5x55 that I used to take this Coues deer.

You can't truly appreciate carrying lightweight rifles until you've learned to shoot them. The key is to take control of the rifle. Heavy rifles require less of your participation. Be a good pedestal and don't wreck the shot, and the rifle will plant the bullet close to point of aim. Rifles that point like wands, on the other hand, must be held, not merely supported. The shot must be pursued, because you may not have

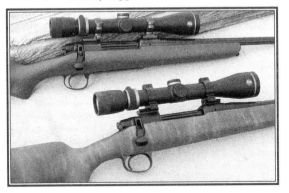

time to wait for the rifle to fire itself. You must do more than bear the weight; you must tame the bounce, subdue the nervous energy between your hands.

To help a light rifle settle down, I favor a leather sling with an adjustable loop. The Latigo sling, from Brownell's of Montezuma, Iowa, has been my choice for decades. I'm

Two Webernick rifles (Rifles, Inc.) show skeletonized bolt handles, very trim stocks.

unaware of any shooting slings that approach it in quality. Its clever design protects your rifle and makes length adjustment a snap. Unlike nylon slings, it will not readily slip from your upper arm. Many shooters prefer bipods; but they add weight and lack versatility. Stoney Point markets collapsible shooting sticks that I like better. For best results, plant the legs well forward and tug the intersection of the sticks toward you, using your left hand to keep the rifle secure on the sticks.

Lightweight rifles can be very hard to shoot accurately if they have rough, heavy triggers. Indeed, unmanageable triggers are largely responsible for the myth that lightweight rifles aren't accurate. A trigger that requires muscle causes rifle movement, sending the shot astray. A consistent trigger that breaks like a slender glass shard is invaluable. I like a two-pound trigger; it's stiff enough to prevent a cold, gloved finger from prematurely tripping the sear. But it's responsive enough that you can easily fire the rifle within a few seconds. Hold any rifle too long, and your muscles will tire, increasing the amplitude of wobble. If your rifle doesn't have a suitable trigger, buy an aftermarket trigger from Shilen, Timney or Bold. In my rack is a .25 Souper from Charlie Sisk. It has a Jewell trigger. This rifle shoots well because it enables me to shoot as well as I can.

The contribution of a good trigger is hard to overestimate. A few years ago I was shooting what may still be the lightest rifle at market: a three-and-three-quarter-pound take-down from Kifaru, International. This wand is built on Remington's Model Seven action, modified to accept interchangeable barrels. My sample included 18 1/2-inch Shilen match-grade fluted barrels in .260 and .308. Changing was easy: twist one out and the other in. Thin-walled barrels get hot quickly, so Patrick Smith, the rifle's designer, gave these barrels a half-length Kevlar sleeve that matches the stock. It's attractive and functional. A screw on the receiver ring

The Kifaru Takedown is as lightweight a rifle as you'll find, and it stows in a backpack!

locks into a detent in the threads so the barrel can't back out. After zeroing with the .260 barrel and a Kahles 3-9x scope, I sat on the ground and snugged my sling. Three bullets went into a one-and-three-quarter-inch cluster at 100 yards. I stood and loosed three more rounds. That group taped three-and-seven-eighths inches. I seldom do much better than that, sitting or offhand. Patrick correctly attributes the rifle's fine performance from hunting positions to its crisp, light trigger.

Balance matters too, of course. Shoulder a best-quality English upland gun, and you'll think it's alive. You don't have to point it because it points itself. Balancing and profiling a rifle must be done at the same time if you are to get that uncanny pointability. It's more art than science, more than just getting to the proper fulcrum. Grip and forend must be relatively straight and ovoid in cross-section, with a slight flare low to keep your hand in place. But neither should be "hand-filling." Rather, they must be slim to allow the rifle to pivot easily and rotate slightly as you bring the rifle to your shoulder or swing on a deer that's moving fast.

You're smart to keep the center of gravity low in lightweight rifles, which means you'll use a trim, lightweight scope mounted tight to the receiver. You don't need a powerful scope for hunting deer anyway, and oversize front lenses are wasted in normal hunting light and at magnifications of less than 8x. I prefer a 4x32 scope for most of my big game hunting. A 6x with a 36mm objective gives you all the power you'll need and all the light your eye can use, even at long range at dusk. Prefer variables? Try a 2.5-8x Leupold VX-III or a Nikon or Kahles 2-7x, or a 3-9x36 Swarovski. Bushnell's 3200 and 4200 lines offer fine value, as does the Burris Fullfield II stable. Mount the scope so you catch a full field when your cheek lies as far forward on the comb as it comes when you shoulder the rifle quickly.

The trend toward lightweight rifles will continue as surely as hunters age. The advent of shorter magnum cartridges have helped fuel it by packing lots of power into small actions. But recoil that leads to a flinch will impair your shooting. For this reason, it makes sense to stick with cartridges that don't beat you up. Truly, few animals get away because rifles or cartridges fall short. Many escape, crippled, because deer hunters shoot poorly. These loads deliver all the reach and power you need for deer, without cracking your scapula or dislodging your dentures.

Lightweight rifles can still shoot tight groups, as this Webernick M70 shows.

Ballistic Performance of Cartridges Best Suited to Lightweight Deer Rifles (LM=Light Magnum)

.243 Winchester		muz.	100	200	300	400
Federal 100 Sierra GameKing BTSP	velocity, fps:	2,960	2,760	2,570	2,380	2,210
	energy, ft-lb:	1,950	1,690	1,460	1,260	1,080
	arc, inches:		+1.5	0	-6.8	-19.8
Hornady 100 BTSP LM	velocity, fps:	3,100	2,839	2,592	2,358	2,138
	energy, ft-lb:	2,133	1,790	1,491	1,235	1,014
	arc, inches:		+1.5	0	-6.8	-19.8
Rem. 100 PSP boat-tail	velocity, fps:	2,960	2,720	2,492	2,275	2,069
	energy, ft-lb:	1,945	1,642	1,378	1,149	950
	arc, inches:		+2.8	+2.3	-3.8	-16.6
Win. 95 Ballistic Silvertip	velocity, fps:	3,100	2,854	2,626	2,410	2,203
	energy, ft-lb:	2,021	1,719	1,455	1,225	1,024
	arc, inches:		+1.4	0	-6.4	-18.9
Win. 100 Power-Point Plus	velocity, fps:	3,090	2,818	2,562	2,321	2,092
	energy, ft-lb:	2,121	1,764	1,458	1,196	972
	arc, inches:		+1.4	0	-6.7	-20.0

6mm Remington		muz.	100	200	300	400
Federal 100 Nosler Partition	velocity, fps:	3,100	2,860	2,640	2,420	2,220
	energy, ft-lb:	2,135	1,820	1,545	1,300	1,090
	arc, inches:		+1.4	0	-6.3	-18.7
Hornady 100 SP boat-tail	velocity, fps:	3,100	2,861	2,634	2,419	2,231
	energy, ft-lb:	2,134	1,818	1,541	1,300	1,088
	arc, inches:		+1.3	0	-6.5	-18.9

Ballistic Performance of Cartridges Best Suited to Lightweight Deer Rifles (cont'd)

Hornady 100 SPBT LM		muz.	100	200	300	400
	velocity, fps:	3,250	2,997	2,756	2,528	2,311
	energy, ft-lb:	2,345	1,995	1,687	1,418	1,186
	arc, inches:		+1.6	0	-6.3	-18.2
Rem. 100 PSP Core-Lokt	velocity, fps:	3,100	2,829	2,573	2,332	2,104
	energy, ft-lb:	2,133	1,777	1,470	1,207	983
	arc, inches:		+1.4	0	-6.7	-19.8
Win. 100 Power-Point	velocity, fps:	3,100	2,829	2,573	2,332	2,104
	energy, ft-lb:	2,133	1,777	1,470	1,207	983
	arc, inches:		+1.7	0	-7.0	-20.4

.243 WSSM		*muz.*	*100*	*200*	*300*	*400*
Win. 95 Ballistic Silvertip	velocity, fps:	3,250	3,000	2,763	2,538	2,325
	energy, ft-lb:	2,258	1,898	1,610	1,359	1,140
	arc, inches:		+1.2	0	5.7	16.9
Win. 100 Power Point	velocity, fps:	3,110	2,838	2,583	2,341	2,112
	energy, ft-lb:	2,147	1,789	1,481	1,217	991
	arc, inches:		+1.4	0	-6.6	-19.7

.240 Weatherby Mag.		*muz.*	*100*	*200*	*300*	*400*
Wby. 95 Nosler Bal. Tip	velocity, fps:	3,420	3,146	2,888	2,645	2,414
	energy, ft-lb:	2,467	2,087	1,759	1,475	1,229
	arc, inches:		+2.7	+3.5	0	-8.4
Wby. 100 Pointed Expanding	velocity, fps:	3,406	3,134	2,878	2,637	2,408
	energy, ft-lb:	2,576	2,180	1,839	1,544	1,287
	arc, inches:		+2.8	+3.5	0	-8.4
Wby. 100 Partition	velocity, fps:	3,406	3,136	2,882	2,642	2,415
	energy, ft-lb:	2,576	2,183	1,844	1,550	1,294
	arc, inches:		+2.8	+3.5	0	-8.4
	arc, inches:		+2.1	-5.1	-27.0	-70.1

.250 Savage		*muz.*	*100*	*200*	*300*	*400*
Rem. 100 Pointed SP	velocity, fps:	2,820	2,504	2,210	1,936	1,684
	energy, ft-lb:	1,765	1,392	1,084	832	630
	arc, inches:		+2.0	0	-9.2	-27.7
Win. 100 Silvertip	velocity, fps:	2,820	2,467	2,140	1,839	1,569
	energy, ft-lb:	1,765	1,351	1,017	751	547
	arc, inches:		+2.4	0	-10.1	-30.5

.257 Roberts		muz.	100	200	300	400
Federal 120 Nosler Partition	velocity, fps:	2,780	2,560	2,360	2,160	1,970
	energy, ft-lb:	2,060	1,750	1,480	1,240	1,030
	arc, inches:		+1.9	0	-8.2	-24.0
Hornady 117 SP boat-tail	velocity, fps:	2,780	2,550	2,331	2,122	1,925
	energy, ft-lb:	2,007	1,689	1,411	1,170	963
	arc, inches:		+1.9	0	-8.3	-24.4
Hornady 117 SP boat-tail LM	velocity, fps:	2,940	2,694	2,460	2,240	2,031
	energy, ft-lb:	2,245	1,885	1,572	1,303	1,071
	arc, inches:		+1.7	0	-7.6	-21.8

.25-06 Remington		muz.	100	200	300	400
Federal 117 Sierra Game King BTSP	velocity, fps:	2,990	2,770	2,570	2,370	2,190
	energy, ft-lb:	2,320	2,000	1,715	1,465	1,240
	arc, inches:		+1.5	0	-6.8	-19.9
Hornady 117 SP boat-tail LM	velocity, fps:	3,110	2,855	2,613	2,384	2,168
	energy, ft-lb:	2,512	2,117	1,774	1,476	1,220
	arc, inches:		+1.8	0	-7.1	-20.3
Rem. 100 PSP Core-Lokt	velocity, fps:	3,230	2,893	2,580	2,287	,014
	energy, ft-lb:	2,316	1,858	1,478	1,161	901
	arc, inches:		+1.3	0	-6.6	-19.8
Rem. 120 PSP Core-Lokt	velocity, fps:	2,990	2,730	2,484	2,252	2,032
	energy, ft-lb:	2,382	1,985	1,644	1,351	1,100
	arc, inches:		+1.6	0	-7.2	-21.4
Win. 115 Ballistic Silvertip	velocity, fps:	3,060	2,825	2,603	2,390	2,188
	energy, ft-lb:	2,391	2,038	1,729	1,459	1,223
	arc, inches:		+1.4	0	-6.6	-19.2

.25 Winchester Super Short Mag.		muz.	100	200	300	400
Win. 115 Ballistic Silvertip	velocity, fps:	3,060	2,844	2,639	2,442	2,254
	energy, ft-lb:	2,392	2,066	1,778	1,523	1,298
	arc, inches:		+1.4	0	-6.4	-18.6
Win. 120 Pos. Pt. Exp.	velocity, fps:	2,990	2,717	2,459	2,216	1,987
	energy, ft-lb:	2,383	1,967	1,612	1,309	1,053
	arc, inches:		+1.6	0	-7.4	-21.8

6.5x55 Swedish		muz.	100	200	300	400
Federal 140 Trophy Bonded	velocity, fps:	2,550	2,350	2,160	1,980	1,810
	energy, ft-lb:	2,020	1,720	1,450	1,220	1,015
	arc, inches:		+2.4	0	-9.8	-28.4

Hornady 129 SP LM		muz.	100	200	300	400
	velocity, fps:	2,770	2,561	2,361	2,171	1,994
	energy, ft-lb:	2,197	1,878	1,597	1,350	1,138
	arc, inches:		+2.0	0	-8.2	-23.2
Hornady 140 SP LM	velocity, fps:	2,740	2,541	2,351	2,169	1,999
	energy, ft-lb:	2,333	2,006	1,717	1,463	1,242
	arc, inches:		+2.4	0	-8.7	-24.0
Rem. 140 PSP Core-Lokt	velocity, fps:	2,550	2,353	2,164	1,984	1,814
	energy, ft-lb:	2,021	1,720	1,456	1,224	1,023
	arc, inches:		+2.4	0	-9.8	-27.0
Win. 140 Soft Point	velocity, fps:	2,550	2,359	2,176	2,002	1,836
	energy, ft-lb:	2,022	1,731	1,473	1,246	1,048
	arc, inches:		+2.4	0	-9.7	-28.1

.260 Remington		*muz.*	*100*	*200*	*300*	*400*
Federal 140 Sierra GameKing BTSP	velocity, fps:	2,750	2,570	2,390	2,220	2,060
	energy, ft-lb:	2,350	2,045	1,775	1,535	1,315
	arc, inches:		+1.9	0	-8.0	-23.1
Rem. 120 AccuTip	velocity, fps:	2,890	2,697	2,512	2,334	2,163
	energy, ft-lb:	2,392	2,083	1,807	1,560	1,340
	arc, inches:		+1.6	0	-7.2	-20.7
Rem. 125 Nosler Partition	velocity, fps:	2,875	2,669	2,473	2,285	2,105
	energy, ft-lb:	2,294	1,977	1,697	1,449	1,230
	arc, inches:		+1.71	0	-7.4	-21.4
Rem. 140 PSP Core-Lokt	velocity, fps:	2,750	2,544	2,347	2,158	1,979
	energy, ft-lb:	2,351	2,011	1,712	1,448	1,217
	arc, inches:		+1.9	0	-8.3	-24.0

6.5/284		*muz.*	*100*	*200*	*300*	*400*
Norma 120 Nosler Bal. Tip	velocity, fps:	3,117	2,890	2,674	2,469	
	energy, ft-lb:	2,589	2,226	1,906	1,624	
	arc, inches:		+1.3	0	-6.2	
Norma 140 Nosler Part.	velocity, fps:	2,953	2,750	2,557	2,371	
	energy, ft-lb:	2,712	2,352	2,032	1,748	
	arc, inches:		+1.5	0	-6.8	

6.8mm Remington SPC		*muz.*	*100*	*200*	*300*	*400*
Rem. 115 Open Tip Match (and HPBT Match)	velocity, fps:	2,800	2,535	2,285	2,049	1,828
	energy, ft-lb:	2,002	1,641	1,333	1,072	853
	arc, inches:		+2.0	0	-8.7	-25.6

Rem. 115 C-L Ultra		muz.	100	200	300	400
	velocity, fps:	2,800	2,523	2,262	2,017	1,789
	energy, ft-lb:	2,002	1,625	1,307	1,039	817
	arc, inches:		+2.0	0	-8.8	-26.2

.270 Winchester		muz.	100	200	300	400
Federal 130 Sierra GameKing	velocity, fps:	3,060	2,830	2,620	2,410	2,220
	energy, ft-lb:	2,700	2,320	1,980	1,680	1,420
	arc, inches:		+1.4	0	-6.5	-19.0
Hornady 130 SST (or Interbond)	velocity, fps:	3,060	2,845	2,639	2,442	2,254
	energy, ft-lb:	2,700	2,335	2,009	1,721	1,467
	arc, inches:		+1.4	0	-6.6	-19.1
Hornady 140 SP boat-tail LM	velocity, fps:	3,100	2,894	2,697	2,508	2,327
	energy, ft-lb:	2,987	2,604	2,261	1,955	1,684
	arc, inches:		+1.4	0	6.3	-18.3
Rem. 130 AccuTip BT	velocity, fps:	3,060	2,845	2,639	2,442	2,254
	energy, ft-lb:	2,702	2,336	2,009	1,721	1,467
	arc, inches:		+1.4	0	-6.4	-18.6
Win. 140 AccuBond	velocity, fps:	2,950	2,751	2,560	2,378	2,203
	energy, ft-lb:	2,705	2,352	2,038	1,757	1,508
	arc, inches:		+1.6	0	-6.9	-19.9

7mm Mauser (7x57)		muz.	100	200	300	400
Federal 140 Sierra Pro-Hunt.	velocity, fps:	2,660	2,450	2,260	2,070	1,890
	energy, ft-lb:	2,200	1,865	1,585	1,330	1,110
	arc, inches:		+2.1	0	-9.0	-26.1
Hornady 139 SP Interlock	velocity, fps:	2,680	2,455	2,241	2,038	1,846
	energy, ft-lb:	2,216	1,860	1,550	1,282	1,052
	arc, inches:		+2.1	0	-9.1	-26.6
Hornady 139 SP boat-tail LM	velocity, fps:	2,830	2,620	2,450	2,250	2,070
	energy, ft-lb:	2,475	2,135	1,835	1,565	1,330
	arc, inches:		+1.8	0	-7.6	-22.1
Rem. 140 PSP Core-Lokt	velocity, fps:	2,660	2,435	2,221	2,018	1,827
	energy, ft-lb:	2,199	1,843	1,533	1,266	1,037
	arc, inches:		+2.2	0	-9.2	-27.4
Win. 145 Power-Point	velocity, fps:	2,660	2,413	2,180	1,959	1,754
	energy, ft-lb:	2,279	1,875	1,530	1,236	990
	arc, inches:		+1.1	-2.8	-14.1	-34.4

7mm-08 Remington		muz.	100	200	300	400
Federal 140						
Nosler Bal. Tip	velocity, fps:	2,800	2,610	2,430	2,260	2,100
	energy, ft-lb:	2,440	2,135	1,840	1,590	1,360
	arc, inches:		+1.8	0	-7.7	-22.3
Rem. 140						
Nosler Bal. Tip	velocity, fps:	2,860	2,670	2,488	2,313	2,145
	energy, ft-lb:	2,543	2,217	1,925	1,663	1,431
	arc, inches:		+1.7	0	-7.3	-21.2
Win. 140						
Power-Point Plus	velocity, fps:	2,875	2,597	2,336	2,090	1,859
	energy, ft-lb:	2,570	1,997	1,697	1,358	1,075
	arc, inches:		+2.0	0	-8.8	26.0

.284 Winchester		muz.	100	200	300	400
Win. 150						
Power-Point	velocity, fps:	2,860	2,595	2,344	2,108	1,886
	energy, ft-lb:	2,724	,2243	1,830	1,480	1,185
	arc, inches:		+2.1	0	-8.5	-24.8

.280 Remington		muz.	100	200	300	400
Federal 140						
Sierra Pro-Hunt.	velocity, fps:	2,990	2,740	2,500	2,270	2,060
	energy, ft-lb:	2,770	2,325	1,940	1,605	1,320
	arc, inches:		+1.6	0	-7.0	-20.8
Rem. 140						
Nosler Bal. Tip	velocity, fps:	3,000	2,804	2,616	2,436	2,263
	energy, ft-lb:	2,799	2,445	2,128	1,848	1,593
	arc, inches:		+1.5	0	-6.8	-19.0
Win. 140						
Ballistic Silvertip	velocity, fps:	3,040	2,842	2,653	2,471	2,297
	energy, ft-lb:	2,872	2,511	2,187	1,898	1,640
	arc, inches:		+1.4	0	-6.3	-18.4

.300 Savage		muz.	100	200	300	400
Rem. 150						
PSP Core-Lokt	velocity, fps:	2,630	2,354	2,095	1,853	1,631
	energy, ft-lb:	2,303	1,845	1,462	1,143	806
	arc, inches:		+2.4	0	-10.4	-30.9
Win. 150						
Power-Point	velocity, fps:	2,630	2,311	2,015	1,743	1,500
	energy, ft-lb:	2,303	1,779	1,352	1,012	749
	arc, inches:		+2.8	0	-11.5	-34.4

.308 Winchester		muz.	100	200	300	400
Federal 150						
Nosler Bal. Tip.	velocity, fps:	2,820	2,610	2,410	2,220	2,040
	energy, ft-lb:	2,650	2,270	1,935	1,640	1,380
	arc, inches:		+1.8	0	-7.8	-22.7

Ballistic Performance of Cartridges Best Suited to Lightweight Deer Rifles (cont'd)

.308 Winchester		muz.	100	200	300	400
Hornady						
150 SP LM	velocity, fps:	2,980	2,703	2,442	2,195	1,964
	energy, ft-lb:	2,959	2,433	1,986	1,606	1,285
	arc, inches:		+1.6	0	-7.5	-22.2
Hornady						
165 SST LM	velocity, fps:	2,880	2,672	2,474	2,284	2,103
(or Interbond)	energy, ft-lb:	3,038	2,616	2,242	1,911	1,620
	arc, inches:		+1.6	0	-7.3	-21.2
Rem. 165						
AccuTip	velocity, fps:	2,700	2,501	2,311	2,129	1,958
	energy, ft-lb:	2,670	2,292	1,957	1,861	1,401
	arc, inches:		+2.0	0	-8.6	-24.8
Win. 150						
Ballistic Silvertip	velocity, fps:	2,810	2,601	2,401	2,211	2,028
	energy, ft-lb:	2,629	2,253	1,920	1,627	1,370
	arc, inches:		+1.8	0	-7.8	-22.8

No matter your choice of rifle and cartridge, deer hunting is most pleasant when the load on your shoulder is light and recoil gentle. You'll stay fresh longer, cover more country–and shoot better too. ■

ECONOMICAL LIGHTWEIGHTS

The mechanics of factory-built bolt guns haven't changed much in the last 40 years, but variations have proliferated. New metals and stock materials have enabled engineers to trim weight without sacrificing strength or lopping barrels too short. Some new bolt rifles have been designed from the ground up as bantamweights. Here are the lightest of the common commercial bolt rifles.

- Browning A-Bolt Micro Hunter, 6.1 lbs.
- Dakota Lightweight Hunter, 6.5 lbs.
- Howa Ultralight, 6.4 lbs.
- Kimber 84M, 5.7 lbs.
- Kimber 8400 Montana, 6.1 lbs.
- Remington Model 700 Mountain Rifle, 6.5 lbs.
- Remington Model 700 Titanium, 5.5 lbs.
- Remington Model Seven AWR (short Ultra Mag), 6.5 lbs.
- Ruger Model 77 Mark II Ultra Light, 6.0 lbs.
- Ruger Model 77/44RS, 6.0 lbs.
- Savage Model 16FSS, 6.0 lbs.
- Tikka Model T3 Lightweight, 6.0 lbs.
- Weatherby Mark V Super Big Game Master, from 5.8 lbs.
- Winchester Model 70 Classic Compact, 6.0 lbs.
- Winchester Model 70 Ultimate Shadow (WSM), 6.5 lbs.

6

RIFLES WITH EXTRA REACH

T he deer was far below the ledge, on a face littered with the blackened debris of a forest fire that had stripped its cover two seasons back. There was no easy approach, and the buck would bed soon. He'd be out of sight as soon as I left the ledge, and would surely vanish before I got another look.

I'd have to shoot from here or not at all.

Draping my jacket over a rock, I laid the rifle across it and knelt behind the scope. Wedged in by boulders, I was steadier than I might have appeared. The reticle in the

I killed this Montana buck with one long shot from a Lazzeroni rifle.

Leupold 4X was death-still. A light breeze played with the fireweed from 10 o'clock. Was it the same downrange? I edged the Model 70 left and pressured it until the crosswire climbed even with the buck's antler. Then I squeezed.

The bullet struck low and right. The buck did not move. I cycled the bolt, corrected and, carefully, fired again. Dust spurted from between the deer's legs, but again it stood still.

Chambering the last round in my magazine, I held farther left and added elevation. At the report, the buck dashed forward, heart shot. A lucky shot, indeed. Long shooting is risky business.

DEER GUNS FOR SHOTS TOO LONG

The trouble with deer is that most of the time they know where you are first. They either hide, then, or go somewhere else. Shooting deer is hard when you can't see them.

If you're a good still-hunter, you'll sneak up on some deer. Hunting from a tree stand, you will ambush a few more. But if you're a trophy hunter, you won't see many of the deer you want to shoot, no matter how you hunt. The reason selective hunters use rifles with great reach is that they know their odds of seeing truly big bucks are slim, and if they see one, they want very much to make the shot. Whatever the yardage.

Big cartridges with fast bullets abound, as do long-barreled rifles to launch them, and high-power scopes to bring distant targets close. Sadly, shooters with the skill to make long shots are still in short supply. No equipment can compensate for shoddy marksmanship. And even ordinary rifles can be used with deadly effect by shooters committed to intelligent, regular practice.

Still, hardware designed for the long shot can give even the best shooters additional reach. Here are a few things to keep in mind when shopping for a cartridge, rifle, and scope to threaten deer in the next township.

It's important to distinguish between rifle and cartridge. The rifle is essentially a detonator, with a sight, and a barrel to help you direct the bullet. The ballistic package you deliver belongs to the cartridge. "I shoot a .30-06" says little about the rifle. All you're naming is the brass cartridge case and, within broad limits, the charge and bullet. "I shoot a .300" says nothing about either rifle or cartridge because there are many .300s.

Enough of semantics. We usually assume a long-range rifle is one chambered for a long-range cartridge. There's no official definition of such a cartridge. For me, it's a round that shoots a deer bullet (say, at least 90 grains) at 3,000 fps or faster, with 400-yard drop of less than 21 inches, given a 200-yard zero. Some of these recoil gently and are well suited to lightweight deer rifles. Ballistic charts for the .243 Winchester, 6mm Remington, .240 Weatherby, .25-06 Remington, .270 Winchester, and .280 Remington appear in chapter 5. But what if you want more velocity, more bullet weight–not to deliver more energy to the target at normal ranges, but to ensure there's plenty for quartering shots at extreme range. Additional speed and weight also make a bullet less sensitive to the wind, so you get less drift. This chart shows a few rounds that offer more than you'd expect from a deer bullet, and perhaps more than you need most of the time.

Ballistic Performance of Long-Range Deer Cartridges
(HE=High Energy, LM=Light Magnum)

.257 Weatherby Mag.		muz.	100	200	300	400
Wby. 115						
Nosler Bal. Tip	velocity, fps:	3,400	3,170	2,952	2,745	2,547
	energy, ft-lb:	2,952	2,566	2,226	1,924	1,656
	arc, inches:		+3.0	+3.5	0	-7.9
Wby. 120						
Nosler Partition	velocity, fps:	3,305	3,046	2,801	2,570	2,350
	energy, ft-lb:	2,910	2,472	2,091	1,760	1,47
	arc, inches:		+3.0	+3.7	0	-8.9
.264 Winchester Mag.		muz.	100	200	300	400
Rem. 140						
PSP Core-Lokt	velocity, fps:	3,030	2,782	2,548	2,326	2,114
	energy, ft-lb:	2,854	2,406	2,018	1,682	1,389
	arc, inches:		+1.5	0	-6.9	-20.2

Win. 140		muz.	100	200	300	400
Power-Point	velocity, fps:	3,030	2,782	2,548	2,326	2,114
	energy, ft-lb:	2,854	2,406	2,018	1,682	1,389
	arc, inches:		+1.8	0	-7.2	-20.8

270 Winchester Short Mag.		*muz.*	*100*	*200*	*300*	*400*
Win. 130						
Bal. Silvertip	velocity, fps:	3,275	3,041	2,820	2,609	2,408
	energy, ft-lb:	3,096	,669	2,295	1,964	1,673
	arc, inches:		+1.1	0	-5.5	-16.1
Win. 140						
AccuBond	velocity, fps:	3,200	2,989	2,789	2,597	2,413
	energy, ft-lb:	3,184	2,779	2,418	2,097	1,810
	arc, inches:		+1.2	0	-5.7	-16.5
Win. 150						
Ballistic Silvertip	velocity, fps:	3,120	2,923	2,734	2,554	2,380
	energy, ft-lb:	3,242	2,845	2,490	2,172	1,886
	arc, inches:		+1.3	0	-5.9	-17.2

.270 Weatherby Mag.		*muz.*	*100*	*200*	*300*	*400*
Wby. 130 Pointed						
Expanding	velocity, fps:	3,375	3,123	2,885	2,659	2,444
	energy, ft-lb:	3,288	2,815	2,402	2,041	1,724
	arc, inches:		+2.8	+3.5	0	-8.4
Wby. 130						
Nosler Partition	velocity, fps:	3,375	3,127	2,892	2,670	2,458
	energy, ft-lb:	3,288	2,822	2,415	2,058	1,744
	arc, inches:		+2.8	+3.5	0	-8.3
Wby. 140						
Nosler Bal. Tip	velocity, fps:	3,300	3,077	2,865	2,663	2,470
	energy, ft-lb:	3,385	2,943	2,551	2,204	1,896
	arc, inches:		+2.9	+3.6	0	-8.4

7mm Remington Mag.		*muz.*	*100*	*200*	*300*	*400*
Federal 150						
Sierra GameKing	velocity, fps:	3,110	2,920	2,750	2,580	2,410
	energy, ft-lb:	3,220	2,850	2,510	2,210	1,930
	arc, inches:		+1.3	0	-5.9	-17.0
Hornady 139						
SPBT HMmoly	velocity, fps:	3,250	3,041	2,822	2,613	2,413
	energy, ft-lb:	3,300	2,854	2,458	2,106	1,797
	arc, inches:		+1.1	0	-5.7	-16.6
Rem. 140						
PSP boat-tail	velocity, fps:	3,175	2,956	2,747	2,547	2,356
	energy, ft-lb:	3,133	2,715	2,345	2,017	1,726
	arc, inches:		+2.2	+1.6	-3.1	-13.4
Rem. 150						
Swift Scirocco	velocity, fps:	3,110	2,927	2,751	2,582	2,419
	energy, ft-lb:	3,221	2,852	2,520	2,220	1,948
	arc, inches:		+1.3	0	-5.9	-17.0
Win. 150						
Power-Point Plus	velocity, fps:	3,130	2,849	2,586	2,337	2,102
	energy, ft-lb:	3,264	2,705	2,227	1,819	1,472
	arc, inches:		+1.4	0	-6.6	-19.6

Ballistic Performance of Long-Range Deer Cartridges (cont'd)

7mm Remington Short Ultra Mag.		*muz.*	*100*	*200*	*300*	*400*
Rem. 140						
PSP C-L Ultra	velocity, fps:	3,175	2,934	2,707	2,490	2,283
	energy, ft-lb:	3,133	2,676	2,277	1,927	1,620
	arc, inches:		+1.3	0	-6.0	-17.7
Rem. 150						
PSP Core-Lokt	velocity, fps:	3,110	2,828	2,563	2,313	2,077
	energy, ft-lb:	3,221	2,663	2,188	1,782	1,437
	arc, inches:		+2.5	+2.1	-3.6	-15.8
Rem. 160						
Partition	velocity, fps:	2,960	2,762	2,572	2,390	2,215
	energy, ft-lb:	3,112	2,709	2,350	2,029	1,744
	arc, inches:		+2.6	+2.2	-3.6	-15.4
Rem. 160						
PSP C-L Ultra	velocity, fps:	2,960	2,733	2,518	2,313	2,117
	energy, ft-lb:	3,112	2,654	2,252	1,900	1,592
	arc, inches:		+2.7	+2.2	-3.7	-16.2

7mm Winchester Short Mag.		*muz.*	*100*	*200*	*300*	*400*
Win. 140						
Bal. Silvertip	velocity, fps:	3,225	3,008	2,801	2,603	2,414
	energy, ft-lb:	3,233	2,812	2,438	2,106	1,812
	arc, inches:		+1.2	0	-5.6	-16.4
Win. 150						
Power Point	velocity, fps:	3,200	2,915	2,648	2,396	2,157
	energy, ft-lb:	3,410	2,830	2,335	1,911	1,550
	arc, inches:		+1.3	0	-6.3	-18.6
Win. 160						
AccuBond	velocity, fps:	3,050	2,862	2,682	2,509	2,342
	energy, ft-lb:	3,306	2,911	2,556	2,237	1,950
	arc, inches:		1.4	0	-6.2	-17.9
Win. 160						
Fail Safe	velocity, fps:	2,990	2,744	2,512	2,291	2,081
	energy, ft-lb:	3,176	2,675	2,241	1,864	1,538
	arc, inches:		+1.6	0	-7.1	-20.8

7mm Weatherby Mag.		*muz.*	*100*	*200*	*300*	*400*
Hornady						
154 SST	velocity, fps:	3,200	3,009	2,825	2,648	2,478
(or Interbond)	energy, ft-lb:	3,501	3,096	2,729	2,398	2,100
	arc, inches:		+1.2	0	-5.7	-16.5
Wby. 139 Pointed						
Expanding	velocity, fps:	3,340	3,079	2,834	2,601	2,380
	energy, ft-lb:	3,443	2,926	2,478	2,088	1,748
	arc, inches:		+2.9	+3.6	0	-8.7
Wby. 140 Nosler						
Partition	velocity, fps:	3,303	3,069	2,847	2,636	2,434
	energy, ft-lb:	3,391	2,927	2,519	2,159	1,841
	arc, inches:		+2.9	+3.6	0	-8.5
Wby. 150 Nosler						
Bal. Tip	velocity, fps:	3,300	3,093	2,896	2,708	2,527
	energy, ft-lb:	3,627	3,187	,793	2,442	2,127
	arc, inches:		+2.8	+3.5	0	-8.2

Wby. 160 Nosler Partition		muz.	100	200	300	400
	velocity, fps:	3,200	2,991	2,791	2,600	2,417
	energy, ft-lb:	3,638	3,177	2,767	2,401	2,075
	arc, inches:		+3.1	+3.8	0	-8.9

7mm Dakota		*muz.*	*100*	*200*	*300*	*400*
Dakota 140 Barnes X	velocity, fps:	3,500	3,253	3,019	2,798	2,587
	energy, ft-lb:	3,807	3,288	2,833	2,433	2,081
	arc, inches:		+2.0	+2.1	-1.5	-9.6
Dakota 160 Barnes X	velocity, fps:	3,200	3,001	2,811	2,630	2,455
	energy, ft-lb:	3,637	3,200	2,808	2,456	2,140
	arc, inches:		+2.1	+1.9	-2.8	-12.5

7mm STW		*muz.*	*100*	*200*	*300*	*400*
A-Square 140 Nos. Bal. Tip	velocity, fps:	3,450	3,254	3,067	2,888	2,715
	energy, ft-lb:	3,700	3,291	2,924	2,592	2,292
	arc, inches:		+2.2	+3.0	0	-7.3
Federal 150 Trophy Bonded	velocity, fps:	3,250	3,010	2,770	2,560	2,350
	energy, ft-lb:	3,520	3,010	2,565	2,175	1,830
	arc, inches:		+1.2	0	-5.7	-16.7
Federal 160 Sierra GameKing	velocity, fps:	3,200	3,020	2,850	2,670	2,530
	energy, ft-lb:	3,640	3,245	2,890	2,570	2,275
	arc, inches:		+1.1	0	-5.5	-15.7
Rem. 140 PSP Core-Lokt	velocity, fps:	3,325	3,064	2,818	2,585	2,364
	energy, ft-lb:	3,436	2,918	2,468	2,077	1,737
	arc, inches:		+2.0	+1.7	-2.9	-12.8
Win. 140 Ballistic Silvertip	velocity, fps:	3,320	3,100	2,890	2,690	2,499
	energy, ft-lb:	3,427	2,982	2,597	2,250	1,941
	arc, inches:		+1.1	0	-5.2	-15.2

7mm Remington Ultra Mag		*muz.*	*100*	*200*	*300*	*400*
Rem. 140 PSP Core-Lokt	velocity, fps:	3,425	3,158	2,907	2,669	2,444
	energy, ft-lb:	3,646	3,099	2,626	2,214	1,856
	arc, inches:		+1.8	+1.6	-2.7	-11.9
Rem. 140 Nosler Partition	velocity, fps:	3,425	3,184	2,956	2,740	2,534
	energy, ft-lb:	3,646	3,151	2,715	2,333	1,995
	arc, inches:		+1.7	+1.6	-2.6	-11.4
Rem. 160 Nosler Partition	velocity, fps:	3,200	2,991	2,791	2,600	2,417
	energy, ft-lb:	3,637	3,177	2,767	2,401	2,075
	arc, inches:		+2.1	+1.8	-3.0	-12.9

7.21 (.284) Lazzeroni Firehawk		*muz.*	*100*	*200*	*300*	*400*
Lazzeroni 140 Nosler Part.	velocity, fps:	3,580	3,349	3,130	2,923	2,724
	energy, ft-lb:	3,985	3,488	3,048	2,656	2,308
	arc, inches:		+2.2	+2.9	0	-7.0

Ballistic Performance of Long-Range Deer Cartridges (cont'd)

Lazzeroni 160 Swift A-Fr.						
	velocity, fps:	3,385	3,167	2,961	2,763	2,574
	energy, ft-lb:	4,072	3,565	3,115	2,713	2,354
	arc, inches:		+2.6	+3.3	0	-7.8

.30-06 Springfield		muz.	100	200	300	400
Federal 165 Sierra GameKing HE	velocity, fps:	3,140	2,900	2,670	2,450	2,240
	energy, ft-lb:	3,610	3,075	2,610	2,200	1,845
	arc, inches:		+1.5	0	-6.9	-20.4
Hornady 150 SP LM	velocity, fps:	3,100	2,815	2,548	2,295	2,058
	energy, ft-lb:	3,200	2,639	2,161	1,755	1,410
	arc, inches:		+1.4	0	-6.8	-20.3
Hornady 165 SPBT LM	velocity, fps:	3,015	2,790	2,575	2,370	2,176
	energy, ft-lb:	3,330	2,850	2,428	2,058	1,734
	arc, inches:		+1.6	0	-7.0	-20.1
Rem. 165 AccuTip	velocity, fps:	2,800	2,597	2,403	2,217	2,039
	energy, ft-lb:	2,872	2,470	2,115	1,800	1,523
	arc, inches:		+1.8	0	-7.9	-22.8
Win. 150 Power-Point Plus	velocity, fps:	3,050	2,685	2,352	2,043	1,760
	energy, ft-lb:	3,089	2,402	1,843	1,391	1,032
	arc, inches:		+1.7	0	-8.0	-24.3
Win. 168 Ballistic Silvertip	velocity, fps:	2,790	2,599	2,416	2,240	2,072
	energy, ft-lb:	2,903	2,520	2,177	1,872	1,601
	arc, inches:		+1.8	0	-7.8	-22.5

.300 H&H Mag.		muz.	100	200	300	400
Federal 180 Nosler Partition	velocity, fps:	2,880	2,620	2,380	2,150	1,930
	energy, ft-lb:	3,315	2,750	2,260	1,840	1,480
	arc, inches:		+1.8	0	-8.0	-23.4
Win. 180 Fail Safe	velocity, fps:	2,880	2,628	2,390	2,165	1,952
	energy, ft-lb:	3,316	2,762	2,284	1,873	1,523
	arc, inches:		+1.8	0	-7.9	-23.2

.308 Norma Mag.		muz.	100	200	300	400
Norma 180 TXP Swift A-Fr.	velocity, fps:	2,953	2,704	2,469	2,245	
	energy, ft-lb:	3,486	2,924	2,437	2,016	
	arc, inches:		+1.6	0	-7.3	

.300 Winchester Mag.		muz.	100	200	300	400
Hornady 165 SST	velocity, fps:	3,100	2,885	2,680	2,483	2,296
	energy, ft-lb:	3,520	3,049	2,630	2,259	1,930
	arc, inches:		+1.4	0	-6.4	-18.6
Rem. 150 PSP C-L Ultra	velocity, fps:	3,290	2,967	2,666	2,384	2,120
	energy, ft-lb:	3,065	2,931	2,366	1,893	1,496
	arc, inches:		+1.2	0	-6.1	-18.4

Rem. 180 AccuTip		muz.	100	200	300	400
Rem. 180						
AccuTip	velocity, fps:	2,960	2,764	2,577	2,397	2,224
	energy, ft-lb:	3,501	3,053	2,653	2,295	1,976
	arc, inches:		+1.5	0	-6.8	-19.6
Win. 180 Ballistic						
Silvertip	velocity, fps:	2,950	2,764	2,586	2,415	2,250
	energy, ft-lb:	3,478	3,054	2,673	2,331	2,023
	arc, inches:		+1.5	0	-6.7	-19.4
Win. 180						
Partition Gold	velocity, fps:	3,070	2,859	2,657	2,464	2,280
	energy, ft-lb:	3,768	3,267	2,823	2,428	2,078
	arc, inches:		+1.4	0	-6.3	-18.3

.300 Remington Short Ultra Mag		muz.	100	200	300	400
Rem. 150						
PSP C-L Ultra	velocity, fps:	3,200	2,901	2,672	2,359	2,112
	energy, ft-lb:	3,410	2,803	2,290	1,854	1,485
	arc, inches:		+1.3	0	-6.4	-19.I
Rem. 165						
PSP Core-Lokt	velocity, fps:	3,075	2,792	2,527	2,276	2,040
	energy, ft-lb:	3,464	2,856	2,339	1,828	1,525
	arc, inches:		+1.5	0	-7.0	-20.7
Rem. 180						
Partition	velocity, fps:	2,960	2,761	2,571	2,389	2,214
	energy, ft-lb:	3,501	3,047	2,642	2,280	1,959
	arc, inches:		+1.5	0	-6.8	-19.7
Rem. 180						
PSP C-L Ultra	velocity, fps:	2,960	2,727	2,506	2,295	2,094
	energy, ft-lb:	3,501	2,972	2,509	2,105	1,753
	arc, inches:		+1.6	0	-7.1	-20.9
Rem. 190						
HPBT Match	velocity, fps:	2,900	2,725	2,557	2,395	2,239
	energy, ft-lb:	3,547	3,133	2,758	2,420	2,115
	arc, inches:		+1.6	0	-6.9	-19.9

.300 Winchester Short Mag.		muz.	100	200	300	400
Federal 150						
Nosler Bal. Tip	velocity, fps:	3,200	2,970	2,755	2,545	2,345
	energy, ft-lb:	3,410	2,940	2,520	2,155	1,830
	arc, inches:		+1.2	0	-5.8	-17.0
Norma 180						
Nosler Bal. Tip	velocity, fps:	3,215	2,985	2,767	2,560	
	energy, ft-lb:	3,437	2,963	2,547	2,179	
	arc, inches:		+1.2	0	-5.7	
Win. 150 Ballistic						
Silvertip	velocity, fps:	3,300	3,061	2,834	2,619	2,414
	energy, ft-lb:	3,628	3,121	2,676	2,285	1,941
	arc, inches:		+1.1	0	-5.4	-15.9
Win. 180 Ballistic						
Silvertip	velocity, fps:	3,010	2,822	2,641	2,468	2,301
	energy, ft-lb:	3,621	3,182	2,788	2,434	2,116
	arc, inches:		+1.4	0	-6.4	-18.6
Win. 180						
AccuBond	velocity, fps:	3,010	2,822	2,643	,470	2,304
	energy, ft-lb:	3,622	3,185	2,792	2,439	2,121
	arc, inches:		+1.4	0	-6.4	-18.5

Ballistic Performance of Long-Range Deer Cartridges (cont'd)

.300 Weatherby Mag.		muz.	100	200	300	400
Federal 180						
Nosler Part. HE	velocity, fps:	3,330	3,110	2,810	2,710	2,520
	energy, ft-lb:	4,430	3,875	3,375	2,935	2,540
	arc, inches:		+1.0	0	-5.2	-15.1
Wby. 150 Pointed						
Expanding	velocity, fps:	3,540	3,225	2,932	2,657	2,399
	energy, ft-lb:	4,173	3,462	2,862	2,351	1,916
	arc, inches:		+2.6	+3.3	0	-8.2
Wby. 150						
Nosler Partition	velocity, fps:	3,540	3,263	3,004	2,759	2,528
	energy, ft-lb:	4,173	3,547	3,005	2,536	2,128
	arc, inches:		+2.5	+3.2	0	-7.7
Wby. 165						
Nosler Bal. Tip	velocity, fps:	3,350	3,133	2,927	2,730	2,542
	energy, ft-lb:	4,111	3,596	3,138	2,730	2,367
	arc, inches:		+2.7	+3.4	0	-8.1
Wby. 180 Pointed						
Expanding	velocity, fps:	3,240	3,004	2,781	2,569	2,366
	energy, ft-lb:	4,195	3,607	3,091	2,637	2,237
	arc, inches:		+3.1	+3.8	0	-9.0

.300 Dakota		muz.	100	200	300	400
Dakota 165						
Barnes X	velocity, fps:	3,200	2,979	2,769	2,569	2,377
	energy, ft-lb:	3,751	3,251	2,809	2,417	2,070
	arc, inches:		+2.1	+1.8	-3.0	-13.2
Dakota 200						
Barnes X	velocity, fps:	3,000	2,824	2,656	2,493	2,336
	energy, ft-lb:	3,996	3,542	3,131	2,760	2,423
	arc, inches:		+2.2	+1.5	-4.0	-15.2

.300 Remington Ultra Mag		muz.	100	200	300	400
Federal 180						
Trophy Bonded	velocity, fps:	3,250	3,000	2,770	2,550	2,340
	energy, ft-lb:	4,220	3,605	3,065	2,590	2,180
	arc, inches:		+1.2	0	-5.7	-16.8
Rem. 150						
Swift Scirocco	velocity, fps:	3,450	3,208	2,980	2,762	2,556
	energy, ft-lb:	3,964	3,427	2,956	2,541	2,175
	arc, inches:		+1.7	+1.5	-2.6	-11.2
Rem. 180						
Swift Scirocco	velocity, fps:	3,250	3,048	2,856	2,672	2,495
	energy, ft-lb:	4,221	3,714	3,260	2,853	2,487
	arc, inches:		+2.0	+1.7	-2.8	-12.3
Rem. 180						
PSP Core-Lokt	velocity, fps:	3,250	2,988	2,742	2,508	2,287
	energy, ft-lb:	3,517	2,974	2,503	2,095	1,741
	arc, inches:		+2.1	+1.8	-3.1	-13.6

.30-378 Weatherby Mag.		muz.	100	200	300	400
Wby. 165						
Nosler Bal. Tip	velocity, fps:	3,500	3,275	3,062	2,859	2,665
	energy, ft-lb:	4,488	3,930	3,435	2,995	2,603
	arc, inches:		+2.4	+3.0	0	-7.4

Wby. 180 Nosler Bal. Tip		muz.	100	200	300	400
	velocity, fps:	3,420	3,213	3,015	2,826	2,645
	energy, ft-lb:	4,676	4,126	3,634	3,193	2,797
	arc, inches:		+2.5	+3.1	0	-7.5
Wby. 180 Barnes X	velocity, fps:	3,450	3,243	3,046	2,858	2,678
	energy, ft-lb:	4,757	4,204	3,709	3,264	2,865
	arc, inches:		+2.4	+3.1	0	-7.4
7.82 (.308) Lazzeroni Warbird		*muz.*	*100*	*200*	*300*	*400*
Lazzeroni 150 Nosler Part.	velocity, fps:	3,680	3,432	3197	2,975	2,764
	energy, ft-lb:	4,512	3,923	3,406	2,949	2,546
	arc, inches:		+2.1	+2.7	0	-6.6
Lazzeroni 180 Nosler Part.	velocity, fps:	3,425	3,220	3,026	2,839	2,661
	energy, ft-lb:	4,689	4,147	3,661	3,224	2,831
	arc, inches:		+2.5	+3.2	0	-7.5

A fast-stepping bullet shoots flat because gravity has less time to depress its flight path over a given distance. You can hit at long range with bullets that scribe steep arcs, but accurate range estimation becomes more critical.

A bullet's trajectory depends on its initial speed and ballistic coefficient (C: a number reflecting its shape and sectional density). C is essentially a measure of how well a bullet cleaves air. A high C value (say, .400 in hunting bullets) indicates a low rate of deceleration, so there is less velocity loss downrange. The more speed a bullet retains, the more energy it carries—and the flatter it flies. A bullet leaving the muzzle at 3,000 fps and holding seventy percent of that speed at 400 yards allows for dead-on aim to 250 yards if you zero at 200. For a point-blank maximum range of 300 yards, you'll put up with greater mid-range deviation: say, four

David Miller makes a science of long shooting during the off-season. He kills far away Coues deer.

inches instead of three for all but the flattest-shooting rounds. (Note that some of the arc values in the chart show 250- and 300-yard zeros.)

Energy is a function of velocity and bullet weight. You don't need a heavy bullet to kill deer. The 180-grain 30-caliber bullets that deliver a ton of energy to 400 yards also make the rifle kick hard. Reduce bore diameter and bullet weight, and you get gentler treatment. Smaller, lighter bullets enable you to keep speed and ballistic coefficient high for flat flight. The smaller powder charges needed to launch them throttle recoil and require less barrel time to burn.

Of course, heavy bullets buck wind better than lightweight bullets at the same velocity. Several of my friends hunt the diminutive Coues whitetail with a rifle in .300 Weatherby. His 168-grain Sierra boat-tails resist drift as well as they defy gravity. You cannot kill game too dead, and there's nothing wrong with a heavy bullet if you can tolerate stiff recoil without flinching.

Most people, me included, get timid after a few blows in the chops from a super-magnum. My shooting improves with mild cartridges. For deer hunting, a .25-06 or .270 is about what I want. The .240, .257, and .270 Weatherby Magnums, with Winchester's .264, also work fine. If elk are on the ticket, 160-grain spitzers in a .280 or 7mm Magnum make sense. The .30-06 is a great long-range cartridge with 150- and 165-grain bullets driven over 3,000 fps. Lighter bullets have such low sectional density that they decelerate like whiffle balls at long range. Heavier bullets equip the '06 for bigger game but have steeper trajectories. The .30 magnums are most efficient with 165- and 180-grain loads. Super-magnums, from Weatherby's .300 and Remington's .300 Ultra Mag, to the 7.82 Lazzeroni Warbird, and .30-378 Weatherby, shoot as flat as the Gobi, with slipstreams that would

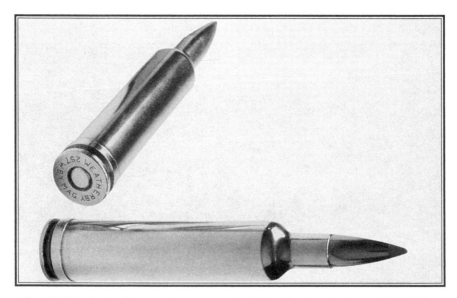

The .257 Weatherby Magnum has great reach. It dates back to the Second World War.

stagger a moose. They're no fun to shoot, even if they do span time zones.

While you can tell all you need to know about a cartridge by looking at ballistics charts, rifles are more enigmatic. You can't say how a rifle will shoot by looking at the catalog specs or even by a close-up eyeballing of the bore. Long barrels are not more accurate than short barrels; in fact, all else equal, the short barrel may group tighter, because it is stiffer. Long barrels do, however, push bullets faster, because they bottle the expanding powder gas longer. Velocity loss or gain per inch of barrel length depends on the load, the ratio of case capacity to bore diameter, and the original barrel length. A .44-40 barrel chopped from 26 to 24 inches won't show

To shoot long, get as close to the ground as you can, and use a sling or bipod.

much difference at the chronograph. Expect measurable loss from a .257 Weatherby barrel given the same treatment. For most long-range deer cartridges, figure 30 to 40 fps per inch between 22 and 26 inches. You want a barrel long enough to get most of the speed your cartridge has to offer, but not so long as to make the rifle unwieldy. The short receiver of a dropping-block single-shot rifle gives you the option of a 26-inch barrel in a relatively short rifle. Barrel fluting is a practical, and now popular, way to pare ounces without compromising barrel stiffness.

Over the past couple of decades a cult has grown up around stand-hunting with "beanfield" rifles in the Southeast, and cross-canyon shooting from log landings in the mountain West. If you sit all day, a heavy rifle is no burden. But big bucks shun exposure. You'll find more of them in places not visible from stands with panoramic views–places you must walk through or climb to. Even if stand-hunting showed me all the deer I wanted, I'd still hike, because traveling in wild country is for me a wonderful part of hunting. So my rifles must be portable.

A seven-pound Winchester Model 70 Featherweight becomes an eight-and-a-half-pound rifle scoped and loaded, with sling. That's an easy rifle to pack. Get much over nine pounds on your shoulder, and mountain passes will seem steep. Bantam-weight rifles typically have short actions that won't handle cartridges designed to reach far, but long-action rifles in the six-pound range are proliferating. Remember that weight can help you steady the rifle against your pulse and gusts of wind. It also absorbs recoil.

Many hunters now install bipods on rifles. A bipod will help you steady the rifle against pulse beat and the wind, but it adds weight and bulk and can bite into your shoulder on long treks. It is hard to set up quickly on uneven ground, and even the models with leg extensions are of limited use sitting and kneeling. Better for me is a Brownell's Latigo sling. Its adjustable shooting loop tames the rifle almost as effectively as a rest. And it puts no extra load on the rifle.

BUCKS BEYOND THE BEANFIELD

You can kill a deer with just about any rifle. If collecting venison or antlers is all your rifle is for, there's no sense paying a lot for one or reading any further here. But for many hunters, a rifle amounts to more than a tool.

A rifle can be art. Engraving and finely checkered French walnut don't help rifles function more smoothly or shoot more accurately, but a deadly rifle made beautiful appeals to many hunters.

A rifle can be a link with the past. That's partly why pre-64 Model 70 Winchesters and early post-war Savage 99 carbines bring a lump to the throat of hunters old enough to remember those times.

A rifle can carry a tradition. So we cherish the battered .30-30 that Gramps used to anchor a buck with antlers the size of a bushel basket the last day of Michigan's 1947 season.

A rifle can reflect our priorities, project an image to which we aspire. So hunters buy rifles bored for cartridges a shade smaller than bowling pins and use extra denture adhesive at the bench.

A rifle can come alive in the hand. Like a maiden's slender palm or the grips on a vintage Harley, a rifle well shaped promises great things with just a touch. You either feel the magic or you don't.

A rifle can, of course, simply shoot accurately. Such rifles don't let on that they're accurate. You can't tell an accurate rifle at a glance, can't pick it from a rack the way you might Gramps' old Enfield or a Biesen sporter or a Weatherby .378. An accurate rifle identifies itself only after you've fired it–and, to be brutally honest, sometimes not then. Accurate rifles won't reveal themselves to inept marksmen. If you can't hold in the same place for consecutive shots, you'll find that accurate rifles scatter bullets as widely as do inaccurate and less expensive rifles. If you don't shoot well, accurate rifles amount to a waste of money.

Because, as a group, riflemen consider themselves crack shots, rifles advertised as accurate sell briskly. Some companies go so far as to guarantee accuracy: one-and-a-half inches at 100 yards, perhaps a minute of angle. Guarantee anything, and you're sure to get product back. A smattering of rifles return to their makers each year, with notes from customers convinced that the hardware is flawed. Patiently, factory technicians punch out additional groups and offer telephone therapy. Convincing the incompetent that they are is lots of trouble. Which is why anyone would be nuts to guarantee half-minute groups.

But Kenny Jarrett does.

Jarrett, 52, is a fourth-generation soybean farmer from Jackson, South Carolina. He grew up on the 10,000-acre Cowden Plantation, then owned by his uncle, J.M. Brown. After high school, Kenny went to work at Cowden. Then, in the late 1970s, he bought a lathe and opened a gunshop. Jarrett's perception of accuracy had already been molded by benchrest matches. Building a rifle that consistently shot competitive groups, he found, was exceedingly difficult.

Texas gunmaker and benchrest shooter Harold Broughton saw promise in the lad and invited him to visit. Kenny still credits Broughton for setting him on track

Pat Beckett shows a 400-yard group shot in practice with a Burris scope and Ballistic Plex reticle.

Kenny Jarrett examines one of his "beanfield rifles," now famous for their accuracy and reach.

to build truly accurate rifles. The next stop was at Jerry Hart's barrel shop. By 1979, Kenny had invested heavily in the gun business and quit farming. His first year building rifles, he grossed $17,000–enough to encourage expansion. Favorable press in the major gun journals gave Kenny the traction he needed to establish himself as an industry icon. A bushy red beard and a golf-ball wad of tobacco, his bib overalls, and Bubba wit all seemed an odd match to machine work demanding tolerances as fine as .0001. At first, that incongruity helped sell stories about Jarrett rifles.

It was the late Art Carter, I believe, who coined the term "beanfield rifle" to describe the deadly long-range effect of those rifles on southern deer. Hunters took notice. By the time Kenny's shop was a decade old, gross sales had topped $500,000, and he had hired 13 people. The 2,200-square-foot shop, built of home-sawn cypress lumber, and roofed with cedar shakes, had sprouted four additions, nearly tripling the space. In 1991, Kenny's least expensive rifle sold for $2,850.

"Lots of people tried to tell me early on that hunters just wouldn't pay for the level of accuracy demanded by benchrest competitors," Kenny told me in an interview then. "I set out to prove them wrong." A champion benchrest shooter himself, Jarrett knew that building such precision into lightweight hunting rifles would be expensive. He also figured, rightly, that for some hunters, accuracy is the defining element of a rifle–even one to be used on targets as big as deer. "It isn't that you need a half-minute rifle to shoot deer," he pointed out. "You don't pay a premium to kill. You pay the extra because accurate is what a rifle should be, and you can't abide a rifle that doesn't measure up."

For years Kenny built rifles on actions the customer supplied, or he'd furnish a Remington 700 or, for large cases, a Weatherby Mark V. After truing the lugs by surface grinding and hand fitting, he chased the receiver threads so barrel and bolt axes lined up perfectly. Kenny used Hart barrels for cartridges of 30 caliber and under. Bigger rounds went in Schneider tubes. Along the way, he developed several of his own wildcat cartridges, from the super-fast .220 Jaybird to the .338 Kubla-Kahn, a .378 Weatherby necked to .33. One of his favorites is the versatile .300 Jarrett, on the 8mm Remington Magnum case. By the early 1990s, Jarrett's shop held 68 chambering reamers. Seventy percent of his customers were then opting for wildcat cartridges, the .280 Ackley getting most play. Kenny also developed a switch-barrel system for the Remington 700.

McMillan provided all the early Jarrett stocks. Kenny did not–and does not–think walnut has a place on an accurate rifle. "Stability is crucial to accuracy," he states simply. "Walnut walks." He pillar-beds all rifles and shoots them to make sure they meet accuracy standards. In 1991, that meant half-inch three-shot groups at 100 yards for rifles 25-caliber and smaller, three-quarter-inch for larger bores. At the time, 85 percent of Jarrett rifle sold wore hunting-weight barrels. Hewing to such strict accuracy standards, and developing loads to deliver that accuracy, limited annual rifle production to about 125.

In 1992, Kenny started making his own barrels, button-rifled in stainless steel.

A requisite for long shooting at deer is an accurate rifle. This Jarrett in .243 Catbird certainly qualifies!

"We learned a lot in those years, rejecting, on average, 27 percent of our barrels." Today, that figure has dropped to six percent, though accuracy standards have become even tougher to meet. Now Kenny demands half inches from even his 30-caliber magnums. Hardware that doesn't pass muster gets tossed. Once, after rebarreling an action several times and scrapping the tubes, Jarrett took a hacksaw to the receiver and hung the split metal over his workbench. No compromises allowed.

During the late 1990s, Kenny Jarrett's rifle business went flat. The rosy flush of publicity that had fueled early sales had died. Some customers came back with repeat orders—one racked $46,000 in Jarrett rifles—but for others, a single expensive, super-accurate rifle was all a marriage could tolerate. At the same time, Kenny was busy designing his own action. Unveiling it to me, he acknowledged that he'd have been better off with an accountant at his shoulder. "It's too good," he shrugged. "I made it too expensive." He wondered, bleakly, if it would ever see production.

Well, it has. The Jarrett action is engineered to offer benchrest accuracy and a smooth-shucking bolt in a magazine rifle that accommodates big hunting cartridges. It is sophisticated and still costly. But it is now available with 90-day delivery.

Not long ago as this is written, I traveled to South Carolina to visit Jarrett's shop and the Cowden Plantation, which Kenny now owns. He operates Cowden as a farm but also leases hunting rights to deer and turkey hunters, and has a 1,000-yard range there to test rifles after they've proven worthy at the 100-yard range in back of his shop. We started the tour where an electrical discharge machine (EDM) and a computer-controlled mill (CNC unit) carve Jarrett receivers from 515 Stainless bar stock, Rockwell 34. The action has clever features, like feed rails specifically designed for each cartridge. They're replaceable, not integral. A collar at the rear of the bolt ensures bind-free cycling. Three evenly spaced lugs offer a lock-up that puts even pressure all around the case head and allows for a low bolt throw.

Stainless barrels are given a copper bore wash to ease passage of the carbide rifling button. The copper must be later removed–not a problem at the Jarrett shop because all bores are hand-lapped. "We want to keep bore diameter within .0001, breech to muzzle," said Kenny. "And we air-gauge every bore to check. Such a tight tolerance makes for relatively high rejection rates, but if a barrel gets chambered, we're very sure it will shoot well. Of course, we don't know until we do the range work. Every rifle gets a proof target. We fire 40,000 rounds a year." He pointed to 55-gallon drums full of brass.

Kenny's son Jay runs the stock shop, where composite shells are precisely fitted to the metal and aluminum pillars and glued in with Marine-Tex, also used in the recoil lug mortise. Conservative, classic profiles, with straight combs and cheekpieces, are typically painted black. "Jay is part of the reason I've kept investing in

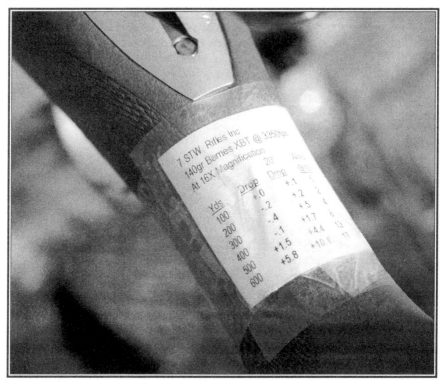

Taping ballistic data to your rifle stock can help you calculate hold for long shots.

the shop," Kenny told me. "He and Rissa, who pretty much runs the office, deserve a shot at this business. They're not only my kids; they produce and sell my rifles." Another son was also about to join Jarrett Rifles.

Final assembly usually includes installation of Jarrett's own muzzle brake. "It's effective because it has plenty of holes and only .001 clearance for the bullet," explained Kenny. We walked through the loading room to the range, where I bellied up to the bench with a Jarrett rifle built on a Dakota 97 action. It was chambered in .300 Jarrett. The brake did indeed work, and though this rifle hadn't been tuned, my first three Ballistic Tips nipped out a half-inch group.

I asked to shoot other rifles, and they were promptly trotted out. A Tactical Rifle in .308, a long-barreled medium-weight customer gun in .243 Catbird (Jarrett's own, a 6mm/.270 that drives 65-grain Shilen bullets fast enough to leave a hole in humidity). And Kenny's own .300, with the 200-grain Bear Claw loads he once used to shoot a huge moose.

Bright, sharp binoculars encourage hunters to hunt farther ahead of their boots.

The first three-shot group from the .308 went under .2 inch.

The first three-shot group from the Catbird measured about .3 inch.

At nearly .8 inch, the Bear Claws seemed naughty; but to miss a moose with a rifle that delivers three-quarter-minute accuracy, you'd have to be shooting at over 4,000 yards . . .

"Wanna shoot long?" Kenny had read my mind. But the wind was up, he warned, and the 600-yard range would be difficult.

Indeed it would be, I concluded, as twice we had to staple backers blown off by gusts that swayed the tops of tall pines and flattened grass beneath them. Still, the wind was quartering, and blocked by a row of trees for more than 400 yards from the bench. Kenny called the breeze as I triggered three shots from the .300. Eight inches. I fired three from the .308, keeping them under five. My reservations about the Catbird's tiny bullets were laid to rest with a sub-four-inch group at 600 yards. Drop, of course, was significant in all cases. "That's why our backer is as tall as an outhouse," Kenny explained. I fell to prone with a tight sling, and fired another group with the .300, correcting with holdover, and doping the wind myself. Two of three bullets landed in the eight-inch target square; the other was a hand's width out.

"Addicting, isn't it?" Kenny grinned.

Indeed it was. A treat too, partly because ranges like the Cowden Plantation's are scarce and partly because few–OK, none–of my hunting rifles can be counted on to shoot three-quarter-minute groups at 600 steps. A truly accurate rifle impresses you the way a truly fast, quick-footed sports car impresses you, or a truly great musician leaves you speechless. It imposes a responsibility too. Knowing the rifle will shoot into one hole, you put your marksmanship on the line. Triggering a Jarrett with Kenny watching, you feel compelled to perform as well as the rifle. Good luck.

The Jarrett product line is smaller than it once was, and the 20-person shop is more efficient. "We can produce 200 rifles a year," Kenny said. "And we want to guarantee 90-day delivery." Quick turnaround is important for cash flow too, he added. "Three of our rifles–the Signature, Windwalker, and Professional Hunter–already account for 90 percent of sales. We are a custom shop, and we'll continue to offer many options, including walnut and laminated stocks soon. But there's no sense slowing production and boosting costs with catalog items that interest only a few people."

Jarrett's customer base is small. "Of 1.3 million rifles sold annually in the U.S., we figure about 5,000 are custom-built," he said, "and our rifles are not on the cheap end of the custom category."

Still, Kenny likes to think his rifles go to people who truly appreciate accuracy and who will use them in the field. "Back in the 1980s, a local youngster saved his summer hay money for three years to buy a Jarrett rifle. I threw in a Leupold scope on that deal."

Kenny Jarrett has shaved his beard and given up tobacco. But he still takes the measure of a rifle in tenths of an inch between impact centers. "It's about all we can do to guarantee first-round hits across big beanfields," he drawled. "It's a good way to size up shooters too."

Postscript: Now Jarrett is manufacturing ammunition built on Norma brass. "We chose Norma for its great reputation," Kenny told me. "The cases are very uniform; the square web is at least as strong as the radiused head from other makers. We already sell handloads to 75 percent of its rifle customers, and we wanted to market ammunition that would match those loads. We picked the .243, .270, 7mm Remington Magnum, .30-06, .300 Winchester Magnum, and .300 Jarrett to start, with a couple of bullet options for each. Probably a Nosler Ballistic Tip and a Swift A-Frame. We've also planned a Safari line, beginning with the .375 H&H and the .416 Remington Magnum."

The new loads meet strict accuracy requirements, so even hunters who don't own Jarrett rifles can expect tight groups. The special 10-round boxes designed for one-handed, no-spill opening. Each includes a card with ballistic data: bullet velocity, energy, trajectory, and wind drift–even sectional density and ballistic coefficient.

Expect to pay a premium for this high-performance ammo. But before you choose cheaper cartridges instead, compare the cost of a box of the best ammunition you can buy with the cost of a deer hunt. And think about what you might pay for one superlative cartridge on the last day of the season, with a big buck cresting a windy ridge three football fields away . . . ∎

7

DEER GUNS FOR DEEP WOODS

I 've seen faster deer. But then, even bucks on a lope can vanish quickly in cover. I levered the 94 Winchester as fast as I could catch aim and managed four shots through the opening. Silence. But in those last two explosions there'd been a dead sound, like an ax biting softwood. Carefully I wound my way into alders, through blackberry tangles that stabbed and tugged like treble hooks. The deer was dead. It was one of few I've killed with repeat shots. I'd swung the carbine too far in front at first, anticipating. But the little .30-30 responded to my corrections instantly and in stride. The final pair of bullets threaded vitals.

FAT BULLETS AT SPITBALL RANGE

Cloverleaf. It's hard to get your first three shots out of the muzzle to kiss on the target. This day, I felt particularly blessed, because that cluster had come from a lever-action .45-70 with a 2.5x scope. The gunsmith, Charlie Sisk, may not have improved on the Marlin's accuracy, but he surely didn't hurt it!

It's one thing to build a rifle with a gaping muzzle. It's another to package it well. Somehow, the British have managed to build elegance into double rifles with bores big enough to swallow young badgers. What's more, these doubles point like shotguns, despite their substantial weight. Americans have become adept at fashioning elegant bolt rifles. Designing muscle into the first lever-action repeaters took decades. Getting the lines and balance just right was yet another chore.

Over centuries of rifle development, bores have gotten smaller. Our biggest bullets now would have looked relatively thin to shooters of even the 18th century. Then, balls of less than half-inch diameter were considered petite. When the first cartridge rifles appeared, black powder and weak breeching limited their effectiveness; thick, heavy bullets made them lethal.

During the middle of the 19th century, many entrepreneurs worked to perfect a repeating rifle. An exception was young New Jersey machinist Christian Sharps, who instead focused on breech-loading single-shots. In 1848, he received his first patent, for a rifle with a sliding breechblock. The first Sharps rifle for metallic cartridges, the New Model 1869, appeared five years before Christian Sharps died of tuberculosis. The New Model 1874 came out the next year. Market hunter George Reighard explained in a 1930 edition of the Kansas City Star how he used his Sharps on bison:

"In 1872, I organized my own outfit and went south from Fort Dodge . . . I had two big .50 Sharps rifles with telecopic sights . . . .

The time I made my biggest kill I lay on a slight ridge, behind a tuft of weeds 100 yards from a bunch of a thousand buffaloes that had come a long distance to a creek, had drunk their fill, and then strolled out upon the prairie to rest, some to lie down. . . . After I had killed about 25, my gun barrel became hot and began to expand. A bullet from an overheated gun does not go straight, it wobbles, so I put that gun aside and took the other. By the time that became hot, the other had cooled, but then the powder smoke in front of me was so thick I could not see through it. . . . I had to crawl backward, dragging my two guns, and work around to another position on the ridge, from which I killed fifty-four more. . . . On that trip, I killed a few more than 3,000 buffaloes in one month. . . ."

The Sharps Rifle Company folded in 1880, largely a victim of its own product. By then, so many bison had been killed that human scavengers would glean more than three million tons of bones from the plains. The only thing deadlier than a Sharps rifle at that time would have been a repeater stout enough to handle its powerful cartridges. Winchester Repeating Arms was by far the country's largest firearms company, with a net worth of $1.2 million. By 1875, ammo output had reached a million rounds per day. Then the declining demand for military ordnance that had helped usher out the Sharps enterprise prompted Winchester to shift direction. To enhance its fortunes in the hunting market, it developed a big, iron-frame version of the popular Model 1873 lever-action. But despite its size, the Model 1876 lacked the strength to handle pressures generated by the .45-70.

In 1883, a Winchester salesman picked up a used single-shot rifle that showed uncommon strength. He showed it to company president Thomas Bennett, who sought out the frontier gunsmith who'd designed and built it. So began Winchester's golden relationship with John Browning. It was to last 17 years and give the company 40 firearms, including the most celebrated of the century.

One of these came shortly after Winchester dubbed Browning's single-shot rifle the Model 1885. John and his brother Matt took to New Haven an idea for a repeating lever gun that would handle the .45-70. The rifle became Winchester's Model 1886, eventually chambered in .33 Win., .38-56, 38-70, .40-65, .40-70, .40-82, .45-70, .45-90, .50-100, and .50-110. The subsequent Model 1892, a petite lever rifle with the

Big bullets loafing at under 2,200 fps won't blast through brush, but they're deadly on deer close up.

86's vertical locking lugs, would spawn the Model 1894, chambered in 1895 for the .30-30, America's first centerfire smokeless round.

The .30-30 had impressive reach. The 94 was lighter and easier to handle than most rifles built for bigger cartridges. It was accurate, too. Sales of the 1886 slipped, and in 1935 Winchester dropped the rifle from its line. Replacing it was the

Model 71, clearly of 1886 lineage but chambering its own special .348 cartridge. The 71, in carbine and rifle forms, with checkered and plain stocks, was the last new exposed-hammer big-game rifle from Winchester in the 20th century. It lasted until 1957, to be supplanted by the hammerless Model 88, with detachable box magazine and a trigger that cycled with the lever. The Model 88 debuted in 1955 and stayed in Winchester's stable for 18 years. Its single big-bore offering, the .358 Winchester, sold only from 1956 into 1964.

In 1978, Winchester modified the Model 94 action to accept the new .375 Winchester cartridge. A thickened rear receiver distinguished the XTR Big Bore from traditional 94s. Four years later, the .307 and .356 Winchester were added. None of these rifles or chamberings are available from Winchester now.

The most powerful Winchester lever-action was the Model 1895, built in rifle and carbine form between 1896 and the end of 1931. Chambered for the .30-40 Krag, .30-03, and .30-06, .303 British, and 7.62 Russian, the 1895 featured a vertical magazine that allowed use of the pointed bullets that gave these potent rounds their great range in bolt guns. The 1895 was also offered in .35 Win., .38-72, .40-72, and the mighty .405 Winchester that Teddy Roosevelt called his "big medicine." T.R. hunted in Africa with a Model 1895 in .405 and found it adequate for dangerous game. While standards have changed since 1910, the .405 is still a powerful round. Hornady offers factory loads for it. Both the 1895 and the 1886 have appeared as limited-edition rifles, manufactured in Japan for Browning/USRAC. So has the Winchester 71.

The powerful .450 Marlin can also deliver tight groups. It's essentially a belted, high-octane .45-70.

During the last decades of the 19th century, in the heyday of Winchester lever-actions, John Marlin came up with a similar–but in some ways, better–lever gun. L.L. Hepburn reconfigured the Marlin 1889 to handle long cartridges. Marlin's Model 1893 appeared first in .32-40 and .38-55, was later offered in .25-36, .30-30, and .32 Special. The Model 1893 became the 93 in 1905, without changes. By the 1920s, it was a favorite among deer hunters. Winchester's Model 94 had a worthy opponent until the Depression claimed the Model 93 in 1936. By then the price had dropped to $25, after more than 73,000 had sold.

Marlin's answer to the Winchester 1886 was the Model 1895, announced in 1896. Essentially a large-frame Model 1893, it was chambered for the .38-56, .40-65, .40-82, .45-70, and .45-90. The .40-70 joined the stable in 1897. In 1912 Marlin added a lightweight rifle in .33 WCF. It held five cartridges and retailed for $18.50.

Marlin exited the Depression by reintroducing its Model 93. The Model 1936 replaced the 93 in 1937. Chambered in .30-30 and .32 Special, it marked the doom

The .35 Remington appeared in the company's Model 8 autoloader a century ago. It's still a gem!

of many traditional black-powder deer cartridges. As Winchester's Model 94 in .30-30 had all but supplanted the elegant 86 and its thumb-size rounds, and the Savage 99 was wooing shooters to the .300 and .303 Savage, Marlin's pitch to hunters in the 1920s and 1930s highlighted smokeless, bottle-necked cartridges of relatively small bore.

Marlin dropped the .32 Special from the 336 in 1964. A year later, the firm announced the Model 444 Rifle, a 336 chambered for a modern big-bore round: the .444 Marlin. Essentially a rimmed .30-06 hull necked to take 240-grain .44 Magnum bullets, the .444 was a Marlin idea. Art Burns and Tom Robinson brought the cartridge to production. Earl Larson at Remington added a 265-grain load in 1980. Renewed interest in the .45-70, and the advent of the .450 Marlin, have drained some vitality from the .444. But it has since been chambered in a special edition of the Winchester 94. The fact that all three are still available in lever rifles belies the assumption that big-bores are dead.

Some of the best, admittedly, have withered. Winchester's .358 cartridge, trotted out in 1955, was chambered in the Winchester 88 and in Savage 99EG and 99R and RS models until they were dropped in 1960. A special run of .358s with distinctive recoil pad came off the Savage line from 1977 to 1980. This compact cartridge has also been cataloged for the Browning BLR, a smoothcycling lever gun introduced in 1966. An exposed-hammer rifle with an exceptionally smooth rack-and-pinion mechanism and a front-locking bolt, it is strong and accurate. Side-ejecting, of course. It was a perfect fit for the .358, surprisingly frisky for its size.

While bullet drop with big-bore cartridges can make hitting difficult at long range, 200-yard shots are not unreasonable with most of them. There's energy aplenty. The .358 Winchester delivers more energy at 200 yards than the .44 Magnum does at 25. Even Remington's lowly

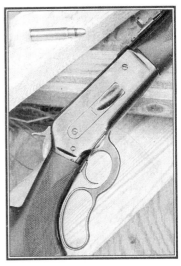

This Model 71 Winchester has been barreled to a wildcat .416/348.

.35 hits like half a ton of bricks at 150 yards. Despite its thick profile, the 265-grain .444 Marlin carries that half-ton to 300 yards, where the flat-nosed .405 Winchester offers even more horsepower. Truly potent wildcats like the .450 Alaskan and .450 Marlin come mighty close to matching the .458 Winchester. Precision? The

Most big Midwest whitetails stick close to woods; long-range rifles are seldom necessary.
CREDIT: EILEEN CLARKE

Markus Wilhelm, CEO of Bookspan, with a good mule deer buck taken in Wyoming. The buck was shot after a long and careful stalk at a distance of about 200 yards as it got out of its bed. Wilhelm was shooting a Dakota .30-06 model 76 with 180-grain Winchester Partition Gold ammo. CREDIT: PETER FIDUCCIA

This fine southern whitetail fell to a Remington bolt rifle fired from a ground blind. Such blinds are often placed at field borders. CREDIT: WAYNE VAN ZWOLL

Two hunters drag a northern buck through the edge cover whitetails favor. Sabot slugs in shotgun-only areas help hunters reach across clearings. CREDIT: JOHN BARSNESS

It's easy to smile over bucks like this, taken by a Remington Model Seven and a Kahles scope.
CREDIT: WAYNE VAN ZWOLL

Peter Fiduccia, host of the Woods N 'Water TV series, with a 16-point buck taken in Saskatchewan, Canada. Fiduccia shot the buck with a Browning BAR .30-06 Springfield rifle with 180-grain Ballistic Silvertip ammo. The buck grossed 207 5/8 and netted 196 5/8 Boone & Crockett points.   CREDIT: FIDUCCIA ENTERPRISES

An improvised rest is always a good idea, no matter the rifle or how easy the shot. Kate Fiduccia, of Going Wild in Kate's Kitchen, takes aim with her favorite deep woods rifle–a Ruger Deerfield Carbine. Kate likes the short barrel and the light weight to carry through the heavy cover where she hunts. CREDIT: PETER FIDUCCIA

The .25 WSSM shoots very flat. It's an ideal deer round for the plains when chambered in this short-action M70 Winchester. Military autoloaders like the M1 Carbine in .30 Carbine, with the various 7.62x39 rifles, offer marginal power and accuracy for deer. Better choices abound.

CREDIT: WAYNE VAN ZWOLL

I shot this fine Coues whitetail at 200 yards in Sonora. My rifle was a modified M600 Remington in 6mm Remington, an excellent all-around deer cartridge.

CREDIT: WAYNE VAN ZWOLL

Jay Cassell, Deputy Editor of Field & Stream magazine, with a dandy 10-point buck he took in the deep woods near the Neversink Gorge in New York's Catskill Mountains. The buck was 100 yards away and walking through a hemlock grove. Cassell used a Browning BBR .30-06 with Winchester Supreme 165-grain Silvertips.   CREDIT: JAY CASSELL

In the Southwest, shots can be long. This beautiful whitetail buck fell to a bipod-equipped bolt rifle.   CREDIT: WAYNE VAN ZWOLL

Sisk/Marlin .45-70 in my rack shoots tighter groups than many of my bolt guns!

As American as the double rifle is British, big-bore lever rifles have staged a comeback. Marlin's stunning success with its .45-70 Guide Gun brought look-alike competition from Winchester. New models borrow heavily from history. Their lean, muscular profile evokes images of the cowboy and the northwoods whitetail hunter, the explorer and the rifleman scrambling to beat elk to a mountain crossing at dawn. In the sweep of a lever well-used, smooth-sounding as the clickety-click of a distant freight train, there's a slice of Americana. Shooters are discovering that lever rifles designed a century ago not only kill deer as handily as bolt guns; they bring us times and places, people, and cultures and events long gone but cherished still.

There's more to a big-bore lever rifle than a gaping muzzle.

Here's a short list of chamberings you'll find in big-bore rifles built by American firms since the .30-30 gave smaller bullets credibility among deer hunters.

Modern Big-Bore Cartridges for Lever Rifles				
Cartridge	Year of Intro	Bullet Weight	Muzzle Velocity (fps)	Muzzle Energy (ft-lbs.)
.348 Win.	1936	150	2,890	2,780
		200	2,530	2,840
		250	2,350	3,060
.35 Rem.	1906	150	2,400	1,920
		200	2,210	2,170
.356 Win.	1982	200	2,460	2,688
		250	2,160	2,591
.358 Win.	1955	200	2,530	2,840
		250	2,250	2,810
.375 Win.	1978	200	2,200	2,105
		250	1,900	2,005
.405 Win.	1904	300	2,200	3,220
.444 Marlin	1964	240	2,400	3,069
		265	2,325	3,180
.45-70	1873	300	1,880	2,355
		405	1,330	1,390
.450 Marlin	2001	350	2,100	3,427

An exhaustive list? Hardly. When I was growing up, the most potent lever guns were Winchester 71s rebarreled to .450 Alaskan (a blown-out .348) by Harold Johnson of Cooper Landing, Alaska. It and similar wildcats like the .450 Fuller and .450-348 Ackley could launch 400-grain bullets at over 2,000 fps! Model 71s are pricey these days. But you can still find 'smiths like Charlie Sisk who work on lever-actions. In Casper, Wyoming, Fred Zeglin fashions takedown Model 1895 Winchesters, replete with XS sights and Scout-style scopes. Wild West Guns makes a specialty of converting big-bore Marlins into takedown rifles called Alaskan CoPilots. You can order many options, including WWG .457 and .50 Alaskan chamberings.

THE NEW BRUSH RIFLES

Before color television, when a McDonald's hamburger cost 19 cents and a gallon of gasoline just pennies more, hunters in my part of the country were still partial to the Winchester 94–which, if memory serves, listed then for about $89. In those days, whitetail deer lived in thickets. They ran fast. You needed a short, lightweight rifle to nail them. Better, we thought, if it was one you could cycle quickly when the first bullet smacked a poplar. Marlin's 336 and the Savage 99 earned followings that rivaled the 94's. A lot of Remington 742 auto-loaders and 760 pumps hung in camps. When Ruger trotted out a .44 Magnum Carbine, budding deer hunters in Mr. Houseman's ninth-grade history class swooned–though at $108, it would have taken their pooled resources to buy one.

Stubby, fast-shucking repeaters still make sense for whitetails, because these deer still live in the brush. In fact, big bucks in pressured areas stay in dense cover. They know bullets fly about in the open. Deer with enormous racks that no one has ever seen before turn up at check stations occasionally, evidence that during rut even veteran bucks who've gone nocturnal make mistakes. And lots of lesser deer fall far from the muzzle in bean patches and stubble. But if you're after more than venison, if grasping big antlers makes you quiver, you must hunt where old deer retreat–where rifles built to shrink distance don't belong.

At least, I used to think so.

The notion that a long-barreled rifle is for long shots and a carbine for short shots is as old as the saw that long-barreled bird guns have more reach than short ones. (When percussion priming was new, some veteran waterfowlers even insisted that flintlocks "shot harder.") Truth is, with modern powders, you don't gain much velocity by adding barrel length beyond reasonable minimums, in shotguns or rifles. The minimums vary, of course; the .44 Magnum and .30-30 lose less speed in carbine barrels than do the .308 or .270. On the other hand, cartridges that aren't efficient in short barrels may have more speed and energy than you need anyway. In 18- or 20-inch carbine barrels, they'll still outperform traditional carbine rounds.

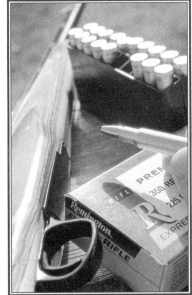

The .350 Remington Magnum has the power for elk as well as deer.

Another common misconception about rifles for thick places is that they must be capable of quick follow-up shots. Truly, I can remember only one time in my years of deer hunting when a fast-firing rifle made a difference. The buck jumped from briars to my left and bounded through an opening in front of me to reach riverbank cover on my right. I fired four times with my 94 Winchester, shortening the lead each time. The last two bullets took him

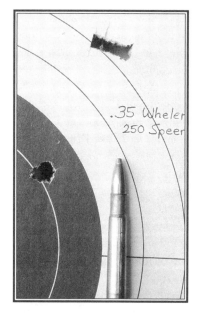

Not even the heaviest bullets can be counted on to penetrate brush straight. This one keyholed.

This buck fell at 35 yards. Most whitetail deer are still shot at under 100 yards.

down. Mostly, deer in cover offer one shot, if any. Recoil, not cycling time, limits your recovery. The important count is aimed shots, not empty cases. With practice, most hunters can keep aimed shots coming as fast with a pump or a lever gun as with an auto-loader. Expert riflemen with bolt guns aren't far behind.

Once, on a bet (was it 25 cents?), a neighbor lad and I squared off with full magazines in our deer rifles. The object: empty them as quickly as we could. He levered his 94 Winchester dry at the same time I spewed the last round from my bolt-action Lee-Enfield. In the woods, we seldom had a chance to fire more than once.

Part of the allure of lever rifles, of course, is their heritage. They're purely American, as much a part of westward expansion as the covered wagon and as symbolic of the cowboy as his Stetson. Yellowed photos of big bucks and lever guns, of Texas Rangers and lever guns, of surplus Willys Jeeps and lever guns, put other rifles in another age. Tradition has always mattered to shooters. But so have big deer on the camp pole. A season or two without a buck to show could test anyone's allegiance to grand-dad's rifle. Where the range was short and the glimpse of a target eye-blink quick, lots of mid-20th-century hunters stuck to their levers. They also began toting auto-loaders and pumps. But that trend soon reversed itself. The swing to bolt-action rifles would last much longer. It was essentially a swing to scopes and long-range cartridges, a concession that Roy Weatherby was right: fast, accurate bullets kill more game.

Now, most whitetails killed still fall well inside the 200-yard mark. Some places, you'll get few shots beyond 50. One reason that bolt-action rifles continue to gobble market share, even where hunters shoot close and fast, is that these rifles have become as nimble as saddle guns. In my youth, commercial bolt rifles like the Remington 721 shared the rack with "sporterized" Spingfields and Mausers. The well-heeled owned Winchester 70s. Loaded, these eight-pound rifles with 24-inch barrels leapt to your cheek with all the agility of a culvert. Steel scopes and mounts made them ponderous. But now the best bolt rifles point more like British grouse guns. In fact, many are lighter in weight than carbines of yesteryear. And because they combine the sound Mauser design with modern steels, they're stronger than many of the heavy bolt rifles that first chambered magnum cartridges. So you can use a flat-shooting, high-pressure round in a rifle that handles like a carbine but delivers the long-range accuracy of a varmint gun.

Not all new bolt rifles excel as woods rifles. Entry-level, meat-and-potatoes turnbolts still weigh seven pounds or more. Barrels typically measure 22 inches for standard rounds, 24 for magnums. But neither the weight nor the length alone disqualify. Some seven-pound rifles seem to point themselves. And Weatherby's insistence on 24-inch barrels for its Ultra Lightweight rifles (to hold velocities high) don't keep these guns from pointing like carbines. More important is the rifle's feel. Most bolt rifles are built to be fired from a rest–whether or not the maker recognizes or admits it. Thick, flat-bottomed forends and tight, beefy grips constrain your hands. Instead of cradling a rifle like you might a slender best-quality 28-gauge, your hands are filled by it. Full contact is a drag on the rifle, which should aim itself. The 94 Winchester does. Its slim forend is free to rotate and pivot in your hand. The long, straight grip has plenty of room to shift to the heel pressure of your

Fast handling matters more than gnat's-eye accuracy at woods ranges.

right hand. If you want a rifle that's quick on target, you want a slender rifle.

You also want one that's perfectly balanced. The proper balance point depends on the length and shape of stock and barrel. But as with a fine shotgun, you'll know good balance when you feel it. The rifle will seem alive. You won't have to muscle it to your shoulder or force the sight onto the target. When you cheek it, the rifle's own inertia, free to guide it in the loose cradle or your hands, will point it where you look. Perfect, slightly front-heavy weight distribution smooths your swing. Shooting becomes the last act of pointing, not a separate effort after you've forced the rifle to obey.

Slim, well-balanced rifles aren't common. And the best aren't cheap. But a few mid-priced rifles, in both walnut and synthetic stocks, make the grade. They're chambered for a variety of cartridges with the accuracy and reach you need for cross-cornfield shots, but they'll jump to your shoulder at the snap of a twig and lock instantly onto a deer's rib. Here's a short list:

Commercial:
- Kimber Model 84M
- Remington Model Seven Custom Shop Synthetic
- Remington Model 700 Titanium
- Ruger 77 Mk II International
- Tikka T3
- Weatherby Mark V Ultra Lightweight
- Winchester Model 70 Classic Featherweight

Semi-custom:
- Brown Precision High Country (Mark Brown, 530-384-2506)
- Ed Brown Custom Ozark (Ed Brown, 573-565-3261)
- Jarrett Walkabout (Kenny Jarrett, 803-471-3616)
- New Ultra Light Model 20 (Melvin Forbes, 304-292-0600)
- Rifles, Inc. Classic (Lex Webernick, 830-569-2055)
- Sisk Rifles (Charlie Sisk, 936-258-4984)

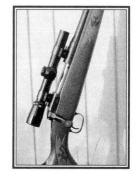

All of these rifles weigh (or can be ordered to weigh) between five-and-a-half and seven pounds with a 22-inch barrel. My preference: six-and-a-half pounds, for a finished weight, with scope, sling, and ammo, of around seven-and-a-half. As for chamberings, I'll stick with ordinary short-action numbers like the .308. In fact, there is no better all-around short-action deer cartridge. Other good picks: 7-08, .260, and .243. If you go the semi-custom route, consider the .358 Winchester and the .250 and .300 Savage. New Ultra Light M20 actions accommodate the .284, 7x57, .257 Roberts, and 6mm Remington. If you

The 2.5X Weaver scope on this Savage 111 is just right for shooting deer in heavy cover.

don't mind a longer bolt stroke and the slightly greater heft of a standard-length action, you can choose the .30-06, .280, .270 or .25-06.

I stay clear of the magnums, because for deer you don't need them–even when you step free of the brush and spot a buck 350 yards off. Magnum rifles generally weigh more because they require long barrels to perform well. The additional blast and recoil delay any follow-up shots and can make you flinch. While the inclusion of 6mm and 25-caliber cartridges in this list might surprise hunters who've been taught to use big, heavy bullets in the woods, my tests show that no bullet can be counted on to travel straight after striking even light brush. Shoot between branches, not through them. A .243 does that as well as a .45-70.

Finding deer is the first step in shooting them. Still-hunters typically get very close shots. *Credit: J.R. Hunter*

Of course, you must see twigs before you can find the space between them. And you must have a sight picture that allows precise aim when all you see of a deer is a grapefruit-size patch of hair. Even in the heyday of saddle rifles, open sights offered little in the way of precision. And they weren't as fast as they appeared. Your eye worked hard trying in vain to focus on rear sight, front sight, and target simultaneously. A receiver sight with a big aperture (like those by Williams or XS Sight Systems) is faster, more accurate. Better still is a low-power scope. I like Leupold's 2½x Compact, the Weaver K2.5 and Sightron's 2½x. No need for variable power, even if you occasionally get a shot at 300 yards. A red-dot sight (or Bushnell's HoloSight) is an option too. My pick: the Aimpoint 7000. Choose lightweight sights and mounts that keep center of gravity and sight-line as low as possible.

Traditional lever-action carbines and fast-firing pump and auto-loading rifles still account for lots of venison each season. In thickets, they're the equal of even modern lightweight bolt rifles. But while the bolt-action has been adapted to woods hunting, carbines bred in the saddle and the sumac are by design less capable when suddenly the woodlot ends and you must shoot accurately across hundreds of yards of crop stubble. A lightweight bolt gun–the new brush rifle–is thus your most versatile choice.

SLUG GUNS THAT SHOOT LIKE RIFLES

The auto-loader had the rough, long trigger-pull characteristic of its breed, but the sandbags made it behave. I managed three careful shots, then peered through the spotting scope. The slugs had chewed one ragged hole. I fired two more. Same hole. To a kid who'd teethed on smooth-bore pumps hurling Foster slugs and cut shells into groups the size of cereal boxes, this new sabbit thing was marvelous indeed.

Not long after that awakening, I replaced "sabbit" with "saybow" in my lexicon, despite derision from locals new to sabot slugs. As shooters have gotten used to launching a sub-diameter slug in a plastic, bore-diameter jacket, their expectations have risen. As rifled tubes have become more common, scopes have enabled shooters to see better and hit more accurately. Terminal performance has improved, too; many sabot slugs are actually big-bore pistol bullets–jacketed and solid-copper hollow-points that mushroom at shotgun velocities but also penetrate predictably.

So are shotguns as deadly as rifles? That depends a lot on gauge and caliber, and the type of ammo in each. Comparing the latest 12-bore slugs with the .270 or .30-06, most hunters say rifle bullets have the edge because they're faster than slugs and shoot flatter. The bullets have higher sectional density than even sabot slugs. That is, they're longer and smaller in diameter for any given weight. A long, slender projectile develops less nose resistance as it plows through the air, and retains velocity better. Most bullets are more aerodynamic in form as well, with point-

Federal sabot loads from a Weatherby shotgun delivered this tight 10-shot group at 100-yards.

ed noses that result in high ballistic coefficients. A long, pointed bullet holds its speed and energy better than a short, round-nose slug. Gravity exerts the same pull on both, but the bullet goes farther per unit of time, so drops less per unit of distance. In sum, rifles reach farther.

All this may be academic as far as you're concerned, however. Most whitetail deer are shot well within the point-blank range of a modern sabot slug–"point-blank" meaning the maximum yardage that you can guarantee a hit in the vitals with a center hold. Point-blank calculations commonly allow a six-inch vertical window–three inches above and three below point of aim. A three-inch vertical deviation seldom lets your shot leak out of the vitals; if you hit three inches high or three inches low, you'll still kill a deer. So smart money is on a "zero" distance that puts your shot just three inches above line of sight a little over half-way to the target (mid-range). With the fastest rifle bullets–for example, a 7mm Weatherby Magnum–you can zero at 250 yards and keep "mid-range trajectory" within the three-inch bracket. Maximum point-blank range is greater by another 60 yards or so–the distance it takes the bullet to fall three inches below line of sight.

A shotgun slug's trajectory is steeper, so this "rule of three" means you have to zero closer. Most

Browning's Buck Special was state-of-the-art until rifled shotgun barrels appeared.

sabot slugs and Foster slugs leave the muzzle at between 1,450 and 1,600 fps (total projectile weight is close to the same, so pressure ceilings keep velocities on par). Magnum three-inch 12-gauge loads can push one-ounce slugs at about 1,750. Remington offers seven-eighths-ounce Foster loads at 1,800 (1,875 for three-inch loads). Winchester has sabot slugs at 1,700 in both 12 and 20 gauge, and a three-inch 12 at 1,900. Still, even very fast slugs are pokey compared to a rifle bullet clocking 3,000 fps. So point-blank range and maximum effective range will be shorter for the shotgun. Ballistically efficient sabot slugs have an edge over Fosters launched at the same speed. Instead of zeroing a Foster slug at 75 yards for a maximum point-blank range of 95 or so, you can program a sabot slug for a center hit at 100, and stretch point-blank reach to 125 paces. Now, 125 doesn't seem far. But it's probably farther than you'll shoot at whitetails most of the time, and–more to the point–it is as far as most shooters can hit regularly from hasty hunting positions. You dump plenty of deer-killing energy that far out. Slugs have enough energy up close to qualify as bear-stoppers in Alaska.

A rifled shotgun is, in fact, a rifle. The ammunition only looks as if it would do well to cough a filbert the length of a gymnasium. Even where the law allows your .30-06, you may in fact be better served with a slug gun. For several reasons.

First, most hunters shoot shotguns more often than they do rifles. Familiarity makes you a deadlier shot. Secondly, shotguns (pumps and auto-loaders) are built

A red-dot sight on a Remington autoloader is a deadly combination in Alabama thickets.

for quick repeat attempts. While the first poke is by all odds your best, fast follow-ups can sometimes help you tag whitetails.

Shotguns are also built to swing. They feel different than rifles. Forends on auto-loaders are bulky, and the gas system adds weight, but the low operating pressures of shot and slug loads permit thin barrel walls, so overall weight up front may be no greater than that of a rifle. You'll get better slug accuracy with beefy barrels, but the super-thick tubes on some slug guns makes them, well, sluggish. If the gun doesn't point well, bench accuracy is meaningless. Ithaca's Model 37 Deerslayer, the envy of all farm lads when I began hunting with slugs, has just the right barrel heft. It's a stiff but agile pipe, rifled one turn in 34 inches. Such is its reputation that Ithaca now builds the same type of barrel as an aftermarket tube for Remington 870s and 1100s, the Benelli Nova, and an expanding list of other popular repeating shotguns.

If you're keen for the ultimate slug gun, a small Midwest firm called Tar-Hunt offers a bolt-action that not only shoots like a rifle, but looks and handles like one. Randy Fritz builds Tar-Hunt guns. He was

Like Tar-Hunt, Savage builds a bolt-action shotgun specifically for slug shooters.

introduced to bench-rest shooting in 1973 and took to it with a passion. By 1981, he had begun building and repairing hunting and bench-rest rifles. In 1988, he established his own company, Tar-Hunt Custom Rifles, and incorporated two years later. "We design and build rifles," says Randy, who also modifies, customizes and repairs many different hunting and bench-rest guns. Tar-Hunt bench rifles have won international bench-rest competitions, even set international bench-rest records.

Randy hunted deer with a rifle in Pennsylvania until 1967, when he moved to New York State and began carrying a slug gun. That's when he got the idea of producing a rifled shotgun. Common now, rifled shotgun barrels were all but unheard of in those days. Randy soon returned to Pennsylvania and, picking up the rifle again, shelved the idea of a rifled slug gun. Then, in 1987, he received by coincidence a 12-gauge jacketed slug and an advertisement for a rifled slug barrel. The concept of the sabot slug, he decided, was marketable. Banking on its future, Randy got busy designing his RSG (Rifled Slug Gun)-12, equipping the prototype in early 1988 with a synthetic stock from McMillan.

Randy had known Gale McMillan for more than a decade at that time, and the two had become good friends. When in 1990 Randy decided to make the original RSG-12 Clip Model slug gun, Gale was running both a synthetic stock operation and McMillan Machine Company. He helped with the Tar-Hunt project in many ways, introducing Randy to industry people who might also assist, and finding OEM parts from suppliers to keep manufacturing costs down. The RSG-12 was introduced in 1991 at the Dallas SHOT show. For the next 11 years (1991-2002), the McMillan

family did 99 percent of the action and stock work for Tar-Hunt rifles. In 2003, due to contractual obligations, another manufacturer handled the actions, albeit McMillan fiberglass stocks remained standard equipment. By then, a 20-gauge RSG had been developed.

"I'd never planned to modify a shotgun to shoot slugs better than a smooth-bore," says Randy. "I wanted to build a rifle to shoot slugs as accurately as any hunting rifle shot bullets." He has designed some RSG-12 guns expressly for the purpose of testing barrel technology and slug ammunition. These RSG-12s have shown him that the accuracy of even expensive sabot loads can vary from lot to lot–also that both lead and plastic fouling will affect accuracy.

Weatherby's SAS slug model handles like a bird gun, but a high comb speeds aim with a scope.

From 1991 to 2000, the RSG-12 had a two-round detachable box magazine with

These two Ontario hunters find the dragging easy on snow. A 70-yard shot killed the buck.

two locking lugs in the center of the action. It weighed eight-and-a-quarter pounds. But through the late 1990s, the profile and mechanical design of the gun evolved. In 1998, Tar-Hunt released a second-generation RSG-12 and RSG-20 with a lighter action, trimmer lines, and a 700 Remington-style stock from McMillan. It has a one-round blind ADL-style magazine, weighs seven-and-a-half pounds, and handles like traditional bolt rifles. The two locking lugs of the current RSGs are at the rear of the action, which was modified in 2003 to accept three-inch ammunition. A 16-gauge version appeared, too. For some time now, the RSG has been offered in both right and left-hand models. Randy recommends Lightfield slugs for all his guns.

An accurate slug gun will perform only as well as you can aim it. A shotgun bead is a miserable sight. I recall aiming with the bald crest of the bead on a Remington 11-48 auto-loader. That metal ball looked as big as a pumpkin against a deer's ribs, and if you didn't "bring 'er down fine," you shot over. The receiver obscured what the bead didn't.

I equipped my first shotgun, an 870 Remington pump, with a Williams receiver sight, and a gold bead front on a long ramp. I had to drill and tap for both. The 16-gauge barrel threw Foster slugs into melon-size groups at 100 yards. Later, I replaced the sights with a 2 3/4x Redfield scope in a Weaver mount screwed to the receiver's side so the scope hung low and centered over the top. Lopping the choked barrel from 28 to 24 inches gave me a whitetail gun as nimble and quick to point as any centerfire carbine, and lightning-fast on repeat shots.

The current crop of accurate slug guns surely justifies scopes. Open sights, still provided on many barrels, are neither as accurate nor as fast as a low-power scope. Even the best open sights hide a lot of the animal. Also, your focus bounces between rear sight, bead and target. A scope brings you a bright, bigger-than-life picture and puts everything instantly in one plane. You'll want a lightweight, low-power scope that won't impair the gun's balance or slip in the rings during sharp recoil. I like standard plex reticles, though a heavy plex is fine. Nikon, Leupold, Pentax, Bushnell, and Sightron market shotgun-specific scopes at reasonable prices. Swarovski's "dangerous game" variables are also excellent.

Shotgun receivers are not as heavy as those of rifles, while the recoil of a 12-bore with stiff slug loads is greater than that of a same-weight .30-06. So secure mounting of scopes can be problematic. One solution has been to use sideplates and the shotgun's own trigger-group pins. But this ploy adds weight and bulk. Steel bushings in alloy receivers enable you to pin scopes atop lightweight guns. But the best solution seems to be the cantilever mount, integral with the barrel. Remington and Weatherby began providing slug barrels with integral cantilever mounts, a great idea. Use the lowest rings you can, and place the scope well forward so you get a full field of view with your face thrust ahead on the comb. ■

8

RIFLES TO REMEMBER

T he hills Daniel Boone called Kaintack still hold deer. Indeed, above the Ohio's nut-brown tides, where sight of smoke from his neighbors pushed Daniel farther west, away from "crowds," you'll see more whitetails than virgin forest could have supported. The swath of alfalfa in front of me was bordered on both sides by hickory/maple woodlots. It fell away into the thick band of willows that fringed the river. I'd been sitting since well before dawn.

I'd seen the first deer early. Its antlers had drifted, white, through the gray screen of willows. He looked very big. But as much as I wanted to shoot, there was no chance. He never stopped.

An hour later, with the sun up, a doe minced out of the woods from the south. A buck followed her into the alfalfa. Both stopped 80 yards from my stand. Eight points. The crosswire settled on his shoulder. But I could tell he was a young deer, with potential. He and the doe walked slowly into the north woodlot.

Acts of charity are properly their own reward. But mere seconds after they'd left, a mature buck emerged, nose to ground on their track. I tugged the Contender's hammer to full cock and whistled softly. The deer stopped, then, as the woods echoed my shot, leaped high in the air, and fled toward the river.

It was the first whitetail I had killed with the .375 JDJ cartridge. But certainly not the first that had surprised a hunter with one bullet in his rifle.

DAKOTA'S M97 HUNTER: AFFORDABLE CLASS

When the late Don Allen was a stock-maker, he indulged a passion for beautiful wood. He and wife Norma built Dakota Arms around M76 rifles stocked in fine walnut. But the exquisite M76, fashioned after Winchester's early M70, is expensive. The M97 Hunter shares many of its features yet costs half as much.

The Hunter's round receiver is machined from bar stock, a cost savings when compared to the flat-bottomed receiver milled for the M76.

Dakota's Model 97 has a streamlined look and a Model 70-style mechanism on a round receiver.

I find the Dakota 97 easy to shoot from hunting positions. It's available in many chamberings.

Like the 76, however, the Hunter has a bolt release that pivots neatly at 10 o-clock on the rear bridge, across from its Winchester-style three-position safety. The Mauser-style extractor gives a mighty tug on sticky cases and affords controlled-round feed. In designing the rifle, Don installed an M70-type trigger because it's "the best trigger ever developed for a big game rifle." I agree. While the Dakota M76 wears a floorplate, the Hunter has none. In my view, blind magazines are the most practical kind. They don't leak water, come unhinged or show blue wear.

Dakota Hunters feature barrels by Lothar Walthar. They're of medium contour on Long Range rifles, 24 or 26 inches long, depending on chambering. The Lightweight version has a slimmer 22- or 24-inch barrel. Rifle weights: 7.7 and 6.3 pounds. The chrome-moly steel wears a satin-blue finish. Machining as well as polish shows great care. All edges are crisp. A deep, neat crown protects the muzzle. The bolt release pivots silently, as if on an axle, and fits almost seamlessly into its slot. The stock hugs the action. Barrel channel relief is even and minimal, as it should be. The classic profile of the black composite stock includes a long grip that's a bit thick up front for my taste.

The first chance I had to shoot game with a Dakota Model 97 came years ago on the last day of an elk hunt in Arizona. A bull broke from his bed below me and dashed across a cedar flat. I slinged up, sat and caught him quartering away at about 170 yards. Brush swallowed the bull right after the shot, but the little 140-grain Nosler Ballistic Tip, kicked out at over 3,300 fps from the rimless 7mm Dakota hull, struck mid-cage. It sailed through the near lung and exited the brisket, cutting the aorta.

More recently, I spent some time on the bench with a Long Range Hunter in .300 Dakota, another in the Dakota line of cartridges based on the .404 Jeffery case. Scoped with a Zeiss Conquest 3-9x40, the .300 shot 180-grain Swift Sciroccos well, averaging 1.1 inches for six three-shot groups. The trigger broke cleanly at three-and-a-half pounds; cycling was smooth and positive. I took that rifle to Wyoming, where it downed a big mule deer. He'd bedded in a deep coulee after foraging just a little too long after daylight. I followed him with the binocular and sneaked up the ravine, peeking over periodically. The shot came at only a few feet as he scrambled up onto the prairie and jetted away. A .30-30 carbine would have sufficed there–but not for the shot I'd made earlier.

My partner had stalked a buck he'd spotted at long range. Swinging wide to get the wind right, he found the deer all right–but the animal didn't present an easy shot. The bullet struck too far back, and in a few seconds any hope for a second try was gone. The deer sped over the crest of a hill onto a north-facing slope. Observing from more than 300 yards to the north, I saw the buck only after the shot; but the animal's irregular gait left no doubt. Just a

This Wyoming mule deer fell to a Dakota 97 in .300 Dakota.

few yards short of vanishing in a brushy cut, the deer stopped. So did my reticle. Resting the horizontal wire on his shoulder, then nudging it forward to allow for the brisk wind, I sent a 180-grain soft-point on its way. He dashed out of sight, but the thud of impact floated back. We found him dead. The flat-shooting bullet had struck exactly where intended, a testimony to the reach of Dakota's rifle and powerful cartridge.

When shooting deer in open country, you'll appreciate an accurate, flat-shooting rifle–and a solid shooting position.

The Dakota Model 97 isn't the cheapest of hunting rifles. But it shows the fit and finish of more expensive guns. It balances nicely in the hand, shoots well, and offers discerning riflemen the tang, trigger, safety, and extractor of early Winchester Model 70s. Specify standard chamberings, belted magnums or one of Dakota's own rounds based on the .404 Jeffery.

H-S PRECISION'S TACTICAL DEER RIFLES

In 1978, Tom Houghton had a degree in chemistry. Instead of getting a job, he started a gun company. "Of course, I couldn't offer a diverse line like Remington or Winchester. And there's no economy of scale with a start-up company." But Tom hoped a few shooters would pay a premium for exceptionally accurate rifles. He found they would. But while another newsworthy

Dakota's cartridge line is based on the .404 Jeffery case; they outperform many belted magnums.

entrepreneur named Kenny Jarrett specialized in big-game rifles, Houghton tapped quickly into the tactical- and varmint-shooting market. Now he manufactures big-game rifles as well, and for a while built a super-accurate bolt-action pistol. H-S catalogs a broad array of synthetic gunstocks, and barrels that have won the allegiance not only of competitive shooters, but ballistics laboratories. "We're the world's leading supplier of pressure, velocity, and accuracy test barrels," said Tom proudly, when I visited his plant a few years ago. "We offer universal receivers, return-to-battery assemblies and a laser aiming system too. You can get an H-S muzzle brake and scope rings, and after-market bottom metal for a Remington 70."

This H-S Precision rifle shows its tactical heritage. H-S makes its own super-accurate barrels.

It's stainless steel, with a detachable box magazine hidden by a floorplate.

Conceived in Prescott, Arizona, H-S Precision came to Rapid City, South Dakota, in 1990. Just a year later, it moved into a 15,000-square-foot plant built specifically for its various operations. The workforce has since grown to 80, now headquartered in a 45,000-square-foot building. Tom's daughter, Tricia Hoeke, and his son, Tom Jr., are active at H-S, which Tricia says is easing out of the ballistics testing done for other firms and the government. "We're very busy

H-S Precision rifles have adjustable triggers, a great boon to deer hunters taking aim at long range.

manufacturing, and our test equipment keeps us in the ballistics business." Tricia says that only about 15 percent of company revenues derive from rifle sales, and that while H-S does sell through wholesalers and retailers, more than half its business has been customer-direct.

Deer hunters owe H-S rifles a look. The rifle line has shifted to accommodate sportsmen, but there's no departure from the close tolerances that have earned military and law-enforcement contracts for sniper rifles. H-S barrels, .17 to .50, are all cut rifled in 416R stainless steel and so accurate that all Pro-Series 2000 rifles up to 30-caliber come with a half-minute accuracy guarantee. Takedown rifles must also repeat to within a half-minute. Few other firms will take such a risk. Committing to even one-minute groups amounts to a self-imposed sentence. It means using the best barrels and ensuring close-tolerance, on-axis assembly of bolt, receiver, and barrel. It means bedding the stock securely and in a channel that won't shift.

Apparently I wasn't horsing the rifle too badly when, recently, I ran ammunition tests with an H-S Precision rifle. This Pro Series 2000, chambered in .223 (one-in-12 twist), routinely drilled out dime-size groups. On a prairie dog shoot, sod poodles unlucky enough to appear in the Leupold scope were blitzed by shiny little Sierra hollow-points. It wasn't long before I vowed a 200-yard minimum and took on the blustery Dakota wind.

Like all Pro-Series rifles, that .223 is built on a stainless action with a two-lug bolt. The bolt handle is silver-soldered to a one-piece bolt body. Its semi-cone head incorporates a face-mounted extractor. A three-position safety and tang-mounted bolt release lever bring to mind the Winchester 70. But the trigger is designed in house and adjusts from 2.5 to 3.5 pounds. Mine was factory-set at the high end–more resistance than I like–but it delivered consistent letoff. A floorplate covers the stainless steel detachable box magazine that feeds a straight vertical stack.

A barrel with .0002 uniformity, breech to muzzle, is part of the accuracy formula (H-S 10x barrels are given a slight radius at the juncture of land and groove

I used this H-S rifle to kill a nice Texas whitetail.

as an additional gas seal). Another ingredient is a rigid H-S stock, built of fiberglass, Kevlar and carbon fiber. Each stock gets an aluminum rail in the barrel channel to stiffen the forend. "Swivel studs attach to the rail, for greater strength," points out Tricia. The stock on my .223 has a deep, vertical grip (ideal for bench or prone shooting), a convenient, adjustable butt plate, and cheekrest. Its forend, shaped to mate with a rest, is nonetheless easy to grasp. H-S offers a Harris bipod as an attachment. The Harris gives you all the steadiness of a bench rest.

The takedown version of the Pro-Series 2000 was designed primarily with tactical shooters in mind, but it's an option many hunters might consider. You can buy it with two barrels of different chamberings, even two bolts so you can carry a .25-06 that converts in the field to a .338 Magnum. Tom tested this rifle by firing five-shot groups one shot at a time, taking the barrel off after each pull of the trigger. Groups stayed under half an inch! This outfit costs a lot; but it's portable, accurate, and versatile. The half-length aluminum hard case that comes with H-S takedown rifles is easy to pack on airplanes and lacks the gunny look that can draw unwanted attention.

"H-S is not really a custom shop," Tricia says, "and we're leaning more and more to producing stock rifles. But we've always tried to accommodate special orders within reason. You can still request any SAAMI chambering that's suited to the Pro-Series action. We offer options in rifling twist and barrel length and can alter stock pull too. We'll supply any stock in our line on any metal that fits it. We accept orders for special paint jobs."

But before you decide a standard-issue rifle from H-S Precision isn't good enough, better shoot one. You may find that half-minute groups bring satisfaction enough!

HOWA–AND ITS ALIASES

The Japanese Howa action, a clean-looking, smooth-working bolt mechanism, is suitable for both standard and magnum cartridges, even modern short magnums. An adjustable trigger and reasonable price prompted Smith & Wesson and Weatherby to use the Howa as the heart of their 1500 and Vanguard rifles, respectively. But you can also get the Howa with its proper roll stamp, from Legacy Sports International.

The Howa's two-lug bolt has a recessed face with plunger ejector, and a stout extractor inletted into the bolt body above the right-hand lug. Upon lock-up, the cartridge is ringed by the bolt head, barrel shank, and receiver, as in the Remington 700. It's a proven design, bank-vault strong. You can get the Hunter with a wood stock, and the synthetic-stocked Lightning, in .223, .22-250, .243, .270, .308, and .30-06, all with 22-inch barrels. Magnums–7mm Remington, .300, and .338 Winchester–come with 24-inch barrels.

The hardwood stock on my Howa rifle in 6.5x55 pre-dates those supplied by Boyds' of Mitchell, South Dakota. Boyds' has become the largest supplier of semi-finished and after-market finished gunstocks in the country. In 1997, after buying

out E.C. Bishop & Sons, Reinhard Fajen shut down, Boyds' bought machines from Fajen's plant, and hired 15 of its employees. A $700,000 computer system helped the company pioneer laser checkering. Now Boyds' lists 600 stocks to fit more than 350 rifles, shotguns, and handguns. As this is written, all Howa wood stocks come from Boyds'.

The 6.5x55 in my rack has the clean, crisp, utilitarian look of 1950s-era commercial Mausers and B-grade Remington 721s. A two-position thumb safety operates on the right side of the receiver. It's easy to use–and quiet. The trigger responded pretty well to my efforts toward a glass-rod, two-pound release. The bolt handle has a sleek sweep and pear-shaped knob that's quick to manipulate. The bolt glides in its race. A hinged floorplate is standard, with a push-button release in the trigger-guard. My

I carried this Howa rifle hunting whitetails in Ontario. It's a 6.5 x 55.

rifle gobbled up every type of 6.5x55 ammunition I could scrounge. This is the only chambering, by the way, that you cannot order in stainless steel as well in blued chrome-moly. Both versions come in wood and synthetic stocks.

The rifle feels solid. In fact, my main criticism is that the stock is beefier than it need be, and the rifle heavier. It weighs seven-and-a-half pounds. Howa people must have seen a market for lighter rifles, because now there's an Ultralight 1500, in .243 chrome-moly only, that scales a pound less. It wears a svelte synthetic stock with a sweeping grip. Barrel length: 20 inches. A 1500 Ultralight Mountain Rifle appeared in 2004. Available with 20-inch barrel in .243, 7mm-08, and .308, it weighs less than six-and-a-half pounds–mainly because the receiver gets extra milling. It would be even lighter if a carbon-fiber stock replaced the hardwood handle (it's painted black). A youth rifle with 12 5/8-inch length of pull is a spin-off of the Mountain Rifle.

My Howa rifle and Nikon 4x scope collected this Canadian whitetail after a long day of still-hunting.

Howa's 1500 Supreme features the same chamberings but with laminated thumbhole or JRS (Jon R. Sundra) sporting stocks. The Varmint Hunter and Lightning rifles, blue or stainless in .223, .22-250, and .308, have husky 24-inch barrels and weigh just shy of nine-and-a-half pounds. A 10-pound Varminter Supreme has a laminated stock with beaver-tail forend. Legacy also offers barreled Howa actions, and Texas Safari Rifles by Bill Wiseman, of barrel-making fame. These feature a contoured cocking piece, three-position safety, Teflon finish, and glass bedding. Magnum versions have ported barrels. You can order other refinements, specify almost any chambering, and replace the synthetic or laminated stock with one of figured walnut.

My first hunt with the Howa came in Ontario. Though rut was in the wind, deer weren't moving past my stand. So I took to the thickets. In half an hour, I found more than a dozen huge scrapes, confirming what my outfitter, Steve Toriseva, had told me: This slice of Canada has some enormous whitetails. "They're beefy, like me." He laughed, then showed me how he won bar bets by touching the top of a door jam with his toe. At nearly 300 pounds, you wouldn't expect that, even from a black-belt. "The deer are lots harder to see." Especially, I thought ruefully, when you're moving on crusted snow.

But the next day I was at it again. By great good luck, I spied a buck through an alley in the trees before the crunch of my step reached him. But as I looked for a tunnel to accommodate my bullet from the sit, he turned away. Hewing to my rule never to shoot an animal in the fanny, I held pressure on the trigger until a slice of rib appeared. The buck was about 120 yards off, and sliding into cover. I fired. An hour-and-a-half later, the tortuous trail ended. My 155-grain soft-point had struck slightly to the right and hadn't driven far enough. It was neither the bullet's fault nor the rifle's. I should have waited for a better angle.

The eight-pointer broke the ice, however, and next day my partner rattled up a heavy-antlered 10. Steve and the crew at Border Country Outfitters were pleased. "Howa bout that!" he grinned, as he put another boot-print over the door.

GOOD KNIGHT! A REVOLUTION!

In-line ignition for muzzle-loaders has been around long enough that every company in the black-powder business has come up with in-line rifles. Even gunmakers of modern bent have caved, marketing muzzle-loaders that look suspiciously like centerfires. Few companies in this hot market will likely stay true to literal interpretations of "primitive weapons."

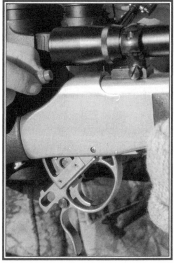

The Knight Revolution accepts a 209 primer in a plastic sleeve you just drop into the breech.

Among the most recent and intriguing of in-lines is the Knight Revolution. The mechanism is best described as rolling block, as lowering the lever swings the firing assembly down. The lever is like that of an 1885 Winchester High Wall, though the breech profile reminds me of that company's 1887 lever-action shotgun. But instead of inserting a cartridge or shotshell, you drop in a Knight Full Plastic Jacket–a small weatherproof cylinder containing a 209 shotgun primer. Then you pull the lever shut and fire. There's a crossbolt safety in the guard behind the trigger.

Of course, you must load first, in the traditional manner. Knight uses 50-caliber Green Mountain barrels for its Revolution. They're round and 27 inches long with a one-in-28 twist, chrome-moly or stainless, your choice. They wear adjustable open sights with fiber-optic inserts. Knight guarantees them to shoot into two-and-a-half inches at 100 yards.

The synthetic stocks come in three finishes: Black, Mossy Oak, and RealTree camo. Walnut and laminated stocks are your other options. Checkering provides for a firm grip, fore, and aft. I'd like the comb nose set a little farther back, and the comb could be taller for scope use. But the rifle handles well and has good balance. It weighs seven pounds, 14 ounces with an alloy ramrod secured by a single guide up front, and a flat spring in the forestock.

Adjustable for weight within a modest range, the trigger mechanism is stout and cleverly designed with the firing mechanism as a unit. You can remove this unit easily: After depressing the under-grip tab to open the action, tug on the flush latch in front of the guard to release the trigger group, which you can dunk in solvent while you swab the bore, now open at both ends. Sliding the unit back in place is a snap.

On a Midwest deer hunt, I got to know Knight's rifle better. A frigid dawn brought the skittering of deer hooves in frosted leaves. Soon the meadow to my front came alive with does and fawns. A young buck sauntered to a copse of ash behind me and bedded. I let him live.

That afternoon, I still-hunted. Late in the day, I stationed myself on a brush pile near new wheat. A doe came by, then another. Far off, more deer drifted from the woods. But not until dusk did a buck appear. A young deer. But this was my only day to hunt. There's a time to shoot, as there is a time to decline shots.

I centered the reticle of the 1x scope on the buck's forward ribs and pulled the trigger. Even as the rifle recoiled, I knew the bullet would strike too far back. The buck humped and ran a few steps. He was 90

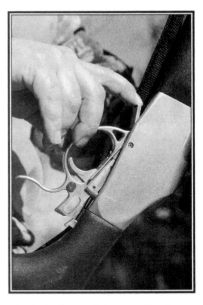

A tab in front of the guard releases the Revolution's trigger assembly for easy cleaning.

yards distant, but with no cover between us I reloaded slowly, shielding movement with my body. The deer moved away as the crosswire steadied–not a good shot. Still, this was a crippled animal. I fired and heard a hit. This time the buck loped off. In gathering darkness, I sprinted after it, reloading on the run. At woods edge, the animal stood briefly. My last bullet downed it.

Loading had been speedy in large part because the primer in its plastic hull was big enough to grasp easily and required only that I drop it, open end forward, into

Big parts and a sturdy frame–the trigger assembly is easily replaced in the Revolution's receiver.

the slot ahead of the breechblock. Much easier than trying to snug a tiny #11 cap on a nipple. A few month later, Hornady would make loading from the muzzle easier still, with an ingenious plastic wallet that holds the sabots and bullets in grooves. Tails on the sabot cups can be pre-threaded with three Pyrodex pellets. You have, essentially, a caseless cartridge, all set to ram down the bore.

Hardly proud of my ragged performance that evening, I was impressed by the Revolution: quick to aim and steady, easy to reload by feel on the chase or scrunched in a blind. It doesn't look like a traditional muzzleloader. Then again, it doesn't look like most in-lines either.

CONTENDER MAKEOVER, WITH MUSCLE

Among men who dreamed of building their own business at the close of World War II was New York toolmaker Kenneth Thompson. From a Long Island garage, he began shipping molds and tools for investment casting. The K. W. Thompson Tool Company moved twice, settling in Rochester, New Hampshire, in 1963. At that time, local woolen mills and shoe factories were struggling, so labor was plentiful and cheap. But seasonal slack in demand for castings sent Kenneth looking for new projects. He found one close to home.

Two years after the Rochester move, toolmaker Warren Center had come to K. W. Thompson, having worked in the factories of Iver Johnson and Harrington & Richardson. In his basement he had been designing a pistol he called the Contender. Tooling up for the Contender meant doubling the size of the Thompson plant, to 20,000 square feet. Both men considered it a good investment, and by 1967 pistols were coming off the line.

The Contender's main attraction was its switch-barrel design, which let the owner easily change from one cartridge to another without having to buy new pistols. The company deftly marketed the gun to shooters who wanted more power, versatility, and accuracy than ordinary revolvers and auto-loading pistols could offer. Initial resistance to the pistol's single-shot limitation was soon overcome. Available chamberings quickly grew to more than 20 cartridges, from the .22 Long Rifle to big-game rounds like the .30-30 and 45-70. Then came accessories: scope mounts, sling swivels, screw-in choke tubes (for the .410 shotgun barrel) and muzzle brakes.

And a rifle. The Condender with a shoulder stock and long barrel helped hunters shoot more accurately. Those who found the .30-30 and .35 Remington pistols a handful in recoil had easier shooting with the rifle.

Now, 40 years later, the Contender G2 has appeared. It's a superior firearm in several ways. The grip angle gives you more clearance, so the opening lever doesn't bite your fingers upon recoil. The grip also seems more comfortable to me. Like the original Contenders, it is walnut and ambidextrous; the broad finger grooves are new. Shooters who teethed on the old model will find this one easier to open. But they won't have to do it as often, as the G2 allows you to lower the hammer and recock it without opening the action. If you prepared to shoot the original Contender, then changed your mind, you had to unlatch, then shut the breech again before the hammer would hold at full cock–a real annoyance if you were stalking game.

The G2 accepts barrels from its predecessor; any Contender barrel will simply snap into place. The G2 will not accommodate barrels from the heavier T/C Encore series. Nor can you switch grips from the original Contender to the new one, though forends are interchangeable.

The G2 weighs a couple of ounces more than its predecessor. You can order a 14-inch barrel in one of 11 chamberings. Some of these appear in 12-inch barrels and in the G2 rifle with 23-inch barrel (also listed: a 24-inch .410 shotgun barrel with ventilated rib). Pistol barrels come with an adjustable open sight and a front blade. Rifle barrels can be had without sights. All are drilled and tapped for scope mounts.

This may be a good place to point out differences between the Contender G2 and T/C's Encore, which preceded it–though not by much. The Encore is essentially a heavy-duty Contender, with a bigger frame. An Encore pistol with a 12-inch barrel weighs 12 ounces more than a Contender of the same configuration. Encore rifles and pistols accommodate barrels larger at the breech end, so they can handle fat cartridges that produce higher pressure than the Contender will comfortably withstand. Besides rounds like the .223 Remington and newer .204 Ruger (relatively high pressure but small in diameter), and the .30-30 and .45-70 (bigger at the base but showing modest pressures), the Encore welcomes cartridges as big as the .270 and .30-06. It is also large enough for a 12-gauge shotgun barrel, which makes it truly versatile. Encore pistols feature schnable forends, distinguishing them at a glance from G2 Contenders. Receiver size and sculpting are also giveaways.

I shot this Kentucky whitetail with a Thompson/Center rifle in .375 JDJ.

While the G2 is the lightweight in the T/C family, it will bottle as much horsepower as you'll need for any deer hunting. In 2005, besides offering .204 Ruger and .410 shotgun barrels for G2 rifles, T/C listed a rifle barrel–and a 14-inch pistol barrel–in .375 JDJ. Developed by J. D. Jones in 1977 for the first Contender, this potent round is fashioned on a .444 Marlin case necked to .375. Wildcatters have used it with deadly effect on elk-size game. In 1984, it accounted for 19 African elephants! Now it's available in factory boxes, loaded with Homady's 220-grain flatnose bullet.

Eager see how the .375 JDJ would perform in the new Contender, I secured a rifle and a pistol and a couple of boxes of the new ammo, loaded by Hornady but head-stamped and boxed with T/C's label. Velocities registered close to the advertised 2,300 fps from the rifle barrel. They averaged 2,070 from the pistol (a bigger drop than I'd expected from this cartridge and a nine-inch reduction in barrel length). Shooting at 100 yards from the bench, I was able to keep bullet holes inside an inch-and-a-half with the rifle. Holding the pistol was more difficult; my best group measured 1.6 inches. Of course, any deer gun that shoots into two inches at 100 yards is accurate enough. If you hold that close under hunting conditions, you're an exceptional rifleman and a marvel with a handgun.

The triggers on both guns were far too stiff for my taste. The pistol's broke at about four pounds, and my RCBS gauge showed a wide range of 58 to 70 ounces. The rifle's trigger pull exceeded the 72-ounce limit of the gauge. G2 triggers are adjustable for over-travel, but not easily for weight or sear engagement, the important components of pull. Aside from that problem, though, the G2s were easy to operate. As on the early version, a switch atop the hammer lets you select the rimfire or centerfire striker. The low hammer spur was easy enough to reach under T/C's 2.5-7x scopes. (The pistol scope offers an eye relief range of eight to 21 inches at 2.5x and eight to 11 inches at 7x. The rifle scope has three inches of eye relief.)

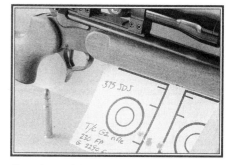

The .375 JDJ, based on the .444 Marlin case, has heavyweight punch. This T/C rifle shoots it well.

Just under six-and-a-half pounds scoped, the G2 rifle was pleasant to shoot. The pistol proved a handful. Boot a 220-grain bullet 350 fps faster than a same-weight .44 Magnum bullet from a maximum charge, and you can expect this gun to hop! The .375 JDJ delivers a ton of energy at the pistol's muzzle and more than 1,500 foot-pounds at 100 yards. You won't think it's brutal when you're shooting at game, but for long sessions punching paper, give me a Contender with a .22 rimfire barrel (the G2 is also chambered in .17 HMR and .17 Mach 2).

The G2's solid, steel-and-walnut feel and simple, sturdy design has carried over from the Contender as it first appeared in Warren Center's shop. As a hunting handgun, it has few peers. A manageable trigger would make it darned-near perfect. The rifle is more fun to shoot with hard-kicking cartridges. Both offer that switch-barrel versatility that helped endear T/C to American sportsmen nearly 40 years ago.

THREE CHEERS FOR TIKKA'S T3!

The moose was motionless as I raised the rifle. Bang! I cycled the bolt and fired again. Offhand, I wished I could throttle that chill north breeze. The crosswire eased into the black again and quivered to a stop. I hurried the pull. Suddenly, the moose vanished behind a concrete wall.

"Eighteen seconds." Under the 20-second limit for three rounds. An electronic scoreboard atop the wall lit up. A nine and two 10s. Better than I could have hoped. The scoring rings, one to 10, were invisible to me, 80 yards off, and mighty small. Credit Tikka's T3 Lite rifle, a sleek six-and-a-quarter-pound wand, this one in .308. The long grip has perfect pitch for offhand shooting, and raised rubber-like panels on grip and forend hug my palms. The shadow lines on forend and butt stock are mainly cosmetic, but my left hand found the slight relief up front a comfortable place to curl fingers. Compared to the discontinued Whitetail, this Tikka has less bulk. Spacers come with each

Tikka's T3 is, in my view, one of the best bolt-action deer rifles available.

lightweight synthetic stock, to give you just the right length of pull.

This Tikka, a third-generation rifle, features the two-lug bolt of earlier models. The recessed bolt face features a plunger ejector and Sako-style extractor. Bolt lift is only 70 degrees, like that of the three-lug Sako 75. While the first Tikkas came in two action lengths, there's only one T3, with two bolt stops to accommodate short and long cartridges. The detachable magazines, feeding a single vertical stack, are of lightweight polymer, quieter, and stronger than traditional metal boxes. They hold three rounds. (Deep five- and six-round magazines are available.) The flush front-mounted magazine latch looks better than the side latch of the Whitetail. You can't load magazines through the receiver, partly because cartridges must be slipped in from the front, partly because the ejection port is small. The minimal cut preserves the rigidity of the receiver. Integral scope mount rails accept 17mm rings; the rifle is also drilled and tapped. Except for the magazine and bolt shroud, and an alloy guard, the T3 action is all steel. A pear-shaped bolt handle is one of four major bolt components. The bolt disassembles by hand. I like the trigger adjustment: from two to four pounds pull with a hex key inserted through the magazine well. There's

The T3's polymer magazines, sized for cartridges of different lengths, feature straight-up feeding.

no sear engagement screw. The two-position safety locks bolt and trigger.

A steel insert in the stock serves as a recoil lug, engaging a receiver slot. The barrel floats. Two of the rifles I shot on that cold range in western Finland (in .308 and .300 WSM) shot about an inch-and-a-half. But Tikka marketing guru Paavo Tammisto assures me that the factory standard is three shots in an inch.

Moose hunters await the drivers in Sweden. The T3 is at home on the whitetail stump too.

Later, on a warm Texas range, I had the change to shoot T3s in .270 WSM, 7mm Remington Magnum and 300 Winchester Magnum, and .30-06. All but the .270 WSM gave me at least two one-inch three-shot groups. Oddly enough, my best targets were shot not off sandbags, but prone, with a tight sling. That's happened before with lightweight rifles, which seem to respond well to sling tension that controls rifle vibration. The .270 WSM was incorrigible. It sprayed three-inch groups no matter what I tried to better them. An anomaly.

You can choose from 13 T3 chamberings: .223, .22-250, .243, .25-06, 6.5x55, .270, .270 WSM, 7mm Remington Magnum, .308, .30-06, .300 Winchester Magnum, .300 WSM, .338 Winchester Magnum. Barrel lengths: 22 and 24 inches, depending on the cartridge. Specify walnut or synthetic stocks, stainless or blued chrome-moly steel.

The problem with even accurate rifles is that they won't help you hit moving moose. Having shot that respectable 29/30 on the standing moose, I had to qualify on the moving target. The moose came at my signal, hurtling along the track as my rifle labored to catch up. The bunkers were suddenly very close, and I almost caught concrete when I fired. The return run gave me fits, as in a jerky swing I tried to shoot with the crosswire on the moose's dewlap. One more trip to the left, and my confidence was shot. I had to repeat three times before corralling shots in the vitals. The expressionless Finn running the range finally shuffled to the line, grabbed a rifle from the rack and as nonchalantly as if he were tossing a Frisbee to his dog, drilled out a 29/30 on the running moose.

The next day, deep in the birch forests of southwestern Finland, I spied a moose. The black form was almost hidden when my crosswire found a pie-slice of black ribs. The .300 bucked, and my 180-grain Fail Safe punched through them. Steam erupted against the shadows, and the moose ran off. But the trail was short. I celebrated the hunt in the traditional Finnish manner, by sitting naked on a wooden bench in a sauna hot enough to steam clams until I was properly drenched, then running down a long dock and leaping into the Baltic Sea. You must do this at least once when hunting in Finland. If you survive, the Finns stop snickering about your running moose scores.

The Tikka T3 has the gunny feel of a fine sporting rifle. It cycles with the oiled-piston ease of a pre-war Winchester Model 70. It also shoots more accurately than most over-the-counter rifles. Add a sear engagement screw to the trigger, and it would be better. Follow Weatherby's lead by installing 24-inch fluted barrels for the likes of the .270 (instead of the current 22-inch), and it I'd like it better still. But as it is, the T3 remains one of the best bargains deer hunters will find. A Sako-quality rifle at a Savage price. ■

9

DEER LOADS TO LOVE

Τ here was no explaining the big buck. Deer like that just don't appear in front of the rifle–surely not in front of my rifle. The other deer, those that had charged out of the thicket at ridgeline, had barreled past me close enough to touch with a flyrod. I'd unwittingly cornered them in a postage-stamp copse of pines. Too steep to draw hunters, the talus slope below was like a moat ringing this promontory.

I could have shot the little buck or turned back after that stampede. The cover was empty. But for some perverse reason, I climbed a few more yards, up past the last tree. The short apron of rock on the cliff face behind the pines had no cover. But there, staring down at me with no place to go, was one of the finest mule deer bucks I'd ever seen. I fired right away, and the .30-06 took him down. Sometimes it pays to go where deer have no business hiding.

A .25 SOUPER . . . AT LAST

"This cartridge is quite similar to the Improved .250/3000 but came at a much later date and did not gain popularity to any degree. It is made by necking the .308 Winchester case to .25 with no other change. Coming after the introduction of such fine and popular cartridges as the Improved .257 and of course the very fine standard .257, it [has] little to recommend it over existing .25 caliber cartridges similar in design and capacity."

The .25 Souper (left) comes close to matching the .25-06 ballistically, from a .308 case.

So wrote P. O. Ackley in his *Handbook for Shooters and Reloaders*, first published in 1962. Well, 40 years later, I disagree. Though the .25 Souper differs little, ballistically, from the .250/3000 Improved and won't match the .257 Roberts Improved, it's a furlong ahead of ordinary .257 Roberts factory loads. In short actions, it is also a better fit than the Roberts, which derives from the 2.235-inch 7x57 case. The .257 (with the 6mm

Alice van Zwoll finds the .25 Souper as easy to handle as it is to shoot.

Remington) is a tad long for actions developed around the 2.015-inch .308 and its offspring. You must seat bullets well into the powder space, negating somewhat the value of the longer hull. Better, in my view, to use a cartridge that matches the magazine when a mid-weight bullet is seated with its base at or near the bottom of the neck.

Drivel, you say. Perhaps. But the hunting cartridge field is so crowded now that we're reduced to conjuring significance from trivialities. If you're satisfied with your .243, .25-06 or .257 Roberts, a wildcat .25 probably has little appeal unless you can be satisfied and curious at the same time. I like those three cartridges, but the .25 Souper stole my heart.

It was a love affair long denied. The late *Field & Stream* shooting editor Warren Page may have written the first text I ever read on this round. The hull seemed nicely proportioned. The useful range of bullet weights and styles appealed to me. So, too, the ease of forming cases. While you can neck down the .308, I prefer to neck up the .243. There's just .014 change in neck diameter–light work for an expander ball. As taken as I was with this cartridge, it was decades before I had one built. Then Charlie Sisk came up with a short Remington 700 action and a 24-inch Lilja barrel with one-in-10 twist. He squared the bolt face, lapped in the lugs, and trued up the receiver face and barrel shank. Before assembling the metal, he installed one of his own recoil lugs.

"It might look like an ordinary Remington washer," he says. "But instead of being stamped out, mine is machined from 416 stainless steel, then bored and surface ground by CNC. The result: a lug that's true and flat and fits the barrel perfectly. Your choice of thickness: .200, .300, and .500. Charlie favors Brownell's Acraglas for bedding, and he used it on this Souper. "My father had an old Farmall tractor whose radiator sprang a leak. Rather than pulling it for repair, we mixed up some Acraglas and dabbed that on the hole. It's held for more than 20 years." Charlie concedes that if Acraglas

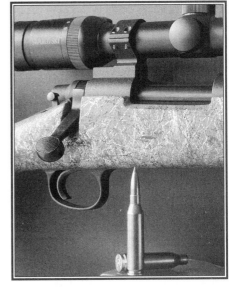

I had Charlie Sisk build his .25 Souper on a Remington 700 short action.

failed as a bedding compound, he'd keep it around only for tractors. But it helps his rifles shoot very well.

This one, in fact, shoots exceptionally well. With a Timney trigger and a Hi-Tech Specialties stock from Mark Bansner, this rifle is easy to control. One-piece Talley alloy mounts deliver a look consistent with the clean, classic lines of this rifle and put the Swarovski 3-9x36 (one of my favorite hunting scopes) right in front of my eye.

Recoil borders on negligible. The rifle feels like a .243 when I launch a bullet. But the .25 Souper accommodates heavier bullets than the .243. It has significantly more capacity than the .250 Savage, a tad less than the .257 Roberts. You can beat the Souper with the Improved Roberts in long actions,

A rifle by Charlie Sisk delivered this group with .25 Souper handloads.

and with the .25-06. But deer won't notice a difference. Here's how this compact wildcat compares to quarter-bore competition, and how it performed with handloads I assembled for the Sisk rifle.

Cartridge	Load	Muzzle Velocity (fps)	Group Size (in.)
.243 Winchester			
	Federal factory, 85 Sierra	3,320	*
	Federal factory, 100 Nosler Partition	2,960	*
6mm Remington			
	Remington factory,100 PSPCL	3,100	*
.250 Savage			
	Remington factory, 100 PSP	2,820	*
.257 Roberts			
	Remington factory, 117 SPCL	2,650	*
.257 Roberts	Hornady factory, 117 SST	2,780	*
.257 Roberts	Federal +P factory, 120 Nosler Partition	2,780	*
.257 Roberts			
	Hornady Light Magnum factory 117 SST	2,940	*
.25-06	Federal factory, 90 Sierra,Varminter HP	3,440	*
.25-06	Remington factory, 100 PSPCL	3,230	*
.25-06	Remington factory, 120 PSPCL	2,990	*

Cartridge	Load	Muzzle Velocity (fps)	Group Size (in.)
.25-06	Hornady Light Magnum factory, 117 SST	3,110	*
.25 Souper	41 IMR, 4064, 87 Hornady	3,335	.75
	43 H380, 87 Hornady	3,200	1.50
	44 H414, 100 Nosler Ballistic Tip	3,170	.05 (best!)
	48 RL-19 100 Nosler Ballistic Tip	3,325	.35
	46 H4350 100 Speer	3,240	.85
	44 W760 100 Speer	3,140	2.00
	40 Vihtavuori N-150 100 Sierra	3,090	.85
	39 Varget 100 Sierra	3,077	1.15
	43 H4350 115 Nosler Ballistic Tip	3,097	1.00
	45 A3100 115 Nosler Ballistic Tip	2,720	1.00
	44 H4831 115 Nosler Partition	2,917	1.10
	46 RL-22 115 Nosler Ballistic Tip	3,030	1.50
	44 WP Big Game 110 Berger VLD	3,145	.75
	44 Vihtavuori N-160 110 Berger VLD	3,020	.35
	47 WMR 117 Sierra flatbase	2,885	.25
	46 WP Big Boy 117 Sierra flatbase	2,730	.75
	45 NMR 120 Hornady	2,945	.35 (2 shots)

*Accuracy with factory loads varies a great deal depending on the rifle used.

During these preliminary trials, the Sisk .25 Souper gave me seven three-shot groups at or under .75 inch. I did not let the barrel cool or clean it. Loads were tested beginning with the lightest bullets and ending with the heaviest. The last 14 shots from a hot barrel showed that this rifle is one of those jewels that wants to shoot. It will get some field time this winter when coyote pelts thicken up. Incidentally, no signs of high pressures surfaced on the Winchester cases or primers. I got no sticky bolt lifts with these loads–though they are near the top end and should be approached cautiously. Ackley, by the way, lists 87-grain bullets at 3,400 fps, a 60-grain at 4,000, both with IMR 4320.

I shouldn't have waited so long to indulge my wish for a .25 Souper.

ARE MORE .270s BETTER?

There's no reason for a .277 bullet. By the time the .270 Winchester appeared in 1925, the 7x57 Mauser was 32 years old. Its .284 bullet–and that of the 7x64 Brenneke, circa 1917–would seem to have been the logical choice for a new hunting round.

But not all having to do with rifle and cartridge design is logical, and perhaps the 7mm's German ancestry figured in. America had, after all, just helped defeat the Kaiser. Probably the diameter of this new sub-.30 big-game number mattered little. The makings for the .270's success were in place: 1) deer hunters freshly enamored of battle-proven bolt rifles, 2) the .30-06 Springfield, with its scintillating reach, and 3) short optical sights that afforded precise aim beyond the reach of traditional deer rounds. Also, smokeless powder, not yet 30 years in the field, was ready to test behind a truly high-speed deer bullet.

When *Outdoor Life*'s gun guru fell for the .270, it already showed promise. Still, Jack O'Connor's writing helped power Winchester's new darling over early bumps, real and perceived. Hunters used to .30-30 bullet action whined that the high-velocity .270 spitzers wrecked a lot of meat. They did–and compared to the .30-30 170-grain soft-nose, still do. The first .270 bullets were particularly troublesome, fragmenting at the breakneck impact speeds guaranteed by a 3,000-fps launch. Winchester initially sought to mollify meat hunters with a 150-grain load throttled back to 2,675 fps. Not surprisingly, nobody bought it. Market response was what you'd

This buck almost sneaked away, but a .270 bullet found a small alley in the brush . . .

expect for fielding a sports car without a high gear. A better solution–stouter bullets–enhanced penetration. More sophisticated bullets followed, ensuring reliable upset across a wide range of impact velocities.

The .270 made its debut in the Model 54 Winchester, replaced in late 1936 by the Model 70. Among the 70's many chamberings, only the .30-06 has proven more popular than the .270. In 1948, Remington introduced its Model 721 bolt rifle in .30-06,

The .270 dates to 1925. This box of Winchester Silvertips isn't *that* old.

.270, and .300 H&H Magnum–at that time the most revered big-game rounds in use Stateside. A decade later, the .280 Remington cartridge had joined them. It withered in the shade of the .270. The 7mm Remington Magnum came along in 1962. Factory loads didn't have much on the .270, but this belted seven was brilliantly marketed, and chambered in the new Remington M700 rifle. The combination sold like hot cinnamon rolls at a Lutheran fundraiser.

Given the 7mm Remington Magnum's success, you'd think Weatherby would have grabbed the headlines early, with its .270 and 7mm Magnums. First available in 1943, they had essentially the same ballistic potential and were loaded by Norma to reach it. But they were ahead of their time. At the end of World War II, hunters still considered the .30-06 tremendously powerful, and the .270 seemed a veritable hot-rod. Also, Weatherby cartridges were proprietary, chambered only in costly Weatherby rifles. By the 1960s, hunters had powered up, and Remington's 700 made magnums common currency among ordinary deer hunters. Here's what the charts say:

Bullet Weight (gr.)	Type	Velocity (fps)	Energy (ft-lb)
.270 Winchester	130 Power Point	3,060	2,702
	140 Fail Safe	2,920	2,651
	150 Power Point	2,850	2,705
7mm Remington Magnum	140 Pointed SP C-L	3,175	3,133
	150 Swift Scirocco	3,110	3,221
	160 Nosler Partition	2,950	3,091
.270 Weatherby Magnum	130 Nosler Partition	3,375	3,288
	140 Nosler Ballis. Tip	3,300	3,385
	150 Nosler Partion	3,245	3,507
7mm Weatherby Magnum	140 Nosler Partition	3,340	3,443
	150 Nosler Ballis. Tip	3,300	3,627
	160 Nosler Partition	3,200	3,638

My Oehler chronograph shows Weatherby's ammunition to perform as advertised, so hand-loaders alone can bring the 7mm Remington Magnum even with these two Weatherby rounds from Norma. Well, that's not quite true: High Energy loads from Federal and Heavy Magnum ammunition from Hornady get Remington's 7mm Magnum within 100 fps. High Energy and Light Magnum ammo also brings the .270 Winchester to 100 fps of the 7mm Remington Magnum! Winchester's Power Point Plus runs right behind.

Bullet Weight (gr.)	Type	Velocity (fps)	Energy (ft-lb)
.270 Win. (Win. PP Plus)	130 Power Point	3,150	2,865
.270 Win. (Hornady LM)	130 SST	3,215	2,983
.270 Win. (Federal HE)	140 Trophy Bonded	3,100	2,990
.270 Win. (Win. PP Plus)	150 Power Point	2,950	2,900
7 Rem. Mag. (Hornady HM)	139 Soft-Point	3,250	3,300
7 Rem. Mag. (Win. PP Plus)	150 Power Point	3,130	3,264

The .270 and 7mm Winchester Short Magnum (WSM) and the 7mm Remington Short Ultra Mag can now be added to that list. The .270 WSM is the first commercial round of that diameter to be offered by a big ammo firm in 60 years. With a case just 2.10 inches long, it does indeed fit short rifle actions, though the body diameter of the case requires magazine changes. The .535 base diameter is essentially a match for magnum bolt faces fitted to the standard .532 bases of most belted rounds. A steep 35-degree shoulder puts fuel capacity close to that of belted rounds. Here are Winchester's factory loads for this potent .270.

Bullet	Muzzle Velocity	Muzzle Energy	Trajectory (yards)			
			100	200	300	400
130 Ballistic Silvertip	3,275	3,096	+1.4	0	5.5	-16.1
140 Fail Safe	3,125	3,035	+1.4	0	-6.5	-19.0
150 Power Point	3,150	3,304	+1.4	0	-6.5	-19.4

I was treated to one of the first prototype rifles, a Browning A-Bolt with 23-inch barrel. Factory-loaded 130 Ballistic Silvertips crossed my Oehler sky screens at 3,290 fps, matching chart speed, even from the relatively short barrel. The 140 Fail Safes left at 3,115, again right on target. Accuracy? That A-Bolt turned out to be one of the most accurate hunting rifles I've ever handled. After bore-sighting, I zeroed the .270 WSM from prone. I've come to trust, even prefer, zeroes established from field positions. You get a true read on the point of impact to expect when you shoot at game. This time, I fired my final two shots prone at 200 yards. Both hit the target's one-inch center ring. A good omen! But repeatable?

My chance to bench this marvel came at Browning's range near Mountain Green, Utah. Two Fail Safes went into a single oblong hole at 200 yards. With no need to shred that target (or to press my luck), I posted another at 300 yards. Three shots later, a one-and-a-half-inch triangle, dead center in the bullseye, stared back through the spotting scope. I can't recall shooting a better long-range group with a hunting rifle. Browning turned down my request to buy the .270 WSM: "It's a prototype. But we'll sell you another." I told them politely I didn't need another hunting rifle but was willing to pay many rubles for this particular rifle. No dice–but I was allowed to keep the hardware for a do-it-yourself elk hunt in Wyoming.

Two weeks later, I was climbing in snow. Declining a shot at the first bull that appeared, a spike, I bungled the stalk on a fine six-pointer 700 yards across a huge basin. On the last day, still-hunting open timber on the cusp of a storm, I slipped into a sizable herd of elk. A young bull appeared 90 yards away. The crosswire moved onto his shoulder crease. He hunched at the shot, sprinted, and fell dead. The storm broke as I rolled him downslope to a flat place. I didn't have a chance to hand-load for the .270 WSM until I'd returned the A-Bolt prototype rifle. Later, with a Winchester Model 70, I used Redding dies to work up starting loads for the round. Because I had no base data, I proceeded cautiously, using data for the .270

Winchester and .270 Weatherby Magnum as goalposts. Percentage differences in case capacity don't translate directly to percentage differences in propellant charge. Performance and pressure can escalate more or less rapidly, depending on burn rate, case shape, bullet weight, and other variables. Powders between H4895 and WW 760 delivered the best results. A better long-range deer round would be hard to find–should you decide the .270 Winchester doesn't go far enough, or that you want to use heavier bullets but stay above 3,000 fps.

The .270 WSM isn't the first to claim high efficiency. One Remington 78 in my rack chambers the .270 Redding, a necked-down .308 introduced to me by Richard Beebe at Redding Reloading. A cartridge that's easy to shoot and nips close on the heels of Winchester's star, the .270 Redding in a Brent Clifton rifle stretched across a wide swath of Colorado prairie one evening long ago to nab a mule deer buck about to make its escape into the oakbrush.

The .270 is perhaps the ideal open-country deer cartridge. Wayne shot this group with factory loads.

Another short but obscure .270 came along in the 1940s, when F.R. Krause of Albuquerque, and Roy Triplett of Cimarron, New Mexico, necked down the .300

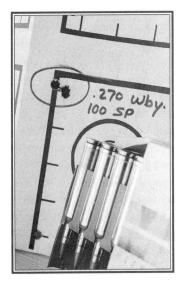

Wayne's Legacy Mauser in .270 Weatherby Magnum delivered this group from bullets clocking 3,400 fps.

Savage. Charles Evans and Bliss Titus also gave their names to this stubby .270. Late-model 99s offered in .308 (the .300 magazines aren't the same length) took the shine off shorter wildcats. The .270 Titus doesn't compete with the 7-08 in modern bolt guns.

One of the criticisms leveled against all .270s is their small selection of bullets. Small is relative. You can shoot only one bullet at a time, and if you can't find a handful of satisfactory .270 bullets amid the dozens now offered by Barnes, Hornady, Nosler, Sierra, Speer, and Swift–not to mention those factory loaded by Winchester, Remington, and Federal–well, you're pickier than me. There could be more .270 bullets around now than there were 7mm hunting bullets in 1962. And, on balance, they're better. Most fall within a narrow but practical weight range; 130 to 150 grains. For deer-size animals, however, 100-grain bullets may be under-rated. A .270 Weatherby Magnum I assembled on a Legacy Mauser action (Shaw barrel, Boyd's stock) shot most bullets well but 100-grain Hornadys superlatively. My first three-shot group with factory ammunition measured under half an inch! While the Weatherby can shoot heavier bullets so fast that at long range they shoot flatter than 100-grain spitzers, there's less recoil with the lightweights. And plenty of killing power.

Best bullets? The .270 established its reputation on deer with ordinary Winchester and Remington soft-nose 130s at 3,100 fps. Those bullets have also taken a lot of elk. Construction matters. One bull I zapped with a fragile 150-grain bullet trotted off because the shoulder stopped penetration. Fortunately, a second hit shattered the animal's neck. Another bull, struck on the run with a 130-grain Nosler Partition, somersaulted–as did one killed by a 140-grain Swift A-Frame that drove from the first rib to the off-side ham. A client once put a 130-grain Hornady through the ribs of a huge six-point bull. The elk reared up, then toppled backward and never twitched. Anyone who says the .270 Winchester is too light for elk, or that .270 bullets won't reliably take big bulls, hasn't gathered much evidence. One Colorado game warden, shooting elk on control missions decades ago, chose the .270 Winchester over other, more potent rounds. He killed hundreds of the beasts.

I suspect one reason this fellow liked his .270 was that it didn't bruise his shoulder or belt him in the chops like rifles chambered to belted magnums. Compared to same-capacity cases with bigger bores, the .270s are well behaved. The .270 WSM's good manners are due partly to bullets of modest weight but also case shape. The short, broad powder column seems to ignite more uniformly and with less violence than a tall stack of propellant. It also permits use of faster powder. Result: less fuel per unit of bullet speed, and less ejecta (unburned powder exiting the case and contributing to recoil).

Compared to 7mms and .30s, there still aren't many .270 cartridges to choose from. But the .270 Winchester, .270 Weatherby, and .270 WSM–with the .270 Howell and wildcat .270 Redding–should be all you need for deer you spot at a distance. Or for just about any animal you'll find in North America.

THE MAGIC OF SEVEN

Numbers can become icons. Between 22 caliber and 35 caliber are lots of numbers designating bullet or groove diameter. Only a few have become standard: .224, .243, .257, .264, .277, .284, .308, .311, .323, .338, .358. The .284, or 7mm, is special because it has become more than a standard. With the .308, it is a most versatile diameter for deer hunting.

You'll find little in the way of black-powder history for 7mms. The obscure .28-30-120 Stevens, a straight, rimmed case, appeared circa 1900. Developed by C.H. Herrick, it was chambered by the J. Stevens Arms and Tool Company in its 44 and 44 single-shot target rifles. Renowned barrelmaker Harry Pope favored it and fitted barrels in .28-30 to other actions. It was said to be an accurate round, better even than the .32-40. But by 1918, Remington had dropped this number from its ammunition list.

These 7mm cartridges are all useful for deer. The 7mm Mauser (center) dates to 1893.

The 7mm really got its start in Europe, where Peter Paul Mauser and his brother Wilhelm designed a turn-bolt military rifle chambered the 7x57 Mauser cartridge (a 7mm bullet in a case 57mm long). The rifle and cartridge were adopted by the Spanish army in 1893. Subsequently, the 93 Mauser and its smokeless round became hugely popular, filling arsenals the world over. Later versions of the Mauser chambered other cartridges, but none have made the jump from battlefield to sporting field as successfully as has the 7x57. The world's finest gunmakers have built magazine rifles and double rifles in 7x57, and many famous hunters have praised it. W.D.M. "Karamojo" Bell used it on ivory hunts, launching long, blunt 173-grain solids that at 2,300 fps loafed through pachyderm skulls. Stateside between the wars, it proved deadly on all manner of thin-skinned game, shooting lighter bullets almost as flat as the .270, and more gently than the .30-06. The 7x57 didn't earn the .270's fanfare, partly because it originated overseas. Also, its listed velocities were considerably lower, due to heavier bullets in standard loadings and pressures kept mild for early Mausers. Its competition steamed up 50,000 psi. Current factory loads (Hornady's Light Magnum in particular) hit hard, and hand-loaders get a big premium when shoveling the coal to the 7x57 in sturdy rifles.

By the time the Spanish Mauser was making headlines, we were already becoming a 30-caliber nation. The .30-40 Krag, adopted by U.S. Ordnance in 1892, was our first small-bore military smokeless round, replacing the .45-70. It was followed a decade later by the .30-03, soon supplanted by the .30-06. In the 1950s, the '06 moved aside for the 7.62 NATO, or .308 Winchester, in the M14 rifle. Not until 1964, with the adoption of the 5.56 Ball Cartridge M19 (.223), did the U.S. Army drift from the .30 bore.

You could argue that the 7x57 had all the markings of an enduring big game round. That with the proper bullets it was as versatile as the bigger .30-06. But not all the early 7mms were as popular as the 7x57, or as promising. In turn-of-the-century England, F.W. Jones designed a cartridge for Sir Charles Ross and the ammunition giant Eley. It was called the .280 Ross and chambered initially in Canadian Ross straight-pull military rifles. A long rimless case launched 160-grain bullets at 2,900 fps, beating the .30-06, which appeared concurrently in the 1903 Springfield. But the Ross rifle was less reliable. And bullets of the day weren't built to withstand the terrific impact of solid hits at nearly 3,000 fps. Hunters used the .280 Ross in Africa on game as big as lions. The hardware and bullets sometimes failed. A few hunters died.

In 1907, English gunmaker John Rigby introduced the .275 Rimless in his magazine rifles. It used a .284 bullet and was very close in dimensions to the 7x57. The original bullet, a pointed 140-grain, was replaced by a semi-pointed 140 after the first World War. The apparent reason for this switch: Rigby's Managing Director was once struck in the head by an 8mm German spitzer, and the bullet bounced off. His faith in pointed bullets was badly shaken! The .275 Rimless spawned a rimmed version for double rifles in 1927. The cases differ in dimensions, and the rimmed round was conservatively loaded. It performed much like the 7mm Rimmed H&H Magnum and Lancaster's .280 Flanged Nitro-Express, said to have been a favorite of King George V. The .280 Rimless Jeffery offered a sleeker profile, more speed. It appeared in 1915, pushing a 140-grain bullet at 3,000 fps. Two years later, Germany's gun genius, Wilhelm Brenneke, trotted out his 7x64. Ballistically the equivalent of the Ross, it had a brighter future in Mauser bolt rifles and with better bullets. The 7x64 (with its rimmed counterpart, the 7x65) looks and acts like Remington's .280, a 1957 introduction. Both these sevens are still manufactured.

During the 1920s and '30s, wildcatters concocted several 7mms on the belted .300 Holland case, and on Charles Newton's big rimless .30. Western Cartridge Company produced, briefly, John Dubiel's .276. An improved version came from Griffin & Howe. The .280 Dubiel, with its .288 bullet, delivered stellar performance from its full-length .300 H&H hull. While Newton's own .280 failed, P.O. Ackley drew some attention to his .276 Short Magnum. Later, A.E. Mashburn fashioned a sharp-shouldered 7mm from the long Holland case. Field & Stream gun editor Warren Page killed a lot of game with this super-charged 7mm. Charlie O'Neil, Elmer Keith, and Don Hopkins followed with their .285 OKH. One version of this cartridge used a flash tube and duplex powder charge. These American experimenters might have been inspired by Holland and Holland's .275 Belted Rimless Magnum Nitro, a shortened, reshaped .375 H&H that appeared about the same time (1912 or 1913). It came in a rimmed version for double rifles. Loaded to unexciting levels, the .275 Rimless Magnum was offered by Western Cartridge in the U.S. until 1939.

In 1944, Roy Weatherby added a 7mm to his new line of wildcats on the shortened Holland hull. Like the .270 and .257, it had rounded shoulder junctures. Though it never became as popular as the full-length .300 Weatherby Magnum, it is in some respects a better cartridge. It shoots as flat, with less recoil. You'll get as much speed from a 160-grain bullet as from a 180 in the larger .30–about 3,200 fps. Luckily for Remington, Roy Weatherby kept a proprietary leash on his ammunition, and no commercial rifles were chambered for the 7mm Weatherby Magnum for 20 years. The 1962 debut of Remington's Model 700 rifle was all the more a hit because its list of chamberings included the brand-new 7mm Remington Magnum. A twin to the Norma-loaded Weatherby in case capacity, it is throttled to SAAMI pressures; hand-loaders get the same performance.

The 7mm Remington Magnum achieved almost instant success, mainly because it was advertised in just the right way. Wyoming outfitter Les Bowman had pointed out to the folks at Remington that what they needed was a cartridge that shot as flat as a .270 but carried more punch—one that developed no more recoil than a .30-06 but reached farther. It would fit standard-length actions, as had the .458, .338, and .264 Winchester Magnums already on the market. The ideal cartridge in his part of the world would be a peppy 7mm a hunter could use for mule deer, elk, and pronghorns. And that is the way Remington promoted its new round. Hunters responded with their checkbooks, while Winchester's .264 Magnum languished. With a case identical to the 7mm Remington's and a bullet just .020 smaller, it deserved better. So did the .280 Remington, which could not budge the similar .270 on sales charts. The 7x61 Sharpe & Hart, a bit smaller than the 7mm Remington Magnum, was chambered commercially in Schultz & Larsen rifles in 1953 but never had support from a major firearms or ammunition company. It is now long defunct.

Lest you think any 7mm doomed by stiff competition, consider those that have since thrived. The 7mm Dakota, on a shortened .404 Jeffery case, gave hunters a handsome round that upstaged Remington's cartridge a bit. The 7mm STW came along in the 1980s, on the full-length 8mm Remington Magnum case. At 3,325 fps, its 140-grain bullet flies 150 fps faster than the same pill from a 7mm Remington Magnum. Predictably, the edge narrows downrange, because the faster bullet sets up greater the air resistance and drag. More drag means a higher rate of deceleration, all else equal. So at 500 yards the 7 STW is only about 110 fps ahead of the 7mm Magnum. And it's 80 fps behind its successor, the 7mm Remington Ultra Mag. Built on a bigger, rimless case, the 7mm UM kicks a 140-grain bullet out at 3,425 fps and shoots

as flat as a Nevada highway. Zero at 250 yards, and you'll see less than three inches of drop at 300, about a foot at 400. This cartridge bit hugely into demand for the STW. So has the subsequent Remington Short Action Ultra Mag, fashioned from the Ultra Mag case to deliver the punch of a 7mm Remington Magnum.

For decades, Winchester resisted the temptation to field a powerful 7mm. As the Ultra Mag series began its ride about five years ago, Winchester engineers were already considering the concept of a short rimless case with the powder capacity of a traditional belted magnum. The .300 WSM came first,

The 7mm-08 in rifles like this short, custom-shop Remington Model Seven, is an ideal whitetail round.

around the time Remington was gearing up to produce its own .300 SAUM. No one doubted that a 7mm SAUM was in the works, but Winchester surprised me when it weighed in with a 7mm WSM. The Remington's case is slightly smaller, to work in a Model Seven action. Performance is nearly identical. I questioned the utility of a short Winchester 7mm magnum on the heels of a short .270 magnum, a cartridge Winchester had all but promised at the .300 WSM's release. After all, a .270 bullet is only .007 smaller in diameter. In fact, prototype 7mm WSM rifles had to be recalled because the cartridges fit in some loose .270 WSM chambers. The solution was to make the 7mm case slightly longer to the shoulder.

As 7mm cartridges grew to meet demands of hunters for greater reach, less celebrated but perhaps more versatile rounds appeared in the shadows. The .284 Winchester came along in 1963, designed to give that company's Model 88 lever-action and Model 100 auto-loading rifles the punch of a bolt-action .270. A rebated hull, fatter, and a bit longer than the .308's, the .284 case holds about as much fuel as a .270's. In same-length barrels, it can be loaded to the same ballistic level. A real boon to short-action rifles, the .284 got only a luke-warm reception from Joe Deerhunter. Savage offered the Model 99 in .284, and Browning bored the A-Bolt and BLR for it. Custom makers dealing with knowledgeable riflemen get most of the .284 business now. Melvin Forbes, whose Ultra Light rifles feature a 7x57-length magazine, has chambered a lot of barrels in .284 and its wildcats. The .284 is a favored parent hull among competitive shooters, who neck it to .264 for 1,000-yard matches. There's less recoil than with .30 magnums; but the 6.5/284 shoots as flat.

In 1980, an unlikely 7mm appeared: the 7-30 Waters. Named for gun guru Ken Waters, who put his ideas into the design, this round is a necked-down .30-30. It was first chambered in Winchester 94XTR rifles. The 7-30 has a shorter neck, sharper shoulder, and more case capacity than its parent; however, you must allow this bullet some barrel time to get advertised velocities (a 120-grain bullet at 2,700 fps).

Three years after the 7-30 slid into Winchester's cartridge lineup, Remington announced the 7mm-08, a .308 necked down. It's an eminently practical design, adaptable to any short-action rifle that handles the .308 and .243. Launching a 140-grain bullet at 2,860 fps, it leaves the 7x57 behind, though the Mauser cartridge is .2 inch longer. Hand-loading can wipe out the 7x57's 200-fps deficit. The 7mm-08 deserves its popularity. The 7mm-08 Weatherby Ultra Lightweight in my rack ranks among my favorite deer rifles. A 140-grain 7mm-08 bullet gallops right alongside the 150-grain from the .280 Remington.

Some hunters talk about the 7mm cartridges as if their bullets have some magical quality—some innate advantage over bullets .257, .277, or .308 in diameter. Not so! It is true that among the most popular 7mm big-game bullets are a handful with extraordinarily high ballistic coefficients. For example, Hornady makes a 162-grain 7mm boat-tail bullet with a ballistic coefficient of .534. Still, the firm's 190-grain .308 Match bullet registers .530. In hunting bullets, you'll get virtually the same arc from a .277 150-grain bullet as from a 7mm 150-grain bullet driven at identical speeds.

A reader once castigated me for writing in another publication that the .30-06 was essentially the equal of the 7mm Remington Magnum. With 150-grain bullets out of the blocks, the 7mm wins. You'd expect it to; it has a bigger case. But comparing the 180-grain '06 bullet with a 175-grain bullet from the Magnum, you'll find the advantage diminishes. In fact, if you pick Hornady's Light Magnum .30-

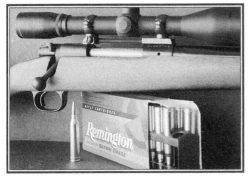

06 load, which launches a 180-grain bullet at 2,900 fps, the Magnum loses in both the velocity category (2,860 fps) and as regards energy (3,361 ft-lbs for the '06, 3,178 for the 7mm). No factory load for the Magnum equals Hornady's most potent .30-06 recipe, or Federal's 180-grain High Energy '06 loads. In fact, potent .270 Winchester factory loads can match what you'll get with the 7mm Remington Magnum.

The short-lived Ranger version of Winchester's M70 was chambered for several rounds, including the 7mm Rem. Magnum.

Of the many 7mm cartridges that have cropped up since 1893, the most useful deer rounds in my view are the 7x57 and 7mm-08. One of the biggest bucks I've taken off the mountain fell to a 145-grain Speer hand-load from my Ruger Number One in 7x57. A 7mm-08 felled an elk for me not long ago. The .280 is a dandy choice too. My Dakota Model 10 is a .280, and I've dropped both whitetails and mule deer with a plain-jane Remington 78 rebarreled to .280 Improved. My rack holds a couple of 7mm Remington Magnums, and I've killed elk with the 7mm Dakota. An Australian buffalo dropped to a 7mm WSM I was toting when he sprinted from a remote billabong. Still, if I were to buy another 7mm rifle soon, it would be chambered for a round of modest size. I'd shoot 140- and 150-grain soft-point or polymer-tipped spitzers–an ideal weight for all-around deer hunting and in .284-diameter at the top of the charts for ballistic form.

There's no magic in the number seven. And Stateside, we hunters are still a 30-caliber fraternity. For deer hunting, however–no matter where–7mm is all you really need to remember.

THE .30-06: STILL ON TOP!

If there's not a .30-06 in your battery, you've probably had to tender an excuse before now. It's not that other deer rifles won't kill as effectively, or that other cartridges aren't as versatile. You own an '06 to pay homage. The cartridge is older than female suffrage. It went to Alaska when miners were still plodding the Chilkoot trail. With the .30-06 we won two World Wars. It was a charter chambering in the Winchester Model 70 three decades after it appeared in uniform. Seventy years later, it is still arguably the most versatile big-game cartridge ever. And it is probably favored by more deer hunters than any other round. You can live comfortably without a .30-06 and without a towel rack in your bathroom. But why would you?

One of my .30-06s is an M1 Garand, a rare bargain from the U.S. government. I have the restocked Springfield that took the moose, and a Model 70 from the 1940s. There's a Remington 721 in the rack, plain and heavy but with that alluring "gunny" feel of post-war rifles I should have collected when they were new and very cheap. My Model 700 in .30-06 is an uncommon version with European styling, manufactured some years ago. I've owned and relinquished quite a few other rifles in '06, most of which I'd buy back. The pre-64 M70 that slipped away for $180 still grieves me. I'd like to own again an early Remington 760 pump rifle, and that M70 Featherweight of the same era. Long-action lever guns don't appeal to me, but I regret passing up a pristine M95 Winchester. And it's a fact that I turned down a Biesen-built .30-06 for . . . well, you'd question my credibility as well as my sanity.

The .30-06 cartridge was conceived in 1900, when Ordnance engineers at Springfield Armory began work on it and a battle rifle to shoot it. The rimmed .30-40 Krag had served ably in the Spanish-American War. But Paul Mauser's 1898 action was in many ways superior to the Krag-Jorgensen, a more costly mechanism.

A prototype rifle emerged at Springfield Armory in 1901. Two years later, the Model

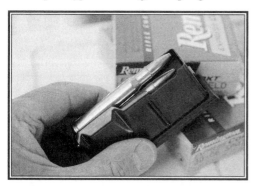

An easy feeder from any magazine, the .30-06 was developed in the 1903 Springfield.

1903 Springfield was in production. Its 30-caliber rimless cartridge headspaced on the shoulder, like the 8x57 Mauser. The .30-03 was longer than both this round and the Krag. Powder capacity and operating pressure exceeded the Krag's. A 220-grain bullet at 2,300 fps made the .30-03 the ballistic equivalent of the 8x57, which launched a 236-grain bullet at 2,125.

About a year after the .30-03 appeared, Germany switched to a new bullet: a 154-grain spitzer at 2,800 fps. At that time, such speed was remarkable. The Americans were obliged to catch up, and in short order they introduced the Ball Cartridge, Caliber .30, Model 1906. It launched a 150-grain bullet at 2,700 fps, increasing probable-hit range. The case could have been left as it was; however, someone decided to shorten it .07, to .494. Of course, this meant that .30-03 chambers were a tad long. Soon .30-03 rifles were recalled and rechambered.

The first bullets for the .30-06 were jacketed with an alloy of 85 percent copper and 15 percent nickel. Satisfactory in the Krag, it did not hold up at .30-06 velocities. Bore fouling rendered the rifles inaccurate. Tin plating reduced fouling, but this practice was abandoned when shooters discovered that, over time, tin "cold-soldered" to case mouths, and occasionally caused colossal pressure spikes. An alloy of zinc and copper in 5-95 or 10-90 proportions proved effective and safe. It became known as gilding metal.

The speedy 150-grain service bullet was supposed to pose a threat out to 4,700 yards. But troops in World War I found the real limit was about 3,400. To increase reach, the Army again changed the bullet, this time to a sleek 173-grain spitzer. Velocity was throttled to 2,647 fps, a minor concession given the substantial increase in ballistic coefficient. Announced in 1925, the new "M-1" round extended maximum range to 5,500 yards. Alas, it also boosted recoil. In 1939, the Army changed bullets once more, to a 152-grain replacement at 2,805 fps. With the "M-2" .30-06 cartridge we fought World War II.

When I was a lad, you could buy surplus military '06 ammo by the bucket. But savvy shooters kept it out of their good rifles. The reason: potassium chlorate primers deposited corrosive salts in the bore. Though Remington developed its non-corrosive "Kleanbore" priming in 1927 (and commercial rounds featured non-corrosive priming exclusively from about 1930), military cartridges were fitted with corrosive FA 70 primers as late as 1952! Corrosive priming, incidentally, does not weaken the case, as does mercuric priming. Conversely, mercuric priming won't damage bores. Since the Korean War, the only domestic .30-06 ammunition to avoid was a run of Western Match cartridges with Western "8 1/2 G" primers. These were corrosive and mercuric.

I still scrounge late-issue .30-06 brass. But I no longer spend hours swaging the primer-pocket crimp on military cases, and for load development I use only commercial brass. Any brand will do; but I don't mix them because case wall thickness, and consequently powder capacity, varies.

There's lots of loading data for the .30-06. Here's some from savvy riflemen who've hunted with it:

Jack O'Conner used 53 grains of IMR 4320 or 4064 behind various 150-grain bullets for 2,950 fps, 56 grains of 4350, and 180-grain bullets for 2,750, 54 grains of 4350 pushing 200-grain bullets for 2,630.

Warren Page claimed fine accuracy with 180-grain bullets and 55 grains of 4350.

Townsend Whelen pushed 180-grain bullets to 2,700 fps with 50 grains of 4064. He also used 58 grains of 4831 with those bullets, and 58 grains of 4350 behind 165-grain boattails.

Ken Waters capped 50 grains of Norma 203 with 180-grain Norma bullets and preferred 52 grains of 4320 with 150-grain Sierras.

Alaskan guide Hosea Sarber, whom Jack O'Conner said had shot more grizzlies than he (O'Conner) had seen, used a 172-grain bullet of unspecified make at 2,700 fps.

Not that you have to hand-load for the .30-06. You can get factory loads with bullets weights of 125 to 220 grains. Remington offers a sabot-style Accelerator, a plastic-sleeved 55-grain .224 bullet that clocks over 4,000 fps. Federal High Energy and Hornady Light Magnum loads deliver extra speed with big game bullets–up to 180 fps more. A proprietary (and costly) two-step loading process delivers the premium within allowable pressure limits. If you're recoil-sensitive but still want to shoot big animals, try Remington's Managed-Recoil and Federal's Low Recoil .30-06 loads. Remington halves the kick by pushing a 125-grain Core-Lokt bullet at

The .30-06 is still the most popular cartridge among elk hunters.

speeds that are standard for 180-grain bullets. Federal gets there with 170-grain bullets throttled back to 2,000 fps. All major suppliers now market .30-06 ammo with controlled-expansion bullets, which include the Nosler Partition, Partition Gold and AccuBond, Swift's Scirocco, and Reming-ton's Core-Lokt Ultra, the Winchester Fail Safe, and Hornady InterBond, Federal's Trophy Bonded Bear Claw,the Barnes Triple Shock X-Bullet.

Without touching a press, you can use a .30-06 for rockchucks, pronghorns, whitetails, The Wimbledon Cup matches and moose. You can hunt with it for brown bears and buffaloes, too. It has the power to stop big beasts up close, with the speed for flat shooting at distant game. And it won't beat you senseless in a lightweight rifle.

The .30-06 is as common as parking meters. Hunters whose luggage has roamed mindlessly for weeks through the shadows of foreign airports can appreciate such ubiquity. You can buy .30-06 ammo in more out-of-the-way places, worldwide, than any other kind of rifle ammunition. When Winchester altered its Model 70 in 1963, it had, over 25 years, offered this flagship rifle in 18 standard

This alpine buck fell to a .30-06, one of the most versatile hunting cartridges ever.

chamberings. Production of .30-06s totaled 208,218–35 percent of all Model 70s made! Incidentally, while standard twist for '06 sporting rifles is one-in-10, Browning 78 and Husqvarna barrels turn one-in-12.

Its versatility and availability have grown despite the proliferation of more potent 30-caliber cartridges and optics that encourage long-range shooting. The chambering of Winchester's Model 70 for the .300 H&H in 1937 didn't dent the popularity of the .30-06. Neither did Roy Weatherby's revamping of the Holland case in the early '40s. But the development during the 1950s of Winchester belted magnums, and the debut in 1963 of Remington's 7mm Magnum, convinced many hunters they could kill more game if they used cartridges bigger than the .30-06. The recent advent of short rimless magnums has kept the .30-06 on the back pages, and while you'll find more than 80 factory loads for it, versatility no longer sells a cartridge.

"I chamber only one or two .30-06 barrels annually," says Lex Webernick, whose Texas shop, Rifles, Inc., puts about 250 rifles a year into the field. "Most of my customers order .300 magnums of some sort. The .300 WSM was very popular for awhile, but shooters are coming back to the .300 Winchester."

Ballistically, the .30-06 compares well with short and mid-length belted .30 magnums. Figure about 200 fps and 300 foot-pounds difference at 400 yards for the same bullet, depending on bullet weight and type. You can make the '06 look better or worse. For instance, fire at 150-grain Nosler Ballistic Tip at 2,910 fps from a .30-06, and at 500 yards it's still clocking 1,245, within 30 fps of a 150-grain Trophy Bonded bullet shot from a .300 Winchester at 3,280 fps. Or match Federal's High Energy 180-grain .30-06 load at 2,880 fps against standard .300 Winchester 180s at 2,970. Given identical bullets in comparable loads and 200-yard zeros, the .30-06 will strike one-and-a-half to two inches lower at 300 yards than a .300 Winchester. That's a smaller slice of target than you'll cover with the crosswire at 300 yards, a much smaller area than raked by my wobble from hunting positions. Bear in mind that the .30-06 is more efficient in short barrels than magnums, afflicts you with less blast and recoil, and fits neatly into actions too slender for WSM rounds or even belted magnums. A magazine box that holds five '06 rounds will take only three belted cases at most, maybe only two WSMs. A Weatherby rifle designed to accommodate five .458 Lott cartridges accommodates eight .30-06 rounds.

It's hard to improve on the .30-06, and when you find something that's better, there's a good chance it derived from the .30-06! The .270 Winchester, popular since its 1925 introduction, and the .25-06, a wildcat hailing from that decade but adopted by Remington in 1969, were among the first examples. Then there's the .35 Whelen, another wildcat given a home in Ilion. The .280 Remington also comes from the .30-06; it's been in production since 1957. Among contemporary wildcats, the .30-06 Improved and .338-06 are more popular than the .375 and .400 Whelen. The 6.5/06 has a small following, as does the 8mm/06.

Pushing the '06 shoulder out to 40 degrees increases case capacity slightly, but you'll gain only 50 to 70 fps for your efforts. I own two .30-06 Improved rifles, both carved from 1903 Springfields. One of them took the biggest elk I've shot, a

Wyoming bull that dropped to a 180-grain Nosler Partition. Certainly, the .30-06 is an elk cartridge. It and the 7mm Remington Magnum proved equally popular in surveys I conducted among members of the Rocky Mountain Elk Foundation. It also ranked among the top six picks of Washington elk hunters 20 years before the 7mm Magnum appeared. A .30-06 with even ordinary 180-grain soft-points will kill elk handily. And it will shoot flat enough for center holds to 250 yards on both deer and elk. At 300, hold on the topline of a deer and the spine of an elk (assuming a 200-yard zero). At 350, aim six inches above the deer, and right on the topline of the elk. At 400, think hard about crawling closer, no matter what your rifle.

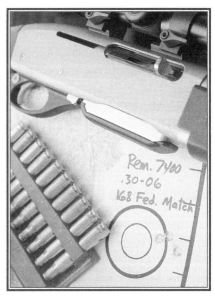

A tackdriver in match guns, the .30-06 showed surprising accuracy in this Remington autoloader.

A 165-grain pointed Core-Lokt behaves much like a 180-grain, though its muzzle velocity is higher (2,800 fps) and its ballistic coefficient lower. At 2,900 fps, the 150-grain Pointed Core-Lokt beats the 180 out of the gate by 200 fps; however, its lower ballistic coefficient narrows the gap down-range. To 300 yards there's less than an inch of difference in point of impact between the 180-grain and 150-grain bullets, at 400 only two inches. But the heavier bullet has a 20 percent weight advantage that translates to deeper penetration. During my youth, some hunters preferred 220-grain .30-06 loads for the biggest game. These days, few riflemen want to sacrifice that much speed. A 220-grain round-nose Core-Lokt starts out at only 2,410 fps. A 200-yard zero requires a three-inch lift at 100 yards. Beyond 200 yards, the bullet drops like a stone: 13 inches at 300 yards, 31 inches at 400. Better to sight this load for a 150-yard zero and limit shots to 250 yards.

While the .30 magnums flatten trajectories, the longest shot I've ever made (or attempted) on deer was with a .30-06. As a hunting guide, I learned to relax when hunters showed up with a battered '06. Often as not, they had shot it a lot and shot it well. Crippled animals were more likely when the hunter was packing a magnum with mule shoes on the butt. One of my hunters, Jack, was a .30-06 fan.

A couple of years ago, I decided to buy a really good .30-06. I discovered that one reason the '06 has lost headline space to magnums is that it's chambered in a lot of cheap rifles and is diminished by association. What if an able gunmaker built an elegant, super-accurate .30-06? Feverishly, I scrounged an action: post-war Model 70 metal that had been part of a match rifle barreled to .308. It had never shot particularly well for me.

I phoned Rick Freudenberg, who had built a .30-338 for me some years back and produced rifles for 1,000-yard and National Match competition. Rick is also a hunter and fashions fine sporting rifles. He invited me to his then-new shop near the I-5 freeway in Everett, north of Seattle. Rick wasn't always this accessible, having spent some of his 50 years in Canada, where he says "there are some very big deer."

Antlers adorn the walls of Rick's machine shop. But if you come just to talk hunting, you'll find that at work he's focused on building accurate rifles. Though he has stocked several in wood, he prefers synthetic stocks: "Mark Bansner's Hi Tech stocks are the best," he says. "They feel good and weigh about 20 ounces–light enough for a featherweight sporter but heavy enough for proper balance in rifles scaling from six-and-a-half to eight-and-a-half pounds with standard barrel lengths."

Rick likes Winchester 70 actions, pre-64s first and current Classics next. He's also built rifles on the Remington 700. Almost all of his custom jobs include Lilja barrels. "Sure, there are other good tubes on the market. But I haven't found any that shoot better than Lilja." He favors a three-groove Lilja with one-11 twist for the .30-06, and commonly gets it to print sub-half-minute groups with Nosler Ballistic Tip bullets.

A pet Freudenberg project is a lightweight hunting rifle with a #4 fluted barrel 23 1/2 inches long. He trims a Remington 700 receiver and flutes the bolt, outfitting it with a Sako-type extractor. The S&K rings and bases add only another ounce, and with a 3-9x36 Swarovski scope (11 ounces), the rifle tips the scales at just six-and-a-half pounds. "I call it the Whitetail Special," says Rick. "Winter camo finish makes it look sharp. You can carry it comfortably on long days, but the barrel is long and stiff enough for fine accuracy."

Jim Spradlin, in Texas Creek, Colorado, finishes metal parts for Rick, using a Teflon-like material that comes in 11 colors. Battleship gray looks good with black stocks and protects metal as no bluing can.

I requested a light blue finish on the .30-06, with a 25-inch, medium-weight barrel. "It'll shoot three-quarter inch," said Rick, months later when he phoned to alert me for delivery. "Let me know how you like it."

I like it a lot. The lines, fit, and finish make it as elegant as a synthetic-stocked rifle can be. The comb puts my eye instantly on-axis with the 6x Burris scope I've mounted low over the bore. The grip is long enough for big hands like mine but steep enough that no one should have any trouble reaching the trigger. If I could whine about anything on the stock, it would be that the forend is a bit thick, and that the ledges either side of the barrel are not exactly the same width.

Rick's barrel contour is just right for my taste, his understated logo there appropriate and not at all obtrusive. He reworked the bolt release and checkered it, a classy touch. The bolt handle had already been given a fine stippling–something I prefer over checkering, which, although it looks better, abrades hands and gun cases and scabbards. I had also stoned the trigger on this rifle before turning it over to Rick, so the pull was a crisp two-and-a-half pounds. The bolt slides smoothly, having already cycled thousands of rounds.

From the start, this .30-06 has wanted to shoot. My first three shots went into three-quarter inch. But in truth I cannot say it's a nail-driver. Often it will start with half-minute intentions, then shake a bullet loose. This recalcitrance is neither unusual nor fatal. The rifle shoots tight enough to kill any deer I target to 400 yards and beyond. On the other hand, it's a custom-built .30-06 with a top-quality barrel, and I'll expect more of it after a reasonable grace period for break-in. I'm confident it will soon corral those occasional fliers that cut one-and-a-half-inch groups from one-holers. Rick prides himself in accurate rifles and has built them for shooters who demand X-ring precision in competition.

A good man to trust with a rifle bored for the best-known big game cartridge of all time.

NOTES ON SHORT MAGNUMS

Since metallic cartridges appeared in the late 1800s, the trend has been to more power in smaller hulls. Several black powder cartridges favored by post-Civil War hunters had cases over three inches long: the .38-90 Winchester and .45-120 Sharps, for instance. Smokeless powder permitted smaller cases, because the propellant was more efficient. The first successful small-bore military rounds, circa 1887 to 1891, had cases less than two-and-a-half inches long: the 7.65 Belgian at 2.09, the 7.62 Russian at 2.11, the .303 British at 2.21. The 8x57 German Mauser hull miked 2.24, our .30-40 Krag, 2.31.

Hunting cartridges followed the trend of infantry rounds. In 1895, the .30-30 (2.04-inch case) was chambered in the Model 1894 Winchester. In 1913, Charles Newton delivered to Savage a new cartridge with a case 1.91 inches in length. Seven years later, Savage announced an even shorter round for its Model 1899 rifle. The .300 Savage hull measured 1.87 inches but packed 10 percent more power than a .30-30.

By this time, British gunmakers had designed several long cartridges for the spaghetti-like Cordite powder. Three became important here. In 1910, Jeffery announced a rimless .404. Rigby's .416 came the following year. In 1912, Holland and Holland brought out its .375 Magnum. The .404 had a rebated case 2.86 inches long, with a .544 base and .537 rim. The .416 Rigby was rimless, with a .586 base and 2.90 overall length. The .375 H&H had a .532 belt ahead of the extractor groove and .532 rim; case diameter forward of the belt was .512. The belt served better than the .375's faint shoulder as a headspacing stop.

Unfortunately for the lunch-bucket sportsman, long cartridges required expensive rifle actions like the Magnum Mauser. Then, in the early 1940s, shorter magnums appeared in the workshop of California insurance salesman Roy Weatherby. He reduced the taper on the Holland case to boost capacity, and cut it to two-and-a-half inches. Necking it down produced the .257, .270, and 7mm Weatherby Magnums. They'd fit any magazine built for the .30-06; however, they were proprietary rounds, available only for Weatherby rifles.

Short magnums became popular Stateside in the late '50s, beginning with the .458 Winchester Magnum in 1956. Two years later came the .264 and .338. Cases measured 2.50 inches–as did the hull of the later 7mm Remington Magnum. The slightly longer (2.62-inch) .300 Winchester Magnum case went commercial in 1963, three years after Norma introduced its .308 and .358 Magnums (2.56 and 2.52 inches).

Even shorter high-performance rounds were already popping up. Olin announced a wide-bodied, rebated .284 in 1963. At the same time, a pair of belted short-action rounds incubated at Remington. The .350 and 6.5 Magnums appeared in 1965 and 1966–in homely 600-series carbines that sold poorly.

On the bench-rest circuit, however, a very short cartridge was about to make history. Competitors Lou Palmisano and Ferris Pindell reshaped the .220 Russian (a necked-down 7.62x39) to form what would become the .22 PPC. That was in 1974; a 6mm PPC would soon follow. From base to 30-degree shoulder, these hulls measured barely over an inch, though basal diameter approached that of the .30-06. Palmisano figured that the shorter powder column would yield better accuracy. Proving the PPC's superiority over the established .222 and 6x47, in a game dominated by one-hole groups, would be tough. But in surprisingly short order, Palmisano and Pindell convinced colleagues to try the new rounds. Two of the top 20 rifles in the Sporter class at the 1975 NBRSA championship matches were chambered to PPCs. By 1980, 15 of the top 20 shooters had a PPC on the line. In 1989, all of the highest Sporter scores were shot with PPCs, plus every one of the top 20 in the Unlimited class and 18 of the 20 best in Light and Heavy Varmint.

In 1992, short rimless magnum rounds appeared in Don Allen's Dakota line. The 7mm, .300, .330, and .375 Dakotas, based on the .404 Jeffery, measure 2.50 to 2.57 inches, but hold more fuel than belted magnums. The .300's 97-grains (water) capacity is just three grains shy of the full-length .300 Weatherby's.

John Lazzeroni's first ventures into cartridge design, in the mid 1990s, yielded a stable of gigantic rimless rounds. Then John embarked on a new project: short cases based on the full-length hulls. Bases for his .243 and .264 short cartridges like .532, standard dimension for an ordinary belted magnum like the 7mm Remington, and same as the head on Lazzeroni's long .257 Scramjet. The short 7mm, .300, .338, and .416 have .580 heads, like their full-length counterparts. John used metric measures to name these hotrods:

- 6.17 (.243) Spitfire: 85-grain bullet at 3,618 fps
- 6.71 (.264) Phantom: 120-grain bullet at 3,312 fps
- 7.21 (.284) Tomahawk: 140-grain bullet at 3,379 fps
- 7.82 (.308) Patriot: 180-grain bullet at 3,184 fps
- 8.59 (.338) Galaxy: 225-grain bullet at 2,968 fps
- 10.57 (.416) Maverick: 400-grain bullet at 2,454 fps.

By then, Winchester had already announced its .300 WSM. Slightly longer and, with a .532 base, not quite as broad as the Lazzeroni Patriot, the .300 Winchester Short Magnum performs like a belted .300

Winchester Magnum (the "short" magnum introduced in 1963 that now seems

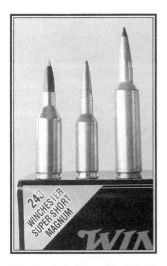

Winchester's Super Short .243 (left), with the 6mm Remington BR and the .270 WSM.

quite long!). At 2.76 inches, a .300 WSM loaded round barely clears the mouth of the .300 Winchester case.

Browning apparently approached Winchester with the idea for the WSM early in 1999. Browning and U.S. Repeating Arms Company redesigned their bolt-action big-game rifles for the .300 WSM, initially loaded with a 180-grain Fail Safe at 2,970 fps and a 150-grain Ballistic Silvertip at 3,300 fps. Though it got the jump on Remington with its first short magnum, Winchester did not then register a 7mm. Remington soon announced a .300 and a 7mm Short Action Ultra Mag, the .300 a ballistic twin to the .300 WSM. Just enough shorter to fit comfortably in a Model Seven action, the Remington rounds hold slightly less powder. Promptly, Winchester followed with a .270 WSM and a 7mm WSM, then brought new meaning to "short" with its Super Short Magnums. The .223, .243, and .25 WSSMs are based on the .300 WSM trimmed from 2.10 to 1.67. Next to the .22 WSSM, a .22-250 looks tall. But there's more capacity in the WSSM case, and the round has a 200-fps advantage over the .22-250. Factory loads include a 55-grain Ballistic Silvertip, a 55-grain Pointed Soft Point, and a 64-grain Power-Point. They kill Texas deer like bolts from Zeus. WSSM cartridges were first chambered in super short-action Browning A-Bolt and Winchester M70 rifles.

I like short cartridges. They're efficient, delivering the velocity of longer rounds with less fuel. A shorter powder column means more complete burning inside the case, which means less ejecta, less recoil. Short cases fit in short actions, for a small weight savings and shorter bolt throw. Given the PPC's history, short cartridges can

The .223 Winchester Super Short Magnum accounted for this Texas whitetail.

be accurate. But these advantages are mainly academic. You likely won't feel lighter recoil or a couple of ounces less weight; you won't notice faster bolt cycling or better accuracy. You might pick up on bumpy feeding, particularly with the Super Short Magnums.

To my knowledge, I shot the first elk ever killed with a .270 WSM and a .300

Winchester and Browning developed extra-short rifle action for the WSSM series of cartridges.

SUM, probably the first killed with an 8.59 Lazzeroni Galaxy. I've shot deer with the .223 WSSM and the 7mm SUM, elk and big African antelopes with the .300 WSM. Australian buffalo dropped to Fail Safe bullets from my 7mm WSM. I like the short magnums as well as the belted magnums whose performance they duplicate, but not a lot better. The WSSMs produce top velocities for their diameters; however, they don't feed as smoothly as traditional rounds. We may not be making cartridges too short yet, but we're mighty close. ∎

SHORT MAGNUM COMPARISONS

Cartridge	Bullet Weight	Muzzle Velocity	Cartridge	Bullet Weight	Muzzle Velocity
.223 Rem.	55	3,240	.270 Win.	130	3,060
.22-250	55	3,680	.270 AHR	130	3,150
.220 Swift	55	3,800	.270 Weatherby	130	3,200
.223 WSSM	55	3,850	.270 WSM	130	3,275
.243 Win.	100	2,960	7mm Rem. Mag.	140	3,150
6mm Rem.	100	3,100	7mm SUM	140	3,175
.243 WSSM	100	3,110	7mm WSM	140	3,225
.240 Weatherby	100	3,400	7mm Ultra Mag	140	3,425
.257 Roberts	117	2,780	.30-06	150	2,910
.25-06	115	2,990	.300 SUM	150	3,200
.25 WSSM	115	3,060	.300 WSM	150	3,200
.257 Weatherby	115	3,150	.300 Win. Mag.	150	3,250

10

BULLETS FOR BIG BUCKS

Bully, we called him. A logger, a bachelor, a consummate outdoorsman. Harold Bullivant drove a green VW bug–1960, if I recall. Its back seat had been removed to make way for flyrods and steelhead tackle, rifles, and assorted ammunition in dog-eared boxes a generation old. Bully had hunted deer when big bucks were common from Oregon's coastal forests to its high desert. Once he had shot at a huge deer that raced by him in scattered ponderosas on the Santiam. His bullet drew no visible reaction. A few seconds later, another shot sounded. Bully's partner had killed the buck with his .30-40 Krag. The hunters dug the first bullet from its swollen neck, just shy of the spine. It was the last time Bully hunted with a .32-20.

Years later, I'd remember that tale as I tracked a deer I'd shot through the forward ribs with a 16-gauge slug. Were blunt bullets ineffective? This shot had been easy, and I'd called it center. Pointed bullets driven fast would have . . . and then I found the deer, not far from where I had expected the big slug to floor it. A heavy slug has no "knock down" power, I concluded. Nor, does a spitzer. Deer die when you destroy vitals. They drop when you shatter the spine. Bully's .32-20 soft-point hadn't reached either. My slug had perforated both lungs.

Last time I saw Bully, he was toting a .30-06 for deer.

FUNDAMENTALS OF DEER BULLETS

Lead bullets that fit the bores of muzzle-loaders are fairly easy to make. Frontiersmen cast their own, and you can too, with a pot and a mold. But the high velocities achievable with smokeless powder generate lead-melting friction in the bore. In the 1890s, bullet jackets became necessary to prevent leading and ensure accuracy.

The lead cores of big-game bullets have a dash of antimony to make them harder. The usual ratio is 97.5 percent lead, 2.5 antimony. A little antimony makes a big difference. Six percent is about the limit in commercial bullets. Sierra uses three alloys for rifle bullets, with antimony proportions of 1.5, 3, and 6 percent. Some game bullets have pure lead cores. Thick copper jackets on the rifle bullets keep soft cores from disintegrating on impact. "Pure," incidentally, means unalloyed. Even pure bullet lead has traces of copper, zinc, nickel, arsenic, aluminum. As little as .1 percent copper can cause hard spots. Core material is commonly cut from lead wire, extruded from bar stock then annealed to prevent expansion during forming. The Barnes X-Bullet and Jensen J-36 feature solid-copper (or copper alloy) construction.

Bullet jackets are born two ways: by "cup and draw" and impact extrusion. Drawn jackets begin as wafers punched from sheet metal. Formed or drawn over a series of dies, they become progressively deeper cups that are eventually trimmed to length and stuffed with lead. The bullet is then shaped and finished off at the nose. Jackets given the impact extrusion treatment begin as sections of metal rods that are annealed and fed into a punch press that slams them into cups with 60 tons of force. Bullets like the Nosler Partition have cavities fore and aft, so must be punched twice. Nosler claims impact extrusion ensures concentricity. Its original machine-turned jackets had a hole in the partition. The hole's location varied.

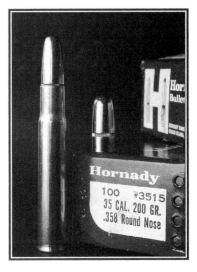

Blunt noses don't limit reach as severely as most hunters think. And many expand beautifully.

Cannelures help the jacket grip the core but serve mainly as crimping grooves. Cannelures have gradually disappeared on rifle bullets. They've been retained on bullets for heavy-recoiling rounds like the .458 Winchester (to prevent bullet creep in the magazine) and on pistol bullets (to keep short, bullets in place and to smooth the cartridge profile for better feeding). Hornady, Winchester, and a few other makers routinely crimp bullets. Most cannelures are rolled on; Nosler cuts the crimp in its 210-grain .338 bullet. Claims that crimping impairs accuracy have not been substantiated.

Jacket and core dimensions must be held to tight tolerances for utmost accuracy. Sierra, renowned for its match-winning target bullets, keeps jacket thickness within .0003 of a standard. The company limits bullet weight variation to .3 grain. Test lots of 168-grain 30-caliber match bullets that don't shoot into .250 inch at 100 yards can send the entire batch back into the production line. Demands on hunting bullets are less stringent, at least in terms of dimensional uniformity and accuracy. Expansion and weight retention are more important in the design of big game bullets.

Remington's Managed Recoil loads feature bonded Core-Lokt bullets.

Properly bonding jacket to core is crucial to making–and marketing–big-game bullets. Hunters have known for some time that bullets must stay in one piece to do the most damage. "Core-Lokt," "Trophy Bonded,"

"Bonded Core" and "Hot-Core" are trade names that play on this theme. Remington's Core-Lokt bullet has an inner belt (from the Peters Inner Belted bullet, which followed the Peters Belted design, with an exterior metal girdle). The Speer Hot-Core process reportedly gives a tight bond because the lead is warm enough to snuggle into every void in the jacket. The other companies don't tell exactly how their superior bonds are formed.

Bullet nose design has a lot to do with how expansion proceeds. Hollow-point bullets are typically used for thin-skinned game. Small cavities and thicker jackets keep hollow-points from fragmenting, but they also make upset less dependable. Among early hollow-points, the Western Tool and Copper Works bullet, with a tiny cavity, had perhaps the best reputation on big game. Westley-Richards offered a bullet with a nose dimple covered by a metal cap that protected the nose and kept the jacket from rupturing too early. DWM's "strong-jacket" bullet had a long, narrow nose cavity lined with copper tubing and capped.

The sophisticate of early hollow-points was Peters' Protected Point. Its jacket enveloped a flat-topped core, the front third wrapped in a gilding metal band, and crowned with a pointed cone. On impact, the flattening nose drove the band down under the jacket. The band initiated and controlled the core's expansion, which split the jacket as it progressed. A Protected Point bullet required 51 operations and three hours to manufacture. Winchester's Silvertip is a cheaper rendition of this design. It lacks an inner band.

Remington put a hard peg in a hollow bullet nose to form its Bronze Point spitzer. Upon striking a target, this peg was driven back into the bullet to start expansion. The Bronze Point opened pretty violently at close range. RWS has counterparts to this design: the TIG (Torpedo Ideal) and TUG (Torpedo Universal) bullets. The TIG's tail section has a funnel-shaped mouth into which the nose core fits like a plug. Expansion starts not only at the nose but at the core juncture. The rear core opens more reluctantly because it's harder. In TUG bullets the joint is reversed: A cavity in the nose accepts a conical protrusion from the rear   section, which acts like a trailing bullet when the nose breaks apart in game. The pointed tail portion resists deformation, penetrating like the trunk of a Nosler Partition.

Bitterroot Bullet Company also uses unalloyed copper for its jackets, which in .338 can be .060-inch thick. The nose of a bitterroot bullet has a cavity to initiate expansion. Bitterroots are long for their weight, requiring deep seating, and a careful eye to pressures bumped by extended bearing surfaces.

Perhaps the best known of bullet-makers specializing in tough bullets is Barnes. This company started in 1939, predating John Nosler's by nine years. Barnes "Original" bullets, from 22 caliber to .600, come in a wide range of weights, some heavier than you can normally get for the caliber. Jackets are pure copper, .032 and .049 inch thick, depending on the application. The jackets have no taper, and the thick ones depend on a substantial jolt to open.

One of America's premier bullet companies, Hornady, has now been in the jacketed bullet business for half a century. The Grand Island, Nebraska, firm began when Joyce Hornady and Vernon Speer, who had been working together, split to seek their own fortunes. By fashioning bullet jackets from spent rimfire casings, they had circumvented war-time metal shortages in the early 1940s. Hand-loaders would, they hoped, sustain a market for jacketed hunting bullets.

Joyce Hornady was quick to spot value in the specialized machinery and tooling dormant in government arsenals after the war. The Hornady plant still uses Waterbury-Farrell transfer presses, manufactured as early as the 1920s and now updated with computerized controls. The rural town has grown, too, since the war, but Hornady is still run by people with Midwest smiles who make time for shooters with technical questions and hunting tales.

Mike Timmerman, Plant Supervisor, says that every bullet run is tested at 100,000-unit intervals–rifle bullets for accuracy, pistol bullets for expansion. "Pistol bullets must not only shoot consistently but open reliably and penetrate. Wide velocity spreads make mushrooming more difficult to control in handgun bullets. Our .38s and .45s are tested at 750 fps and 1,500, the .454 Casull bullets at 1,000, and 1,600. Those velocities work for muzzle-loaders too. We use some pistol bullets as sabot projectiles in muzzle-loaders."

Mike shows me a rugged one-hole group. "We shoot four five-shot groups with rifle bullets. The average must meet our standards. For .30s it's .600 at 100 yards, for .17s it's .400. The 6mms come in at .450, the .338s at .750. We have more stringent standards for match bullets: .350 for .22 match. We check 'em more often too: every 30,000 units. Our 30-caliber match bullets are tested at 200 yards. They have to shoot inside .800."

Chief Ballistician Dave Emary says that jacket design largely determines expansion. "Nose cavity dimensions and bullet hardness matter too," he adds.

Hornady gets its lead in ingots, which are melted and formed into cylindrical blocks about the size of a roll of freezer paper (but heavier!). A massive press squirts

I took this eastern Washington buck with a Hornady softpoint from a .280 Improved.

these cylinders, cold, through dies to form the wire that's then cut into bullet lengths. Antimony content is specified at purchase, from zero to six percent. Most bullet cores have three percent antimony. Jacket cups are punched out of sheets. "Jacket concentricity is vital to accuracy," Dave emphasizes. "We hold it to .003."

Like many of Hornady's 140 employees, Dave Emary is an active shooter. His high-power rifle skills earned him a coveted spot in the President's Hundred at Camp Perry. Before coming to Hornady, he worked with artillery, "shooting five-pound bullets at 7,000 fps and 12-pound bullets at 6,500" from 90mm and 120m cannons.

Hornady's Spire Point soft-points have been a mainstay of deer hunters for decades. Now the firm also makes A-Max (Advanced Match Accuracy) spitzers for competitive shooting. The V-Max, introduced in 1995, share the A-Max's plastic nose insert. Its very thin jacket has explosive effect on small animals. The SST (Super Shock Tip) plastic-nose bullet for big game followed. "We got the SST designation from an old 1950s Hornady bullet board," explains Director of Sales Wayne Holt. "Its now our premier deer bullet." The Hornady InterBond is really a bonded version of the SST, for use on tough game.

Some shooters might question the need for new soft-point bullet designs, given the broad selection now at market. But new product is as important in the bullet industry as in the automotive business, and customer expectations change. For example, bullet weight retention has become a common measure of bullet performance in big game. So, though Hornady's soft-points have a lethal record, there's reason to build them to keep more of their original weight.

Hornady production lines supply hand-loaders and companies that assemble ammunition. They've also been equipped to load ammunition, a growing part of the business. Says Dave Emary: "We launched our Light Magnum line in 1995 after I saw at Olin-St. Marks how to concoct these super-powerful loads. It was a good move, and we plan to expand the Light and Heavy Magnum stable." Shotshells and .22 rimfire ammo is probably not on the horizon. Nor is the .17 HMR (Hornady Magnum Rimfire) or .17 Mach 2, both of which were largely developed in Emary's shop. "We supply CCI/Speer, Eley and Remington with .17 bullets. The loading machines are a huge investment."

Hornady profits from its wide selection of high-quality deer bullets. Lowell Hawthorne has been a ballistician there 18 years. He tests bullet prototypes in the lab, below a rack of gleaming Hart and Schneider barrels screwed onto M70 and M700 receivers: the test battery. A three-point free-recoiling machine rest fills the mouth of a 200-yard shooting tunnel, where ballistic coefficient is derived from starting and ending velocities. Some bullets, like .348s for Winchester's Model 71, are tested from the shoulder. Dave shows me a cloverleaf group from a well-worn 71.

I ask about a large instrument. "That's a Heise Gauge, a hydraulic device for calibrating chamber pressure," says Dave Emary, explaining that it has a transducer with a quartz crystal. Pressure registers through electrical discharge.

Dave points out that peak pressure as commonly measured in copper units (CUP) is not sufficient because it tells nothing about the pressure curve. "Time matters. You can boost velocity by extending the peak of the curve forward without making the curve higher." He says that a strain gauge falls short because it can't be calibrated to a standard in the manner of the Heise. Dave allows that hand-loaders can detect high pressure levels by measuring case web expansion. "But a .001 bulge at the web can become .005 a touch farther forward. It's best to measure forward, because you get more reaction from the brass."

Typically, he says, you start to pierce primers at about 70,000 CUP, and get blown cups at 80,000. Pressure that's high enough for most shooters to notice is already well above SAAMI spec. "We get higher speed from Light and Heavy magnum ammo by pushing the pressure curve forward so the peak occurs when the bullet is three inches out. The powder has four percent more nitroglycerin than ordinary double-base powders. Surface deterrents slow the intitial burn so the bullet doesn't outrun the burn so soon."

The Light Magnum line includes popular rimless rounds, and the .303 British. "The .303 has a great record on big game," Dave says. "And we still get lots of orders for 174-grain FMJs from Australia." The Light Magnum load features a 150-grain Spire Point bullet at 2,830 fps.

Hornady manufactures between 60 and 70 percent of its cartridge cases in house.

Hornady bullets reflect Dave's experience at the 1,000-yard line. He points out that bullet design is an exercise in compromise. "Though it would reduce drag in the barrel, lengthening the nose to shorten the shank gives the nose greater leverage if it swings off the bullet's axis in flight," he says. A long nose also mandates a more gradual curvature forward of the shank–which increases the odds for misalignment in the throat, and for subsequent yaw. "A short transition is best, so the bullet is forced quickly into full contact with the rifling." Dave says he likes to keep the ratio of bullet bearing surface to diameter at 1.5 or higher, though nose type and other variables also affect that ratio.

He adds that the "secant ogive" nose profile of Hornady's traditional Spire Point bullets reduces their nose weight. "Tangent ogives generate a more rounded form," he explains. "We've used the secant ogive for years to minimize air friction. It does not necessarily mean a sharper junction between the conical and cylindrical sections of the bullet; however, it can appear that way." (Secant and tangent refer to the point from which an arc, whose radius is measured in calibers, scribes the outline of the bullet nose. The tangent measure is perpendicular to the bullet axis at the cylinder/cone juncture. Secant measurements are taken from behind that point.)

Do Hornady bullets ever come back? "Yes, but they shouldn't." Dave points to long shelves full of red boxes. "We cull our bullets severely, even for surface blemishes. The rigid testing just doesn't allow substandard bullets or ammo out the door." He smiles. "Well, they do go out the door, I guess. Employees get the seconds."

Perhaps that's one reason the average shop tenure at Hornady is 12 years.

"What happens when a customer insists he's got bad bullets?"

Dave laughs. "One of those characters phoned me not long ago to say his bullets wouldn't stay closer than three inches. He seemed to know a little about shooting.

Because he was also local, I asked him to bring his rifle to the plant, expecting I'd have to suggest major gun work. When he came in, the first thing I did was load up some of his bullets and take his rifle to the test tunnel. It shot into three-quarter inch. To his credit, he took it gracefully. Not all customers do. Shooting can be an ego thing."

STICKING WITH THE OLD SOFT-NOSE

At the swamp's west end a grassy slope climbed to a corn field, now a shag carpet of tattered gray stubble anchored by crusted snow. I stood on the slope, shivering in the raw, Michigan wind. Then good sense got the better of me. From here the

view was grand, but any deer the drivers pushed from the swamp would see me and duck back in. Besides, the marsh border would afford a windbreak.

I didn't make it down the hill. Branches snapped. Seconds later, a deer jetted from the swamp and scooted up the hill. I fired as the bead passed its brisket–did the head sag just a little? Seconds later came the flat pop of Joe's .30-30. Still shivering, but now with excitement, I raced over the hill and toward Joe, a scarlet plaid beacon in the stubble sea.

"Nice buck!" I gasped, mustering enthusiasm. I'd never shot a buck.

Joe smiled. He'd taken lots of them. "There's another over there." He pointed. "It just cleared the rise and dropped."

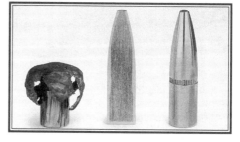

Remington's bonded Core-Lokt Ultra bullet is one of many CE bullets on the market now.

Winchester's Power Point is one of the most effective deer bullets ever designed.

I'd kill other bucks with soft-nose bullets like the Winchester Power-Points in my .303 SMLE that day. They'd pile up bigger game too, with monotonous efficiency: the Montana elk, the British Columbia moose, a huge eland in Zimbabwe.

You hear a lot about controlled expansion bullets now, bullets with long names and special jackets and complex innards that allow them to upset without fragmenting, then to penetrate without losing weight.

We're told they smash through bones and muscles that would stop ordinary soft-nose bullets.

The trouble with bullets tough enough to let the air out of a Caterpillar engine block is that they're expensive. Besides, for deer hunting, I've never found them necessary. Even with quartering shots, you can kill as cleanly–and sometimes more quickly–with an ordinary soft-nose. That's because a bullet shedding its weight and speed and energy midway through game is scrambling the vitals.

I shot my first deer with a .303 SMLE like this, using a Winchester softpoint bullet.

Our preoccupation with retained weight is ill founded. There's not much left of a grenade after it detonates, but a grenade that stays in one piece doesn't do much damage. I once watched a hunter shoot a big bull elk at 250 yards with a .30-06. The elk took the bullet too far back, but the shot angle brought it to the off lung. Within seconds that bull was on the ground. A post-mortem confirmed that the 180 Hornady was pretty well minced.

"Not much left," mumbled the hunter, inspecting it.

"No," I said. "But that tattered bullet just gave you a whopping big elk. Be kind."

Elk test deer bullets. But I've seen dozens shot dead with ordinary soft-points. A big bull tipped over backward and died after one shot through the lungs with a 130-grain Hornady from a .270. Another mature bull collapsed from a hit with a 145-grain Speer, courtesy of a .280 Remington. One fellow I know has killed a lot of elk with factory loads in a .250 Savage. Another uses 100-grain Hornadys in a .25-06. Deer cartridges with deer bullets can be deadly on bigger game.

Power Point Plus ammo features oxide-coated Power Point bullets at elevated velocities.

Full expansion is better than pass-through penetration when you hurl a soft-nose through the slats from the side, and side presentations are most common. Any expanding bullet that drives through the lungs will kill, but you may get shorter blood trails following the violent upset of relatively soft or fragile bullets. Those with stout jackets, bonded cores, and expansion-limiting devices give you an edge in heavy muscle and bone—and won't open prematurely on thick hide. However, kinetic energy lost as a deep-driving bullet exits the animal is energy not used in the destruction of vital tissue.

Proponents of strong bullets argue that bullets are driven faster now than when soft-points like the Winchester Power Point and Silvertip, and the Remington Core-Lokt and Bronze Point were top choices. High impact velocities mean bullets are more apt to fragment during upset. That's true. It's also true that a bullet stopping short of the vitals is much less desirable than one so strong it zings through without putting on much of a blossom. In the early days of high-velocity rifles, bullet-makers had to experiment to get the right jacket and core materials, then taper and fit the jacket correctly. Some of those first bullets blew up on a deer's near-side skin; others didn't open at all. But in time, reliable upset would be taken for granted, More options ensued: hollow-points, polymer-tipped bullets, and bullets that looked like soft-noses outside but were bonded or had mid-section jacket dams inside.

Nosler's Ballistic Tip started a trend toward polymer-tipped bullets.

"It's hard to make an all-purpose hunting bullet," points out one ballistician, who'd as soon remain anonymous. "An ordinary soft-nose comes close. Polymer tips are sporty but a pain to make. To ensure deep penetration, the jacket must be thick to slow setback of the tip on impact. Thick jackets are harder to keep concentric. So are complex jackets."

Rich Maccholz of Sierra Bullets insists jacket concentricity is the key to bullet accuracy. "Sierra's MatchKing shoots tiny groups because we take extra care with jackets. We allow .0003 thickness variation at the bullet base, .0010 at the nose. Jacket tolerances for Pro-Hunter (flat-base) and GameKing (boat-tail) bullets are almost as tight: .0005 at the base, .0015 at the nose. Weight limits for match and hunting bullets are the same: .3 grains maximum variation on finished bullets. Maximum run-out is the same too: .0001 at the nose." Sierra makes its own jackets, using two to five draws to bring the cupronickel from strip to cup. Most Sierra bullets go to competitive shooters "because they shoot a lot," but the hunting line is extensive.

Hornady's Dave Emary agrees that jacket concentricity is important. "Another thing to mind is the distance between center of gravity and center of pressure. It's hard to measure because it's only there when the bullet is moving. For a bullet that flies point-on, CP doesn't matter. But if there's lift or yaw, a CP that's far from CG affects stability." A tapered heel or boat-tail moves the center of gravity back, away from the center of pressure. "That's one reason flat-base bullets commonly shoot as well as or better than boat-tails. Another is that flat-base bullets are easier to keep uniform; there's one less angle on the heel. And when the shank of a flat-base bullet clears the muzzle, there's no tail for powder gas to wag." On average, says Dave, flat-base bullets go to sleep sooner in flight.

"Most bullets that expand readily and reliably in deer can be made to shoot very accurately," says Rich Maccholz. "Thin gilding metal jackets and a lead core allow ballisticians plenty of freedom in nose design. We're not so constrained by length limits as we would be with thick jackets or solid-copper bullets. The more lightweight material you have in a bullet, the longer it will be for its weight. At some point you have to reduce bullet weight to get the design you want, or put up with a bullet that's too long to stabilize in the rifling or must be seated so deep as to reduce powder capacity." He adds that heavy bullets can be very accurate. But the heaviest bullets have the rounded noses and steep ogives that shooters associate with lots of long-range drop.

The bullet's tip has less to do with accuracy than does a uniform base. And it has almost no effect on trajectory. "If the meplat, or bullet tip, is less than 15 percent of the bullet's diameter, you won't get any flatter flight with a sharp bullet," says Alan Corzine, a ballistician for ATK (Federal). "The ogive or curve of the bullet from about one-tenth inch back from the tip to the shank matters more. Nose form and ogive don't affect accuracy, only trajectory." He concurs with Emary that round-nose bullets often fly more accurately than spitzers.

Federal features several bullet types in its Premium ammo, like the Nosler Partition shown here.

To test the effect of nose shape on accuracy, I once cut the noses off several .338 bullets halfway down the ogive. Bullet shanks were crushed in the jaws of my tool. Though now of different weights, and leading with ragged mouths, the bullets still shot into three inches at 100 yards.

Blunt bullets sometimes penetrate straighter than pointed bullets. Any deformation resulting in an unevenly weighted front or a lopsided ogive will cause the bullet to stray. Blunt bullets may drive more consistently through light brush, but this is difficult to prove because it's nearly impossible to hit branches exactly the same each time in trials. I have found that both pointed and blunt bullets deflect on thumb-size limbs so badly that targets 12 feet behind show keyhole hits well off the mark.

Round or blunt bullet noses helped define the first smokeless cartridge profiles during the 1890s. Holdovers from the black-powder era, when most shooting was short and bores large, blunt bullets made a lot of sense in the tubular magazines of early lever-action repeaters. Then came World War I. Germany's 8x57 service round first featured a 236-grain round-nose bullet at 2,125 fps. Our .30-03 with its 220-grain round-nose edged it at 2,300 fps. But soon German troops got a 154-grain Spitzgeschoss bullet at 2,800 fps. The U.S. Army countered with a 150-grain pointed bullet at 2,700. Shooters have since hewed to spitzers.

A round-nose bullet has a weight advantage over pointed bullets of the same length, so it yields higher sectional density. But at long range drag eats momentum, which is why spitzers are more popular. Round-nose bullets can't battle drag as well, so they decelerate faster. A bullet losing speed is also losing energy. Because round-nose bullets clock slower times downrange, they drop farther per unit of distance. For example, a 180-grain Nosler Ballistic Tip kicked from a .30-06 at 2,700 fps crosses the 500-yard mark still clocking 1,887. Swift's A-Frame, a soft-nose bullet with a mid-section dam that drives deep into heavy game and delivers a picture-book mushroom, has slipped from 2,700 to 1,648 fps at 500 yards. Indeed, the Ballistic Tip brings almost as much energy to 500 yards as the A-Frame does to 400!

Now, polymer-tipped bullets do not always fly flatter than soft-nose bullets. The 150-grain Sierra GameKing loaded by Federal to 3,110 fps in the 7mm Remington Magnum reaches 500 yards traveling 50 fps faster than a Nosler Ballistic Tip of the same weight, launched at the same speed. Nor are polymer-tip bullets necessarily your most accurate choice. During a visit to Hornady's plant, I noticed a stack of targets with one-hole groups. They were shot with regular soft-nose bullets.

I like accurate bullets, and one year had to choose between an ordinary soft-point and a controlled expansion bullet for an elk hunt. The soft-nose shot tighter and I loaded it. Days into the hunt, as we came down a steep trail horseback, a bull elk popped up across a draw and ran. I piled off Paint and yanked the Model 70 from its scabbard. The bull was quartering away, just shy of the timber when my shot reached him. The trees swallowed him up. Fearing the worst and wishing I'd picked a stouter bullet, I hurried to the track and followed it, rifle ready. The elk lay dead just a few yards into the trees. The Power-Point had struck in the middle of the ribs and angled forward across the top of the heart. It was balled up in shoulder muscle on the far side. About what old-timers would have expected from ordinary soft-nose bullets, before myriad new designs grabbed our imagination.Image 10-11

I was reminded, as we field-dressed that elk, of the hunter in turn-of-the-century British Columbia who'd bought a box of .303 Savage soft-points for his new lever rifle and proceeded to kill 18 big animals, including two grizzlies, with those 20 cartridges. A pretty good testimonial for the soft-nose.

SOFT-NOSE SMORGASBORD

Ordinary soft-nose bullets are still deadly. Even animals the size of moose die quickly when shot through the ribs with bullets designed before television. Here are some popular bullets that cost less (and sometimes shoot more accurately) than bullets with special expansion-control

The Savage 340 with ordinary softnose .30-30 ammunition is still a deadly deer combo.

devices. On deer-size game, they commonly give you quicker kills.

• **Federal Soft-Point.** This Federal-produced bullet supplants the Hi-Shok in the Classic line of ammo—now named the Power-Shok line. It is offered in round-nose, flat-nose, and spitzer form, in diameters .224 to .375. Currently, some Speer bullets are available in Power-Shok ammunition.

- **Hornady Interlock and Traditional.** The reputation for fine accuracy that attended the company's flagship Spire Point carries over to the Interlock. Inner jacket belting holds the lead core in place during upset. The round-nose traditional versions show fine accuracy and upset on deer at modest ranges.
- **Remington Core-Lokt.** In both round-nose and pointed form, this veteran may have killed more big-game animals than any other soft-point. It has an internal belt to help hold the core in place and is available in many weights. The Core-Lokt expands over a wide range of impact speeds and drives deep.
- **Sierra GameKing.** Long renowned for superior accuracy and flat flight downrange, Sierra boat-tail bullets open violently. I've seen lightning-like kills on deer from these soft-points. The 250-grain .338 and 300-grain .375s have extra-heavy jackets.
- **Speer Hot-Cor.** The huge selection of these solid performers adds to their popularity. You'll find weights not available elsewhere, even .366 spitzers for that 9.3mm rifle. Traditional soft-nose construction and a sleek profile make Speer Hot-Cors ideal for long shooting at deer-size game.
- **Winchester Power Point.** This 40-year-old soft-point might well be considered an archetype. It has no special features, save the nose notches on its tapered jacket. They ensure quick expansion. The Power Point has recently been moly-coated for stepped-up loads in Winchester Power Point Plus ammo.
- **Winchester Silvertip.** For years the firm's heavy-game bullet, Silvertip got a more fragile nose cap in the 1960s. This bullet now opens more easily—sometimes even easily than the Power Point. Expect sure kills with rib shots. Weight retention doesn't match that of bullets built to penetrate.

JUST IN CASE . . .

If you hunt where oblique shots at elk-size game are common, you'll want a cohesive bullet that plows a long furrow. You'll pay more for it, so before you spring for a controlled-expansion bullet, consider velocity. If you aren't pushing 3,400 fps, you don't need bullets that hold up to impact speeds of 3,200 fps. A fellow at Nosler once told me that the only reason the company offered a Partition-style 170-grain .30-30 bullet was to appease retailers. "They needed a complete line of .30-30 bullets, and they didn't want to deal with a lot of suppliers." Here's a list of the tough bullets.

- **Alaska Kodiak:** This bonded-core bullet delivers double-diameter upset, superior weight retention. Jackets are of drawn gilding metal, not pure copper.
- **Barnes X:** A solid-copper hollow-point, this bullet is long for its weight. Weight retention of 95 percent or more means you can get penetration with lighter weights and higher starting speeds.

- **Hornady InterBond:** This bonded, polymer-tipped bullet has an inner-belted jacket to help control upset, which is relatively violent. A sleek ogive gives it a flat trajectory.
- **Lapua Mega:** The copper jacket of this bullet has a wide inner belt to hold core to jacket. Mega is available in Lapua ammunition. Its round nose profile is consistent with European tradition.
- **Norma Oryx:** I used this bullet in Norway. It typically expands to double diameter before peeling back, the bonded core preventing separation and yielding a retained weight higher than 90 percent.
- **Norma TXP:** This is the Swift A-Frame, renamed by Norma for marketing. A partitioned core of pure lead is Nosler-like in cross-section. The front end is cold-soldered to the jacket.
- **Nosler AccuBond:** To stay competitive in a market enamored of polymer-tipped bullets that Nosler itself popularized, the company now offers a bonded version of its Ballistic Tip.
- **Nosler Partition:** Developed in 1947 by John Nosler, this classic bullet with two-piece core has a dam that stops expansion, guarantees penetration by the heel. Loss of the nose is common in tough game.
- **Remington Core-Lokt Ultra:** Designed for the high-speed impact of Ultra Mag cartridges, jackets on C-LU bullets are 20 percent heavier, the belts 50 percent thicker. Weight retention: 80 to 90 percent.
- **Speer Grand Slam:** A flat meplat atop a long, sleek ogive, and a cannelure groove distinguish this bullet. The thick rear jacket arrests expansion. I've had it come apart in elk shoulders.
- **Swift A-Frame:** Developed by Lee Reed on the Nosler Partition design, this bullet has a bonded front end that gives it better weight retention. Expect a wide, deep wound channel, picture-book upset.
- **Swift Scirocco:** This sleek polymer-tipped bullet has great flight characteristics. But the bonded core and thick jacket hold it together in tough game. I've shot it through 6-inch spruce trees.
- **Trophy Bonded Bear Claw:** Developed by Jack Carter and now loaded by Federal, this bonded soft-point is among my favorites because it mushrooms broadly but doesn't fragment. Not streamlined.
- **Winchester Fail Safe:** This black-oxide-coated bullet has a lead core capped by a steel insert in the heel, a solid-copper front with a hollow nose. It flies flat, penetrates deep. Weight retention: 95 percent +.
- **Winchester Partition Gold:** Based on the Nosler Partition, this bullet has a longer shank section to boost weight retention, and a steel cap at the rear of the dam to control bulging there at impact.
- **Woodleigh Weldcore:** Made in Australia and distributed by Huntington's in Oroville, CA, this is not a sleek bullet, but weight retention runs to 95 percent after broad upset. It's available in very heavy weights.

SLUG STORY

"What's a cut-shell?" The willowy teenager was, by all indications, new to hunting.

The proprietor peered over grimy reading glasses. Thick as an oak, with massive arms and a bull neck, Mike wore a perpetual grimace behind iron-gray stubble shaded by a Tigers cap.

"A cut-shell is a poor man's slug," he explained, slipping off the glasses to better focus his glare. You take a knife and score the hull around the wad. When you shoot, the whole front half of the shell goes out the muzzle. The hull acts like a shot cup put in backwards, so the shot stays together for a few yards."

"Doesn't sound very accurate."

"Isn't. Not safe either. You're squeezin' a big plug of shot, wad, and hull through the forcing cone and choke."

"But don't slugs have to squeeze down in a choke too?"

"Well, yes. But not that much. Besides, a slug is pretty much pure soft lead, and it has ribs on the sides that mash down easily in the choke."

"I thought those ribs were to make it spin."

"Nope. The ribs you see on most slugs don't help much with spin. What makes a slug accurate is its heavy nose and hollow base. The weight's all forward. Think of a shuttlecock or a spear. They're not as accurate as rifle bullets, but they fly pretty straight over short distances. A slug's base is hollow, to expand to fill the bore–like Minie balls soldiers used during the Civil War. Of course, in a rifle that idea makes more sense than in a shotgun, where you have a wad in front of the powder. There's probably some set-back as the slug gets going, like tires squat when you pour the coal to a hot-rod." Mike looked at the gangly youngster. "Ever do that?"

But the kid wanted to know more about slugs. "What's a Foster slug?"

"What we've been talkin' about." Mike explained that Karl Foster was a Winchester ballistician who came up with his slug about 1933. "The only other kind of slug I know of is the Brenneke. That came out of Europe in about 1895. We didn't see it here until after World War II. It's got ribs like the Foster, but the wad is screwed onto it, and there's no hollow base."

It was 1963, and coming up on deer season. In southern Michigan, deer hunters couldn't use rifles. The relatively short reach of shotguns made them safer where farms were small and cattle grazed between woodlots. The most coveted guns among farm boys back then were Ithaca's Model 37 Deerslayer pump and Browning's Auto 5 Buck Special. Both came with short, cylinder-bore barrels and iron sights. These were costly smooth-bores. Most of us youngsters carried the same cheap shotguns we used on pheasants. You had to take a fine bead with a bird barrel, or the slug would strike high at 50 to 75 yards, where a lot of the deer were shot.

Some remarkable shooting was done with the worn pumps and auto-loaders pulled from mudroom racks in Michigan's rural hinterlands come deer season. One farmer I know killed a buck, offhand, at 147 paces with his 16-gauge Remington 11-48. "It was the last of the 10 shots Bill and I threw at that deer," chuckled Harvey. "It had to be good."

In this enlightened time, we might not feel justified launching slugs from a smooth-bore at deer that far away. But there's no question that the lumbering Foster in a 12- or 16-bore repeater could reap venison as far as you could hit it. Almost nobody used buckshot. We were dimly aware that "buck" was popular in the Deep South, where hounds chased deer at full throttle past waiting hunters. Michigan woods could be as thick as Mississippi swamp; but sometimes you needed a slug's greater reach, to tag a buck crossing a field or peeking at you from the far side of a thinning.

Ironically, most deer-load development in my growing-up years was to boost the effectiveness of buckshot. Super-heavy charges of hard, plated shot were nested in granulated plastic buffer to cushion them during launch so they stayed round and flew straight. If you hunt where shots are typically short, modern buckshot is a deadly choice. It's important to pattern several loads, so you can pick the shot size and charge weight that works best in your gun. Double-ought and triple-ought shot offer a lot of energy per pellet, but pattern density matters, too.

It wasn't until the 1980s, with the advent of rifled shotgun barrels and special-purpose scopes, that slugs began to dominate the "new products" pages of ammo catalogs. Now Mike's slug lecture would be longer. He would note that Foster slugs still account for 60 percent of all slugs sold. But then he might say there are better choices: "Sabots. Saybows. It's French for a projectile within a projectile. Sabot slugs are smaller than the bore, and they come in bore-diameter capsules that fall away leaving the muzzle."

The kid: "What's good about sabots?"

"You can make a sabot slug just about any shape, and you can reduce the weight because you don't have to fill up a big bore. Less weight means faster, flatter flight. Now, you may not care about long shooting. Maybe you want all the weight you can get for close shots in thickets. Sabots that weigh as much as Foster slugs are the answer. They penetrate better because they're skinnier and have a higher sectional density. The sabot's main advantage, though, is that plastic capsule. You can fire it in rifled barrels that spin it for better accuracy. You can't shoot a hard lead or jacketed slug in thin-walled rifled shotgun barrels at high speed because the friction could cause too much pressure. Soft lead would strip. With sabots, there is no mark on slug or bullet."

"Bullet?"

"Some sabot slugs are actually bullets. For example, Nosler's pistol bullet for the .454 Casull goes into Winchester's newest sabot shotgun loads . . . "

The shift to sabot ammunition began when California-based Ballistics Research Institute (BRI) developed an hour-glass-shaped slug in a two-piece plastic sleeve split along its length. It was designed for police use but by the mid-80s had been packaged for deer hunters. I remember shooting prototype rounds through a Benneli autoloader with a rifled barrel, and coming up with a one-hole group at 50 yards. I was mightily impressed with the new ammunition. So were folks at Winchester, who later bought BRI. Federal followed with its own hour-glass slug.

What kept the sabot from burying the Foster slug? Well, the Foster shoots as accurately or even more accurately in smooth-bore barrels. It flattens readily in deer, opening a bigger wound channel than the slender sabot slugs. Not every shotgun can be fitted with a rifled barrel. And a lot of casual hunters choose not to spend the money for a rifled tube. Besides, sabot slug ammo costs considerably more than shotshells loaded with Foster slugs (in my youth you could buy a box of 25 Super-X slugs for $5).

In 1993, a small New Jersey firm announced a "Lightfield Hybred" sabot, an almost-bore-diameter slug in a thin-walled, two-piece capsule. Designed by Tony Kinchen, the new Lightfield expanded readily and proved deadly on deer-size game. Like the Brenneke Magnum, this slug had an integral wad. Another New Jersey shop, Gun Servicing, was at that time testing .45 ACP pistol bullets in a 12-gauge sabot cup. And Remington was about to intro-

The BuckHammer slug from Remington is surprisingly accurate, and packs a wallop.

duce the first commercially successful bullet-shaped slug: the 50-caliber Copper Solid. It had a notched hollow nose to initiate expansion, but the light body of a deer later proved unable to cause upset. So Remington revamped the slug, using softer metal. By then Barnes had unveiled its Expander MZ bullet, developed for muzzle-loading rifles but promptly added to the slug market. Federal adopted this 50-bore solid copper hollow-point for its Premium slug ammunition in, if I remember correctly, 1997. That was the year that Hornady shouldered its way into the slug market with a sabot design. A new Hornady slug, the 300-grain .486 H2K Heavy Mag, appeared two years later.

The turn of the millennium brought a new Brenneke sabot slug to the PMC line. This rural Nevada firm loads the one-ounce slug to 1,600 fps. Winchester earned the spotlight about the same time, with a 385-grain Partition Gold hollow-point bullet pushed from a 12-bore shotgun at 1,900 fps. This Nosler bullet delivers more than a ton and a half of energy at the muzzle, and at 200 yards it still has 1,500 foot-pounds—more than a .243 Winchester, a 6.5x55 or a .300 Savage! So much for the image of the slug as a pumpkin ball, lethal only as far as you can throw a rock!

Of course, ballistic performance depends not only on slug design, but its weight and the load in the shell. When I was young, only 12- and 16-gauge shotshells were thought suitable for deer hunting. The 20 (then as only a two-and-three-quarter-inch shell) drove a slug as fast as a 12 (to 1,600 fps); but its lower ballistic coefficient resulted in quicker deceleration, with an attendant loss in energy. At 100 yards, where a one-ounce 12-gauge Foster slug still carried 1,255 foot-pounds of energy, the 20-bore slug managed only 835. The 12 at 100 yards hit like a .30-30 bullet at 125 yards, while the 20-gauge at 100 yards mustered only the snap of a .30-30 at 250. The .410 with its quarter-ounce slug at 1,775 fps, churned up just 770 foot-pounds at the muzzle, and was down to 435 foot pounds at 50 yards. That's about as much as the .30-30 delivers at 500 yards!

But while the .410 is still out of the running as a whitetail round, some modern 20-bore slug loads make sense. Here's a performance comparison of slug types and loads from Federal, which has the most extensive line of slug ammunition. (Similar slugs from Remington, Winchester, PMC, and Brenneke offer comparable velocities and energies.)

Type	Gauge	Shell Lgth.	Slug Wt.	Velocity			Energy		
				Muzzle	50	100	Muzzle	50	100
Barnes Sabot	12 ga.	3"	438	1,525	1,390	1,270	2,260	1,870	1,560
	12 ga.	2¾"	438	1,450	1,320	1,210	2,045	1,695	1,420
	20 ga.	3"	325	1,450	1,320	1,200	1,515	1,250	1,040
Hydra-Shok Sabot	12 ga.	3"	438	1,550	1,340	1,180	2,335	1,750	1,345
	12 ga.	2¾"	438	1,450	1,260	1,120	2,045	1,545	1,215
	20 ga.	3"	275	1,450	1,230	1,070	1,285	920	705
	20 ga.	2¾"	275	1,400	1,190	1,050	1,200	860	670
Hydra-Shok HP	12 ga.	2¾"	438	1,300	1,110	1,000	1,645	1,205	865
	12 ga.	2¾"	438	1,610	1,330	1,140	2,520	1,725	1,255
Classic Sabot	12 ga.	2¾"	438	1,450	1,260	1,120	2,045	1,545	1,215
Classic Foster	10 ga.	3½"	766	1,280	1,080	970	2,785	1,980	1,605
	12 ga.	3"	547	1,600	1,320	1,130	3,110	2,120	1,540
	12 ga.	2¾"	547	1,520	1,260	1,090	2,805	1,930	1,450
	12 ga.	2¾"	438	1,610	1,330	1,140	2,520	1,725	1,255
	16 ga.	2¾"	350	1,600	1,180	990	1,990	1,075	755
	20 ga.	3"	325	1,680	1,340	1,110	2,055	1,310	890
	.410	2½"	109	1,775	1,348	1,080	770	435	275

Notes: Hydra-Shok Sabot and Classic Sabot slugs are of the hour-glass type; in Premium loads, they are copper-plated. The Barnes Sabot is a hollow-point muzzle-loading bullet of solid copper. Range is in yards, velocity in feet per second, energy in foot-pounds. One ounce = 438 grains.

You can glean some useful information from this chart. First, the most sophisticated sabot slugs do not deliver the meanest punch up close. A one-and-a-quarter-ounce Foster slug from a three-inch 12-bore shell generates a ton-and-a-half of smash at the muzzle, 40 percent more than the three-inch Barnes Sabot load! Secondly, there isn't a lot of difference in muzzle velocity across gauges and slug weights. If you ignore the .410 and drop the heaviest 10-gauge slug and slowest 12, you get a real horse race. All the others leave the gate at 1,400 to 1,680 fps, most between 1,450 and 1,600. Differences in slug weight among gauges translate to energy differences downrange.

Another thing to notice is that for all its machismo at the muzzle, the Foster slug gets tired in a hurry. In fact, that powerful one-and-a-quarter-ounce magnum

12-bore load can't match the Barnes Sabot for energy at 100 yards. Over the length of a football field it loses 470 fps to the Sabot's 255, giving up all of its 850 foot-pounds of initial advantage. The Hydra-Shok (hour-glass) Sabot slugs can't maintain speed like the Barnes, but they don't decelerate as fast as Foster slugs either.

It's worth noting that the plain two-and-three-quarter-inch 20-gauge Foster load outperforms the newer Hydra-Shok sabot in the three-inch 20-gauge hull. More speed, more weight, more energy, even at 100 yards! Why would anyone pick the sabot? Better accuracy from a rifled barrel, perhaps.

Among slug types, the trajectory of the Barnes bullet is the flattest. Zeroed at 100 yards, it hits two inches high at 50 and three inches low at 125. Hydra-Shok slugs arc half an inch higher at mid-range and strike almost an inch lower at 125 steps. Foster slugs don't warrant a 100-yard zero, because they would climb too high between 50 and 70 yards. Better to zero closer if you're shooting Foster slugs. A 50-yard zero will keep you within two vertical inches of your aim out to 75 yards. At 100 yards those slugs land about five inches low. If the gun shoots Fosters accurately, it makes sense to zero a little farther out—say 70 yards. That way you'll be able to hold center on a deer's shoulder to 100 yards and be sure of a solid hit. Foster slugs can kill farther than that, but shot placement becomes a problem.

A slug with no counterpart in the chart is Remington's BuckHammer, introduced in 2002. It is a homely projectile, with the profile of a soup can. Remington gave this flat-nose, large-diameter lead slug a short sabot collar at the heel. The collar, which snaps onto a nipple extending from the slug's base, stays attached in flight. "It could fall off, as we've demonstrated in tests," admits one company engineer. "But if it did, the slug would fly straight anyway. Has in tests." Though it hardly looks accurate, BuckHammer will outshoot Foster slugs and holds its own against other sabot ammo. My first three shots from a Remington 1187 at 100 yards stayed well inside two inches. Like Remington's Solid Copper and Core-Lokt Ultra Slugs, BuckHammer is meant only for rifled barrels. The lead is harder than in Foster slugs, but gelatin trials yield double-diameter upset.

Perhaps the most surprising thing about BuckHammer is how well it holds up in flight. This one-and-a-quarter-ounce oil drum leaves a two-and-three-quarter-inch 12-gauge shell at 1,550 fps—and is still traveling 1,145 fps at 100 yards, where it delivers 1,600 foot-pounds of energy. In comparison, a one-ounce Foster-style Slugger launched at 1,680 fps reaches the 100-yard mark at 1,045, with just two-thirds of BuckHammer's payload: 1,060 foot-pounds. Core-Lokt Ultra, a 385-grain slug started at 1,900, outperforms BuckHammer downrange mainly because energy calculations favor high velocity. The larger BuckHammer will be deadlier in many cases. It is heavier than the Copper Solid slug and, matches the three-inch Copper Solid load in foot-pounds carried to 100 yards. Despite its blocky shape, BuckHammer flies relatively flat, dropping only three-and-a-half inches at 150 yards from a 100-yard zero. That's roughly the arc you'll get from a standard Copper Solid load, or the three-inch Foster-style Slugger.

Buckhammer comes in 12- and 20-gauge shells, two-and-three-quarter- and three-inch. The three-inch 12-bore slug weighs one-and-three-eighths ounces and churns up over 3,200 foot-pounds of muzzle energy–more than generated by a 180-grain .30-06 bullet. Both 20-gauge slugs weigh a full ounce. The three-inch load packs more punch at 100 yards than any 12-gauge Foster load! For all the performance, BuckHammer ammunition costs less than Remington's other sabot shotgun slugs.

How much energy is needed for a quick kill? Not as much as is commonly thought. The slug kills by destroying vital tissue. The more you destroy, the quicker the deer will expire. The main thing is to put that slug where it will scramble the vitals. Dumping a ton of energy in the wrong place can leave you with only a blood trail. A 20-gauge slug sending 700 foot-pounds through a deer's lungs will put out the lights.

Because slugs are big and heavy, some hunters assume they'll hit like a cement truck and literally throw a deer to the ground. That can happen, but generally it's when you shatter the bone structure that supports the deer, or destroy its spine. In my experience, a lightweight, high-speed expanding bullet from a .243 gives more dramatic results than the pile-driver punch of even a 12-gauge slug. One mule deer I shot through both lungs with a 16-gauge Foster slug showed almost no reaction. It ran off as if unhurt. I found it dead within 60 yards. Other hunters have told me they've seen deer drop as if flung down by the impact of a big slug. Soft slugs that flatten and stay inside the animal can give quicker results. For that reason, and because whitetail deer do not require a deep-penetrating slug, I prefer sabot slugs that upset readily. Foster slugs don't have to expand to plow a big channel; they're still a great choice for close shooting!

The accuracy of Foster slugs from smoothbore barrels can vary a great deal. I sawed the full choke off my Remington 870 16-gauge pump years ago and mounted a 2 3/4x scope. My expectations for rifle-like groups were unfulfilled. At 80 yards the gun would keep Foster slugs inside a six-inch circle–but it had shot almost that well with the choked barrel! The notion that open chokes yield better accuracy than tight chokes makes sense, but individual guns don't always follow this rule.

BuckHammer upset shows why this Remington slug is deadly on deer at ordinary ranges.

Rifled barrels and sabot ammunition deliver better results. Most barrels are rifled one-in-24 to one-in-34. The fixed-barrel bolt-action shotguns by Savage, Mossberg and Marlin can outshoot autoloaders and pumps with lightweight, interchangeable barrels. Still, I'll pick those over the bolt-action shotguns, which seem a bit unwieldy. It matters not to me whether a shotgun punches three-minute groups or makes all slugs jump through one hole, because I'm not going to use a shotgun at long range. While bullets from sabot loads can be deadly at 200 yards and even a bit further, slugs are at their best in the thickets, where ranges are measured in feet, not furlongs. That's where hunting whitetails is most fun too!

A lot has been written about shotgun slugs driving undeflected through thickets that would turn a Panzer. My tests with 12-gauge Foster slugs showed deflection to be less than that of rifle bullets typically used for deer–150-grain .280 bullets to 250-grain .35 Whelen bullets. But thick screens of sagebrush still turned the slugs. Holes in the targets showed that some also flattened and otherwise deformed. Tipping was evident too. So, while beefy projectiles are less susceptible to deflection than small, lightweight bullets, you can't shoot confidently through dense brush or tree limbs. If you're trying to tag a running deer, it's still sound policy to ignore the trees and concentrate on the vitals, just as you block out the alders when you paint a rocketing grouse with shot. It is truly the only way to hit! But you are also smart to pass on shots that put lots of brush between you and your target. If the slug deflects, a crippling hit may result. I count on shooting through the delicate stuff, and on losing my slugs or bullets to any tree that gets in the way. Those half-inch branches are what annoy me. Too small to block the target from view, they won't intercept a slug. But they're big enough to turn it.

Whether you're new to slug shooting or a veteran shotgun deer hunter reconsidering your options, it's a good idea to test various slugs and loads in your gun. To do a good job of that (and to give yourself the best chance on the hunt), you need a proper sight. An aperture sight like the Ashley or Williams with a flat-faced, angled bead up front works better than open sights. A low-power scope with a bold reticle is probably best on shotguns with the reach of rifled bores. A 2 1/2x like the Weaver K2.5 is my pick. Mount the scope low, either on a cantilever base or directly to the receiver.

As with rifles, dry firing with a shotgun helps you hone shooting skills. So do sessions with light shot loads at "rabbit" targets on sporting clays courses. And if you're firing Foster slugs through a smooth bore, you'll want to try one of the "light recoil" slug loads offered by several manufacturers. They're not as effective as full-power loads for deer hunting, but they enable you to practice without developing a flinch.

Forty years ago, I listened raptly as Mike explained slugs. He'd have a lot more to talk about now. ■

11

SIGHTS AND SCOPES

I heard the rocks clatter. "Bucks!" Vern could see them scramble–up, up the face toward a saddle yet unlit by dawn. I sat, tried to throttle a racing pulse, and tugged the sling taut. The angle was so steep, I almost tipped over backward.

Vern's rifle cracked. Frantic now that I could no longer see the deer, I had no place to move. The trail was no wider than a skateboard, and the mountain dropped off steeply below. Great rock outcrops and whitebark pine blocked my view uphill. Swiveling, I poked the .270 toward an open slice of talus. There!

The second buck was just shy of the saddle when it paused–smack against the crosswire of my 2 1/2x Alaskan. The last ounces came off the trigger just as Vern fired once more. The two deer died within a few feet of each other. We field dressed them in the first light of the first day.

METALLIC SIGHTS STILL MAKE SENSE!

Few hunters use iron sights these days; almost all deer rifles are scoped. During its first years of production in the late 1930s, Winchester's Model 70 had no provision for scope mounts, but now most versions of the 70 wear no sights. Still, remarkable shooting is possible with iron sights, and some people have worked magic with them. People like Annie Oakley and Ad Topperwein.

Phoebe Ann Moses, born in a log cabin in Darke County, Ohio, in August 1860, endured a hard childhood. But subsistence hunting would propel her to fame. She shot her first game, a squirrel, at age eight. Soon Annie began shooting quail on the wing with her .22, and dominating turkey shoots. Then, at a local match, she beat visiting sharpshooter Frank Butler–who apparently did not know that his opponent would be a 15-year-old girl. A year later they married, and Annie joined Frank's traveling show under the stage name of Annie Oakley. Sioux Chief Sitting Bull called her "Watanya cicilia," or "Little Sure-Shot." When exhibition shooter Captain A. H. Bogardus left Buffalo Bill's Wild West Show, Annie got on the docket, aiming into a mirror to shoot over her shoulder at glass balls Frank threw in the air.

Petite at 100 pounds, and sweet-tempered, Annie became an audience favorite. The German Crown Prince, later to become Kaiser Wilhelm II, asked her to shoot a cigarette from his lips. She obliged, then allowed in the wake of World War I that a miss might have changed history. Annie shot coins from Frank's fingers and split playing cards edgewise with bullets. In 1884, using a Stevens .22 at an exhibition in Tiffin, Ohio, she hit 943 glass balls out of 1,000 tossed. She could make one hole in the middle of a playing card, firing 25 shots in 25 seconds with a .22 repeater. Johnny Baker, another Wild West Show marksman, tried for 17 years to outshoot Annie Oakley–and never did. "She would not throw a match," he said ruefully. "You had to beat her, and she wasn't beatable."

Annie used iron sights for exhibition shooting. At age 62, after an automobile accident crippled her, she could still hit with rifle bullets 25 airborne pennies in a row.

Equally amazing were the stunts of Ad Topperwein, born in 1869 near New Braunfels, Texas. With a .22 Winchester 1890 pump rifle, Ad began his career shooting aerial targets. He had little use for hunting or paper bullseyes. Ad later replaced the 1890 with a Winchester 1903 auto-loader, then with its successor, a Model 63. In 1887, at age 18, he landed a job as a cartoonist in San Antonio. Ad honed his marksmanship during off-hours and wound up shooting for a circus. In 1894, he used a rifle to break 955 of 1,000 clay two-and-a-quarter-inch disks tossed in the air. Dissatisfied, he repeated twice, shattering 987 and 989. Clay birds proved too easy; he broke 1,500 straight, the first 1,000 from 30 feet, the last 500 from 40. By his late 20s, Ad was also a showman. After firing at a washer tossed aloft, he'd tell onlookers that the bullet went through the middle. Challenged by the audience, Ad would stick a postage stamp over the hole for another toss, then perforate the stamp. He could hit the bullet of an airborne .32-20 cartridge without tearing the brass.

Winchester hired Ad Topperwein when the tall, slim, blue-eyed young man was about 27. He would shoot for Winchester for 55 years. There he met Elizabeth Servaty, who worked in the company's ballistics lab. They married in 1903. To audiences thereafter, she became "Plinky," a superb shot in her own right. In 1916, she blasted 1,952 of 2,000 clay targets with a Model 12 shotgun. She once ran 280 straight. Ad preferred rifles. Holding a Model 63 with the ejection port up, he'd fire a cartridge, then nail the airborne empty. He could riddle five tossed cans before any hit the ground. His artistic ability showed in Indian heads drawn on tin with up to 450 .22 bullets fired at the headlong rate of a shot a second.

Topperwein's exploits sparked competition. Doc Carver (who had no medical background) shot 11 Model 1890 Winchesters over 10 days, 12 hours a day, to break more than 55,000 of 60,000 two-and-a-half-inch glass balls tossed in the air. The second time, he missed only 650. B.A. Bartlett eclipsed Carver's record. Shooting for 144 hours, he shattered 59,720 of 60,000 balls. Ad Topperwein responded. In 1907, at the San Antonio Fair Grounds, he uncrated 10 Winchester 1903 rifles, 50,000 rounds of ammunition, and 50,000 wooden blocks cut two-and-a-quarter x two-and-a-quarter inches. After running out of blocks and ammo, Top got resupplied and resumed shooting. He stopped after 120 hours, 72,500 tosses. He had missed just nine targets. Once, he ran 14,500 straight. His record stood until after World War II, when Remington salesman Tom Frye began flailing at wood blocks with Nylon 66 auto-loaders. Frye missed two of his first 43,725 targets. When he finished with the incredible score of 100,004 out of 100,010, an aging Topperwein wrote to congratulate him. Ad died at age 93, nearly 18 years after losing Plinky in 1945.

Iron sights may be the natural choice for aerial shooting, but they're also amazingly precise. Thirty years ago in Mishawaka, Indiana, I stepped to the firing line for a go at a spot on the U.S. Olympic Team. In the middle of the black scoring area that appeared as a dot at 50 feet was the real target, a 10-spot the diameter of a finishing nail surrounded by a nine-ring you could obliterate with a single .22 bullet. Centering the black in the sight, I had to assume my precisely zeroed Anschutz rifle and its super-accurate Eley ammunition would deliver 10s. To reach the final qualifying stage, I'd have to fire the equivalent of a one-hole 60-shot group in a bullseye I couldn't even see! Luck was with me that day, my prone position as good as it's ever been. Fifty-one bullets took out the dot in the middle, and the other nine cut deep into

Big apertures are appropriate for whitetail rifles like this Marlin carbine.

nine-ring. A .45 pistol bullet would have covered the group.

The best iron sights for bullseye shooting are an aperture (peep) rear and a globe front with an insert that's the equivalent of a scope's reticle. For a long time, my insert was an orange plastic disc with a hole in the middle just big enough to admit a narrow rim of white around the black target. The hole's bevel showed dark, for a crisp sight picture. An aperture rear sight is also a good deer-hunting sight, though you'll want a bead rather than a ring up front, for quick aim at big, irregularly shaped targets. You'll also want a wide-open aperture in the rear, to help you find the target right away and to deliver more light to your eye. On a hunt, you may be compelled to shoot in shadow or failing light. I've taken the aperture out of the Redfield sight on one of my M70s; now the threaded hole serves as my aperture. It is more precise than it appears, because my eye automatically puts the front bead in the middle. That's where most of the light is.

A long sight radius (distance between the sights) increases precision. The closer the aperture is to your eye, the smaller (and more accurate) it can be. Field of view, depth perception and brightness are all greatest when your eye crowds the aperture. That's why rifles for 19th-century Schuetzen matches had tang-mounted rear sights. Winchester and Marlin lever rifles and single-shot hunting rifles routinely wore tang sights before scopes became so popular; now Cowboy Action shooters have rediscovered the value of these long-stemmed Marbles and Lyman "peeps." Cocking-piece sights on bolt-action rifles have become as rare as crank-handles on automobile engines; however, they're among my favorite sights because they're close to your eye and compact. (On hard-kicking rifles like the Winchester

This open sight is on a high ramp because the rifle is stocked for scope use.

71 in .348, any tang sight can put the aperture too close to your eye. Receiver-mounted peeps still have a place!)

My first hunting rifle, a restocked .303 SMLE, had a barrel-mounted Williams open sight with a shallow V "African" notch. It proved faster than the popular U or deep V notches and didn't obscure the target as much as buckhorn or semi-buckhorn sights then common on lever rifles. I still like the shallow V, with or without an eye-catching white center-line. It's popular on double rifles. So is an "Express" sight with folding leaves zeroed for different yardages. I prefer a single fixed leaf filed to a 100-yard zero. Then there's no choosing the wrong leaf, or having the right one collapse during recoil or rough handling. An open sight is properly a close-range sight. Few marksmen shoot well enough with one to justify its use beyond 150 yards. With a single rear notch, you should be able to hold center and count on a lethal hit on deer out to at least 150 yards.

Whether you have an open sight or aperture sight on a hunting rifle, the front sight should be big enough to catch your eye right away, even at the expense of precision. There's no magic bead size, because barrel length affects apparent size and subtention. There's no perfect bead material or color either. I like ivory, except in snow. Gold works well against a variety of backgrounds. Fluorescent sights are very fast, but under bright conditions get fuzzy. In shadows they can give you a halo effect, much like that of a street lamp at night. Too much brightness not only blurs sight edges; it can hide the target. Even metal beads can degrade a sight picture by scattering light. Avoid spherical bead faces, as they reflect incident light off the edge, shifting the bead's apparent position and causing you to miss. A bead should be flat-faced but angled toward the sky to catch light.

Redfield's Sourdough front sight featured a square red insert, angled up. You could employ it as a bead or a post. A black steel post can get lost against thick timber. It also mandates a 6-o'clock hold–fine for bullseyes on white paper but obstructive on game and slower than a bead you can slap on a target.

Someone is always cooking up new iron sights. Friend Bob Fulton has experimented with globe sights on hunting rifles. His Ruger Number One in .411 Hawk has a globe front sight holding a clear plastic insert etched with a crosswire. The rear sight is a modified Krag. At the end of the 27-inch barrel the flared rear end of the globe sight fits almost perfectly in the aperture of the rear sight. There's a thin ring of daylight around the globe so you can tell instantly if it's out of center.

"It's a good sight against mottled backgrounds," says Bob. "Unlike a blade, the vertical and horizontal wires obscure almost none of the target. The sight picture is like that of a scope."

Bob has also built barrel-mounted rear aperture sights. The rear sight on his Winchester 95 has a platinum-lined ring arcing over the factory notch. "That's the fastest sight I've ever used," he told me. "It accounted for piles of jackrabbits when I was, stationed in the Southwest. Surplus '06 ammo was cheap!"

Some innovative sights have gone commercial, like the "Little Blue" peep sight, a dainty folding aperture that screwed to the back of a Redfield scope base as an auxiliary sight. Alas, it is no longer made.

There's nothing wrong with a standard Lyman or Redfield or Williams receiver sight and a gold bead over the muzzle. Traveling to Alaska some seasons back, I carried only one rifle: a 1903 Springfield with a Lyman rear aperture sight and a fine gold bead up front. With that old .30-06 I made a one-shot kill on a moose at 120 yards, and toppled a Dall ram at 70. A scope would have allowed me to shoot at longer range–but it also would have denied me the thrill of a sneak. Iron sights give you a feeling of personal contact with the game, more intimate than one artificially conjured in a lens. It's similar to the feeling you get stalking animals with a bow and arrow.

The XS sight on this Charlie Sisk rifle in .450 Marlin has a wide-open aperture for fast aim.

A few years ago, a tall, rough-hewn Texan handed me a Marlin lever rifle with a perforated peg perched on the receiver. Its stem threaded into a small block that dovetailed into a larger base block and moved across it for lateral adjustment. To raise or lower the sight you simply screwed the ring out or in. "How about that, partner?" he bellowed. "Kinda slick, huh?" It was indeed slick. So was the front blade, angled like a Sourdough but all the way to the base and with a white line down its middle.

The Texan founded Ashley Outdoors to make his sights, then left. The company has grown and now goes by the name of XS Sights. It builds aperture sights and front blades for all manner of rifles. I use them on my Marlin Guide Gun and on a Mauser 98. They seem to me near-ideal sights for hunting deer in cover, though I still prefer the Sourdough or flat-faced beads up front. The XS white line does stand out in dark conditions, and against a light background the entire blade is easy to see.

The key to hitting with any sight is practice. Here are some things to keep in mind after you zero:

Focus on the front sight. Your eye can't focus at three distances simultaneously, so it's best to get a sharp view of the middle image. That way, you won't have to put two fuzzy images together. The rear sight can be out of focus and the target not quite as clear as you'd like; you'll still hit center if the front sight is distinct and in the proper relationship to the other two images.

Remember that every shot is practice, and that the more you shoot, the better you'll shoot if you take care with every sight picture and let-off. Sloppy shooting is just practicing bad form. Gifted shooters like Topperwein make disciplined marksmanship look casual. Honestly, good shooting takes focused effort—more

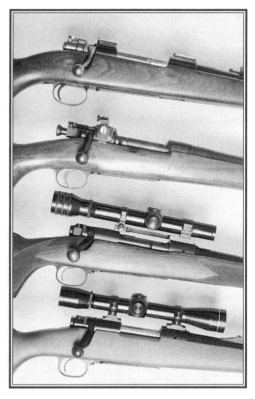

From top: Mauser with open sights, Springfield with receiver sight, Winchester 70s with 2 3/4x and 6x scopes. For most deer hunting a scope works best; stay with magnification of 6x or less.

with iron sights than with a scope because your eye must do more work.

Don't assume that a scope will always help you shoot better. Scopes help mainly when a target is too small or indistinct to see clearly. Iron sights take weight off the top of your rifle, improving its balance and enabling you to aim more quickly. Irons are also less affected by the snow and rain that cloud scope lenses.

Finally, remember that the world's best-known hunters used iron sights. Jim Corbett, for instance. The famous slayer of man-eating tigers began his career waiting for jungle fowl on the bank of a ravine. Suddenly, he spied movement close by. A leopard! It sprang. Jim fired as the cat sailed over his head and vanished in brush. He reloaded and followed the trail. So confident was he of his rifle and his ability that when he saw the leopard's tail ahead, he grabbed it and pulled the dead animal out of a thicket. Such cool, deliberate action up close would save him many times later, when, at night, he sat alone near tiger baits. Jim killed the great Muktesar man-eating tiger at a range of just two yards!

Sometimes scopes are simply superfluous.

LITTLE SCOPES WITH A BIG VIEW

If bigger were always better, the most affluent of us would be living in gymnasiums and driving cement trucks to work. But many hunters buy the biggest scope they can find. Here's why I don't:

A big scope is heavy.

A big scope has lots of inertia, which can wrest it free of the rings' grip during recoil.

A big scope must be mounted high above the bore, forcing you to crane your neck to aim.

A big scope doesn't fit in saddle scabbards designed for more useful sights.

A big scope costs more than a small scope of the same quality.

Most big scopes are big because they deliver high magnification, which restricts field of view and limits eye relief, the distance from your eyeball to the ocular lens. It's easier to make scopes with generous, non-critical eye relief if magnification is low. Modest magnification also delivers a bigger exit pupil–that pencil of light you see when you hold the scope at arm's length. Exit pupil diameter is a measure of light transmission. So low power gives you a brighter image for any given objective diameter. Or, from another angle, lenses that transmit as much light as your eye can use are smaller when magnification is low. In my jaundiced view, about the only thing good you can say about a big, powerful scope is that you get adequate brightness with more detail in the sight picture. But the high magnification that gives you the detail, besides shrinking field and eye relief, shows you so much wobble as to impair your trigger squeeze. You are more apt to botch a shot because of too much magnification than because you have too little.

I recall guiding a hunter to a huge bull elk. When the animal appeared a few yards away, it was in the company of other bulls. "Shoot the second from the right," I hissed. My client couldn't comply because his 2 1/2-8x scope had been set at the top end. The field was too small for him to see all the elk. They got our wind and galloped off before he could put the crosswire on one. Two of those bulls would have cleared Boone & Crockett minimums.

Years earlier, 4x scopes had helped me kill a deer and a pronghorn with shots at over 400 yards. I had come to like the low profiles and light weight of these sights, and of 2 1/2x models with no front bells. They looked good on rifles and slid into scabbards like Peacemakers into gun-fighting leather. They were inexpensive and lightweight and could be mounted very low so a rifle pointed like a shotgun. The modest magnification made for bright images in the thickets I prowled for elk. When guiding others, I cautioned them to keep variables set at low power: "You'll always have time to turn that dial up for a long shot, but a short shot must be taken right away."

As scopes have become bigger and more sophisticated, I've stuck with low-power, fixed-power models. When 30mm tubes with battery warts for illuminated reticles make the news, I report it but keep my old-fashioned sights. The 50mm objective, touted to increase brightness, does just that–if you have the dial set at 8x or above in dim light. A 42mm objective gives seven-power lenses an exit pupil diameter of 6mm, about all a healthy eye can use. I didn't need 8x glass for precise aim at deer. Under most field conditions magnification higher than 6x seems to me a liability.

By some measures I'm an anachronism, still struggling with our television's remote control. But I'm proudly old-fashioned when it comes to scopes. By far the most useful big-game sights are still those of modest proportions and power. Though lately the number of fixed-power scopes cataloged as standard rifle sights has diminished, Compact Scopes, Turkey Scopes, Slug Gun Scopes, Muzzleloader Scopes, Rimfire Scopes and Scout Scopes have appeared for people who expect to shoot game inside 200 yards. Were they to tally their hits over many hunting seasons, most hunters would find that killing shots commonly happen much closer than that. When I was guiding elk and deer hunters, I discovered that beyond 200 steps, the probability of lethal first-round hits dropped by half. Besides, if you consistently botch sneaks beyond the 200-yard mark, your hunting skills need polish.

What about that occasional long shot? You're hardly handicapped with a 4x. I've killed deer well beyond 350 yards with a 4x. For most big game hunting, in fact, a 3x scope is my pick. A couple of years ago, I hunted into a big herd of elk spread across a charred mountain face. Wind and scatterings of cows prevented me from closing on the mature bull on the herd's far side. I backed out, climbed onto a parallel ridge and slinged up in prone next to a ridge-top rock. When the bull fed into my crosswire, he was 300 yards out. I could have turned up my 3-9x Leupold VX-II, but didn't. Instead, I laid the intersection just under his backline and squeezed. The .358 Norma punched me hard, but in the settling scope field, I saw the bull collapse. The 250-grain soft-point had struck within a couple of inches of where I'd intended.

No, you can't aim as precisely with a low-power scope, but under field conditions, you can't aim precisely with any scope. A bigger target image comes with more pronounced reticle movement; you just see more clearly what low magnification won't tell you. It's more than you need to know most of the time.

I have shot one deer with a 20x scope. It was a Coues buck, a dainty creature about the size of a collie. It appeared in the purple light of dawn at the base of a hill, ghosting through desert scrub. I dropped to my belly, snapping the bipod legs forward on the David Miller rifle. The shot alley was tiny at ground level, and the buck hadn't reached it yet. I guessed the range at 400 yards. As the deer stepped out of the brush into the scope field, the vertical wire came even with his first rib. I inched the intersection up what I took to be 16 inches and fired. The 168-grain Sierra from the .300 Weatherby hit exactly where I had hoped it would, 410 paces away. That would have been a hard shot with a 4x scope, and if you're hunting coyotes and 'chucks at long yardage, of course you'll use a high-power sight. But for most big-game hunting, the smaller models have the edge.

A word on field of view, often touted as the biggest benefit to using scopes of modest power. Field of view varies among models of the same magnification

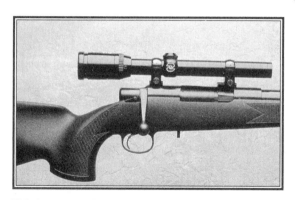

This low-power Zeiss is a fine scope, but it's mounted too high and too far back.

because optical systems differ in their design. You can increase field of view by shortening eye relief, but few hunters would appreciate that trade-off if they got bumped by the scope in recoil. Long- and intermediate-eye relief scopes for pistols and barrel mounts on rifles and shotguns have smaller fields of view than sights designed for receiver mounts. As expected, 4x scopes in this list have smaller fields than do 2.5x models. But they're still bigger than the field you'll see with a variable cranked to 9x (around 12 feet), 12x (10 feet) or 14x (eight feet). Figure 24 feet or more for a 4x, and you have enough room to lead a whitetail buck with his afterburners on. More than enough to pick one animal from a group.

The Swift 1x scope delivers a panoramic view, as do other 1x models (also called 0x because they do not magnify). I do not care for them. Some magnification is helpful, and up to 3x or 4x you can aim as quickly as with a wide-open aperture sight. Also, magnification of less than 2.5x shows you the barrel on most rifles. That can be distracting, and it's why I'm not keen on low-power variables. If you must have a variable, make it a 2-7x or 2.5-8x. On the low end, you'll be fast enough to shoot deer that burst from the shintangle a car-length away. And you'll have power aplenty for shots across soybean fields or sage flats.

What about low-power scopes or mid-power variables with 30mm tubes? By themselves, oversize tubes do not yield brighter images or bigger fields of view. They do allow for more sight adjustment if the scope's erector assembly is the same dimensions as that used in one-inch tubes. Many are. Of course, you do not need extra feet of adjustment to zero most hunting rifles.

There's no ideal weight for a rifle scope. Good glass can be heavy, and you want the scope to be durable too. My rule of thumb: a hunting scope with mount should weigh no more than 15 percent of the rifle's bare weight. So on a seven-pound rifle, you're allowed a sight that weighs up to 16.8 ounces. Trim rifle weight to six pounds, and you get a ceiling of 14.4 ounces. Steel bases and rings use up several ounces; alloy mounts like those by Talley weigh as little as an ounce apiece. Though my rule is arbitrary, it keeps overall rifle weight reasonable and center of gravity low between your hands where it belongs.

A lot of game is killed with rifles wearing big scopes. Almost all of it could be taken with smaller scopes that cost less and make rifles carry easily and point fast.

AIMPOINT OF SWEDEN

The forest reminded me of westside timber in my home state of Washington. Towering conifers hid a gray sky that leaked rain to a black forest floor already soggy. I could have been stalking blacktail deer. But then I caught the faint moan of a hunting horn.

Now I could hear the voices of the cheerful Danes pushing the highland. I dabbed the sight's rear lens with an already-saturated Kleenex. Closer they came, and suddenly a dark flicker of movement winked between alders on the swamp's edge.

At 100 yards, in the rain and with lots of brush in the way, I couldn't tell if it was a bull or a cow, but it was surely a moose. I looked for a calf. Cow moose were legal game on this hunt only if they were without calf. The animal had vanished by the time it was clear no calf would follow. I pivoted to cover the forest, where the alders gave way to big trees, and where open understory might give me another glimpse.

There! But the moose had almost passed me, crossing at 90 yards, before I could find a shot alley. Then I saw the antler, which wouldn't have mattered, except that here a bull that carried between five and 10 total points was protected. I could shoot a forkhorn. The red dot of the sight probed the gaps between the black boles as pieces of moose slipped between them. The animal stopped once with its shoulder exposed, but not the antler. Then I saw the antler again and decided to shoot and found no vitals. Just as the moose was about to vanish, angling away through the gloom, it paused one more time. The dot glued itself to the shoulder, and I triggered the .30-06. Instantly the bull lunged forward, a rear hoof coming up just a little higher than normal. It was a good sign.

I didn't move, because here in Sweden you didn't leave your stand until the drivers converged or you heard the final three blasts on the hunting horn. Finally they came. I raced over to where the moose had stood and saw the great animal dead a few yards down the trail. The Blaser's 165-grain bullet had hit a tad farther forward than I'd called, but still well within the boiler.

It was the first moose of the day at Claestorp, the first game I'd ever shot in Europe.

The notion of shooting driven game didn't appeal to me at first. I don't like to stand still for long in the woods, and I don't like other people doing my hunting for me. But the expansive forests of central Sweden give the game plenty of options. I saw moose sneak away from the drivers and sprint between the standers. A huge wild boar, which would have been the hunt's finest trophy, seemed to vanish in the mist.

Swedes hardly need to apologize for shooting a few moose. A few years ago, when the big-nosed deer were at a population peak, there may have been more moose in Sweden than in all of North America! Roughly the size of California, Sweden had to trim moose numbers. With typical Scandinavian care, it did. Closely managed on privately-controlled ground, moose and other big game thrive north of the rich coffee-colored soils that nurture sugar beets and other cash crops east of a line between Malmo and Hoganas.

You can hunt big game with lots of cartridges, but the not-surprising favorite among Swedes is the gentle 6.5x55. Next comes the .30-06, then the .308. From what I could determine, almost all of Sweden's moose harvest is taken with one of these cartridges. Mauser rifles are favorites. So are big scopes. Hunting wild boar from stands at the edge of night, Swedish hunters value pie-plate objectives.

"But you certainly don't need high magnification on drives," one rifleman told me before the hunt, seeing that I'd borrowed the Blaser with its Aimpoint sight. "In fact, I like a sight with no magnification at all, even for the qualification target."

The qualification target, I found, was the life-size print of a moose on a frame that ran under motor power along a track. Scoring rings on the vitals were invisible from the line, 100 yards distant. The drill: Load with four rounds. Call for the target and fire once at the moose as it pauses. Then cycle the bolt and fire as the moose scoots along the track to. Call for the target again, shoot once more at the standing moose and finally as it repeats its run in the opposite direction. You fire all shots off-hand, for a possible score of 20. I managed 18 once, but not the first time.

There's no reason you shouldn't net 20. Unlike a real moose, the target runs smoothly and at a set speed. There's no brush in the way. But the Swedes assured me that many hunters failed to keep all shots in the scoring rings. Offhand is evidently as tough a position in Scandinavia as it is Stateside.

I found in shooting the target, and then in killing the bull moose, that Aimpoint's red dot sight was my best bet. Never fond of gadgets and wary of anything that requires batteries, I had to give this sight high marks. In the dim forest, that dot shone like the North Star on a frosty night. It was easy to pick up, and no matter where it appeared in the field of view, I could be assured the bullet would go there. I proved

Aimpoint made the first successful red dot sights, and is still widely believed to make the best.

that at the range, moving my head to different positions on the stock. I found the key to precision was keeping the dot at its lowest visible setting. Many shooters dial up brightness to give themselves the equivalent of a brake light. As the dot gets brighter, it appears bigger, hiding the target. There's a halo effect that reduces resolution around the dot. And your eye's pupil constricts, impairing its ability to see anything but the dot. Dark conditions call for a very low setting–#4 was my choice on the nine-station dial of the Aimpoint–while in bright light a higher setting is necessary for you to see the dot at all.

Frankly, I hadn't given red dot sights much thought until the trip to Sweden. But after a couple of days at Claestorp, I was convinced this sight is one of the best you could choose for a whitetail rifle.

Red dot sights are available from several companies now. But the idea was pioneered in Sweden back in 1975 by Gunnar Sandberg, inventor and entrepreneur.

Sandberg formed the Aimpoint Company shortly thereafter. In 1976, it comprised four people. One of them was Kenneth Mardklint, who graciously agreed to talk with me at Aimpoint's modern Malmo facility. It's an upscale place. He pointed out that the company designs and specs everything for its sights, but outsources most of the 60-odd components. "It's more cost-effective that way. Of course, we assemble and proof all the sights here." The facility has state-of-the-art optical testing devices.

"The first red dot sight we called the single-point sight," said Kenneth. "You saw the dot with one eye and the target with the other. You couldn't see through the sight at all!" In 1975, the first-generation Aimpoint Electronic appeared, with windage and elevation adjustments under the three-quarter-inch tube, so it sat high on Weaver-style bases. "Its five light settings were all too bright for a dark day," Kenneth laughed. "We produced only 2,000 of them." Two years later an improved version came out, with more latitude in the brightness dial and no detents. A year later, the second generation of Aimpoint sights made its debut. It featured a better diode and a detachable 3x or 1-4x lens. It was the first Aimpoint sold in the U.S.

Aimpoint refined its "G2" sight and in 1983 brought out the Mark III, with internal adjustments and a dot that automatically dimmed for dark conditions after it was adjusted to the eye in daylight. The Aimpoint 2000 arrived in 1985. Unlike its predecessors, it had no base. The one-inch tube could be mounted like an ordinary scope. Long and short versions were manufactured to accommodate various ring spacings on rifles and handguns. Stainless finish became available for the first time.

In 1987, Aimpoint came out with its Model 1000, designed as a penny-wise alternative to the 2000. It offered nine click-stop light settings and an integral Weaver-type base, with less costly electronics than the 2000. That year Aimpoint also introduced a red dot bow-sight. It fared poorly at market, because there is essentially no bowhunting in Sweden, and U.S. bowhunters weren't sold on it.

In 1989, the Aimpoint 3000 supplanted its predecessors. Its battery case was much smaller, so this sight was lighter and more compact than the Model 2000. It featured 2x magnification, a one-inch tube with an extension for wide ring spacing on rifles. The company dropped the automatic brightness adjustment in this sight. Though the 3000 is still available, it was upstaged in 1991 by the 5000, which is really a 3000 with a 30mm tube. Field of view increased by 20 percent. In 1998, Aimpoint announced the XD (extreme duty) diode in the 5000. It generated three times the brightness of the old diode, using a fifth of the current. Battery life jumped from 100 to 500 hours. The technology was carried over to the 5000 Comp, introduced four years earlier specifically for handgun competition. In fact, the XD diode was engineered for the target range, where shooters needed a bright but "clean" dot on white paper in mid-day light. Hunters benefited from the switch. The #6 setting on an XD sight is as bright as the #9 (highest) setting on a pre-XC model.

Incidentally, one difference between the Comp and hunting-style 5000 is the brightest setting on the dial. It is right next to the "off" position on the Comp, but farthest from "off" in a standard Aimpoint. Intelligent.

Kenneth and the firm's U.S. representative, Mike Kingston, assured me that

Aimpoint is a widely-recognized name in the red-dot sight industry, but pointed out that fame is a mixed blessing. "Aimpoint has been unlucky in that some shooters think of it as the only red-dot sight," said Mike. "Like Xerox became a synonym for copier. Trouble is, not all sights or copiers are made to equal standards. Aimpoint's sight costs more than most red dots produced by companies following our lead. That's because Aimpoint is expensive to produce. It's a better sight, hands down."

The main difference, he explained, is in the front lens, whose red tint means it reflects red light so the dot appears brighter. That's a common feature. What isn't so common is the compound objective lens, which corrects for parallax. A single lens up front will still reflect the dot produced by the diode in the rear bottom of the tube. But the angle of reflection varies. The Aimpoint's doublet brings the dot back to your eye in a line parallel with the optical center of the instrument. Not so the single lens. Its reflective paths spread fanlike as your eye changes position behind the sight. Result: If the dot isn't centered in the sight, you'll have parallax error at distances other than the one for which the sight was parallax-corrected. The farther your eye is off-axis, the greater the error. With an Aimpoint, if you see the dot, you will hit where the dot appears to be.

The field of view of an Aimpoint 3000 is about the same as that of a 4x scope. How so? Well, the 1x Aimpoint has a straight tube and is not designed to maximize field. You don't need extra field if you have no magnification, because there's plenty of woods around your target anyway. While the 4x has an edge in resolution, it gives each eye a different perspective downrange. You can't shoot with the scope as well with both eyes open because there's an area you see with your left eye, immediately around the field of view, that's invisible to your right. And the images differ in size. Your eyes can't believe what they're seeing–so you squint. The Aimpoint's field border is simply a narrow shadow caused by the sight's body. You can shoot as you might with a shotgun bead, both eyes wide open.

Except in models with magnification (I prefer those without), Aimpoint red-dot sights impose no limits on eye relief. Your eye can be two inches back, or 10, and you'll see the same field. The dot is there for you, too, in the same apparent focal plane as the target. There simply is no faster sight. And if you keep dot brightness at low settings, you'll shoot as accurately as you can hold under hunting conditions. A couple of hunters who have used Aimpoints have told me that they lose precision beyond 100 yards. My shooting suggests that 200-yard kills should be easy. That's about as far as you'll zero a big-game rifle, or as far as you'd fire at animals without the benefit of magnification.

Early red-dot sights were heavy and hard to mount. The detachable magnifiers added length and decreased eye relief, while reducing precision (in the rear focal plane, they magnified the dot too!). Battery life was limited. But the advent of XD Aimpoints, which have wider fields but weigh less than the molded-body models of the 1980s, make this sight a practical choice for hunters.

Aimpoint's newest rendition, the 7000, is a smoother, "prettier" sight, with a diode that offers 20 times the battery life of previous LEDs. A standard 3V lithium

This Aimpoint, on a straight-pull Blaser rifle, is parallax-free with almost unlimited eye relief.

camera battery will give you a visible dot for 20,000 hours on the low setting. That's a lot of hunting! Figure 1,000 hours at the highest setting. Batteries go to work only when the dot switch is on, and according to Kenneth, they last the same number of hours whether you use the sight intermittently over 10 years or leave it on for weeks. The Comp 7000 has double the range of windage and elevation adjustment of earlier sights–four meters at 100 meters. That's more than 140 inches at 100 yards!

As you might expect, Aimpoint has courted military and police contracts. The Comp M and ML are heavy-duty sights for service rifles and pistols. Band-pass coatings on objective lenses suit them for use with night-vision equipment. The first two stops on a night-vision red-dot sight dial bring you no red dot. It's there but invisible to the unaided eye. Military sales account for a whopping 75 percent of revenues at Aimpoint. Mike Kingston added, however, that if you left out the considerable commitments to the U.S. and French armies, Aimpoint's hunting market share would be bigger. Currently, Aimpoint exports hunting sights to 40 countries, equipping one of every 10 Swedish hunters using optical sights.

No Aimpoint sights are nitrogen-filled. "It's not necessary," said Kenneth. "From the beginning we've advertised our sights as submersible. First with caps on, but now with caps off. Aimpoints don't fog, and they don't leak." After two days under near-constant rain in Sweden's forests, I'd seen no evidence of either. The only moisture problem I had came on the last afternoon, just before dusk, in a swale overhung by dripping conifers. The rain drove through them, and I tucked the Blaser under my arm to keep water off the Aimpoint's lens. My body heat eventually fogged the outside of the lens–but I didn't think about that until a branch snapped. Moose! The first was gone before I could raise my rifle. The second paused behind a tree 70 yards off. Hastily I rubbed the condensation off the lens with my thumb. Still, it was like looking through a bass pond: black moose in black timber behind a sheet of rain thick enough to part with a power saw. A crosswire or ordinary dot would have vanished in the murk. But that red dot stood out immediately. I fired. The moose bolted back toward the horn.

When the drivers came, I expected them to have found a kill. None had. "We'll bring the dogs," one said. Tracking dogs are not only popular in Sweden; the law requires that big-game hunters have quick access to them. Still, I paced in the wet as the dog handlers waited for an hour for the woods to "get quiet" –as rain washed the trail and darkness descended. "If you hit the moose, the dog will find it," said one. "Don't go near where the moose was. Your scent will confuse the dog."

It was near flashlight-dark when we harnessed up a couple of Norwegian hounds. The older dog went to work like a setter on a hot pheasant track. Over a knob, down into the swamp. Then she hooked back toward where I'd shot the moose. Surely the drivers that came through would have seen a carcass . . .

"There she is." The dog handler pointed. In a narrow, water-filled depression lay the cow, belly down, her hump blending with the swamp grass and hidden from the side by tangles of brush. I'd never have found her. She had been shot squarely through both lungs and had obviously died on the run, falling where even seasoned woodsmen only a few yards apart had passed her by.

The dog tore a little hair from the hump. I let her.

A DEER HUNTER'S ALL-AROUND SIGHT: THE 3-9X

Channel surfing is a good way to find out what you're missing on other networks while ensuring that you'll miss most of what you wanted to watch. It's the inevitable result of limitless choice. Delightful, choice. It confirms your freedom. You don't have to stick with this; you can go to that. Nobody can pin you down; you've the

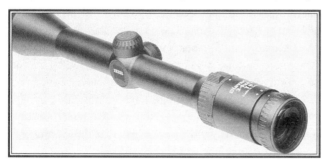

option of foiling all predictions, eluding those who would pigeonhole you or plant you where you might not want to be a few years from now. Or months. Or minutes.

Zeiss Diavari and Conquest variable scopes give shooters brighter, sharper images than their forebears could have imagined.

Sorry. That's the best explanation I can find for the American shooter's infatuation with variable scopes. Fear of the fixed is, I'm afraid, a terminal affliction. Once you've turned that dial, a scope without one seems incomplete. What if the animal is far away? What if it is running? What if it is partly hidden? What if the light isn't good? What if there's mirage? Collectively, shooters have accepted the notion that there's a proper magnification for every target and shooting condition, and that you're stupid if you don't buy instant access to that magnification. I've about given up trying to convince anyone otherwise.

The 3-9x Leupold, here in silver finish, is one of the most popular scopes among big-game hunters.

Scope companies have left anachronisms like me little selection in fixed-power sights. Gone are the lightweight 4x and 6x models by Zeiss and Swarovski, swept away by an avalanche of variables. My pouting was to no avail. "The 4x and 6x models generated only about one percent of our total sales in 1997," Swarovski's Jim Morey tells me. "When the 6-24x50 PV came out, we sold five times as many of those scopes as both of the small fixed-powers put together. And the 6-24x is a very costly sight."

Americans are like that. Something that becomes popular suddenly becomes very popular. Surveys of hunters I took a decade ago showed that more of them used Leupold 3-9x Vari-X II scopes than all other 3-9x scopes combined. Leupold enjoyed hearing that–all the more because 3-9x variables outnumbered by a wide margin every other scope option. In fact, the 3-9x arena is still where scope makers find their success or lament their failure. Among hunters, no magnification range is more popular.

How did the 3-9x come to merit such loyalty? Is there magic in those numbers? A quick review of rifle-scope history can help explain.

The first receiver-mounted scopes were designed by and for hunters used to shooting with iron sights. As early as 1887, Cummins had built a "Duplex Telescope Sight," the first U.S. scope to feature achromatic lenses and internal adjustments. You could specify magnification of 3x to 18x. Long eye relief let hunters mount the scope ahead of the receiver on top-ejecting rifles.

Viable receiver-mounted hunting scopes date, roughly, to the turn of the last century. In 1901, the J. Stevens Arms and Tool Company bought the Cataract Tool & Optical Company and began building its own scopes. Legendary barrel-maker H.M. Pope claimed his 5x, 16-inch Stevens scope helped him see at dusk after other shooters were obliged to quit. By 1907, Stevens catalogs showed several scopes.

With a power range of 6x to 11x, the Multiscope became the first variable with a sliding erector system. It retailed, with adjustable mounts, for $42. Stevens also listed a 3x "Reliable" that weighed just four ounces! In Europe, Zeiss had a modern-looking hunting scope on the market in 1904.

Winchester began selling scopes in 1909. The A5 had adjustable objective and ocular systems in its three-quarter-inch tube and could be ordered with a variety of reticles. At the time, 5x magnification served for target shooting. Winchester also sold 3x and 4x "B" scopes before the 1930s ushered in new scope makers–most of whom disappeared after World War II.

Bill Weaver built the prototype for his first scope by hand when he was 24. Introduced in 1930, the 3x Weaver Model 330 sold for $19, complete with a spring-steel mount that resembled an oversize paperclip. The three-quarter-inch tube had internal adjustments: one-inch increments for windage, two-inch for elevation. A flat-topped post came standard, but you could order a crosswire reticle for $1.50. Lighter in weight than contemporary German scopes, Weaver's was also less expensive. Its price and reliability made domestic competition wince.

While Bill Weaver can be said to have introduced American riflemen to scopes, Professor A. Smakula of the Carl Zeiss firm gave shooters the world over a brighter image. Smakula discovered that by coating lens surfaces with a thin layer of magnesium fluoride, he could dramatically boost light transmission. The Third Reich prevented publication of Smakula's findings until 1940; after that, coated lenses were widely adopted. Germany's Schott Glassworks became the first company to use multiple lens coatings. A three-layer process was in place before the end of World War II.

Stateside, scope makers were proliferating. Rudolph Noske designed a sight that John Amber of *Gun Digest* and fabled gun writer Elmer Keith liked very much. Available in 2 3/4x and 4x, the Noske "A" had a seven-eighths-inch tube and a whopping six inches of eye relief. It listed for just over $50, a tidy sum in 1939.

Lyman's famous Alaskan appeared in 1937. Lyman had bought rights to Winchester's scope line in 1928, and to Stevens scopes a year later, modifying the Winchester A5 to build the Lyman 5A. The 3x Lyman 438 resembled an early Stevens model. Both these Lyman sights featured achromatic lenses by Bausch & Lomb. The $50 Alaskan resembled the Noske with its seven-eighths-inch tube. It had B&L glass and five inches of eye relief, with one-minute internal windage and elevation adjustments. Unlike many smaller scope firms, Lyman survived the war, which put Alaskan scopes in the hands of U.S. snipers. Wray Hegeman, the Alaskan's designer, followed up with the 4x Lyman Challenger in 1948, the 6x, 8x, and 10x Wolverines in 1953.

By the mid-1950s, surviving scope firms had grown by improving their products. The seven-eighths-inch steel tube was supplanted by one-inch alloy housings. More precise, more positive windage, and elevation adjustments followed. Reticles were strengthened and designed to stay in the optical center of the scope throughout the adjustment range. Contrary to Old World practice, American firms placed reticles in the second (rear) focal plane so they stayed one apparent size throughout the power range of a variable scope. Advocates of first-plane reticles, still popular in Europe, point out that these subtend a constant measure on the target, whatever the power, so you can more quickly use them as range-finding devices. Front-plane reticles also eliminate point-of-impact shift when you change power on variable scopes.

Better seals reduced fogging, but the problem persisted until, in the 1950s, nitrogen gas was injected into scopes that were then sealed at the factory. This gas prevented condensation from temperature changes within the scope. At the same time, scope rings were split to allow installation without removing turret or ocular housing. Disassembling a scope to mount it had been a common practice before the advent of sealed tubes.

The 4x emerged as the most popular scope among post-war deer hunters. It offered a 30-foot field of view at 100 yards, and plenty of magnification for long shots. The Weaver K4 sold for less than $50 in my youth. Perched on Savage 99s, Winchester 70s, and Remington 721s, it helped slay truckloads of deer.

Variable scopes appeared decades before fixed-power scopes became either fool-proof or popular.

A 1926 Zeiss catalog in my file carries the logo of Carl Zeiss, Jena. It lists 1x Zeileins and 2.5x Zeilklein scopes for $25 each, the 4x Zeilvier at $45, the 6x Zeilsechs for $52. An 8x Zeilacht cost $60. Variable 1-4x Zeilmulti and 1-6x Zeilmultar scopes retailed for $66. All of those scopes were very expensive, given the purchasing value of the dollar at the time. It would be some time before rifles were given high combs and fitted with reliable mounts. But visionaries like Bill Weaver and the folks at Bausch and Lomb knew there was a future in variables. The B&L Balvar arrived before the company adopted internal adjustments.

Not long ago I shot a Kentuchy whitetail with a borrowed rifle. It was a Thompson/Center G2 Contender, in .375 JDJ. Though I had time to boost the power, I killed the animal with the scope at 3x, its lowest setting. Later, I'd use a T/C scope on a Contender pistol in 6.8mm Remington to shoot another deer. Again, the dial stayed at the bottom end. Two years ago as this is written, I used a Leupold VX II 3-9x40 on a Mauser rifle in .358 Norma Magnum to shoot an elk. I had climbed hard to stay with a herd that was moving in and out of charred lodgepoles at dawn. Just shy of heavy timber, I flopped prone and snugged my sling. In a lemon haze, the bull appeared about 300 yards off. I let my breath half out and pressured the trigger. He swiveled to reach a clump of grass, and when the crosswire got rubbery-still high on his ribs, I finished my squeeze. The elk went down right away–not a step. The sound of impact floated back.

That was a hunt made to order for a 3-9x: sneaking through conifers, then setting up for the long poke. But I never turned the dial. With the scope still at 3x, the bullet hit a couple of inches from where I'd intended. Frankly, that was no surprise. A few weeks earlier, I had challenged a colleague to a one-shot match. The target: an ear-plug tacked above a bullseye target. Prone, with a 2 1/2x scope, I allowed that he might win from the bench with his 3-9x cranked to the top end. I couldn't see the plug, so had to use the bullseye as my reference. His first shot and mine both landed a little over half-an-inch from the plug. We fired again, and he must have nudged the rifle a bit, because the bullet struck an inch off. Mine hit closer.

For targets as big as deer and elk, 2½x or 3x magnification is no handicap. A broad, bright field and generous, non-critical eye relief help you find the animal quickly. Wobble is not unnervingly visible. Recovery from recoil is quick, should you need a second shot.

Turn up the power, and field shrinks. So does exit pupil, that bundle of light reaching your eye. At 3x, a 3-9x40 scope offers an exit pupil of 13mm, about twice as big as your eye can use. At 9x, that sight delivers a 4.5mm exit pupil, small

This Bushnell variable is properly mounted low and well forward on the Weatherby rifle, a lightweight six-lug Mark V in .25-06.

enough to limit apparent brightness at dawn or dusk or in deep shadow. With many variables, you'll also notice a shortening of eye relief as you boost magnification.

What you don't have to worry about these days is point-of-impact shift when changing power. I recently tested 27 variable scopes, shooting at low and high magnification, then recording movements in group centers. Fewer than half these scopes showed any perceptible shift–and only a couple moved the group a minute of angle. You can dismiss any lesser shift, because you can't keep all your shots anywhere near that close from hunting positions. It's a good day indeed when I can hold all my shots inside an inch from the bench.

Some hunters say that even if you can't hold the rifle still, 9x–or 10x or 12x or 16x–delivers greater precision. Not necessarily. I've shot many sub-minute groups from the bench with 3x scopes, and many dismally ragged groups with high magnification to help. In my view, magnification assists only when the apparent wobble is already inside an acceptable area of impact. When wobble is greater, high power only makes the inconsequential and uncontrollable movements of the reticle more distracting. In the iron sight stages of small-bore prone competition, scores can be as high as in the any-sight stages–during which shooters typically use 20x scopes. With iron sights, you cannot see the bullseye, only the largest of several black scoring rings around it. With a scope, you can quarter the bullseye. Properly designed and expertly used, iron sights and low-power scopes don't have to show you the impact point if the target is plain and you know where in the sight picture your bullet will strike.

Some hunters say that 9x is useful for judging antlers and finding twigs in the bullet's path. I used to say that was a job for binoculars. And it is. But when you've a small window of time or space for a shot and can ill afford to lose position to use your binocular, a high-power scope can be a boon. Last fall, after a long sneak on a bull elk in oakbrush, I bellied to an opposite bench and slinged up. There was little room to move in the thicket that provided my cover. The elk was alert, and in brush thick enough that at 5x I wasn't sure if I could get a bullet to the ribs. I turned the variable scope to 12x and found that, indeed, branches screened the vitals. I waited, ready to fire. Eventually the bull moved, and the 12x glass showed a football-size alley. Carefully I squeezed the trigger. At the report, the animal lunged forward, then crashed to earth.

It's clear that in that situation, I'd have been ill equipped with my beloved 4x scope.

Variables also make sense on multi-purpose rifles–say a .25-06 that's a deer gun in autumn but harasses coyotes in January and rockchucks in June. And there's probably no better power range than the 3-9x. Here's why.

You should never need lower magnification than 3x. With it you'll quickly find a deer as it dashes across your front at 50 yards, where field of view is 17 feet (three times the length of a deer). You'll shoot offhand easily at 3x, the crosswire almost as still as an iron sight as it shows you the consequential dips and hops but doesn't unnerve you with the jitterbugging of a reticle at 9x. In the dimmest light, even very small 3-9x objective glass (32mm, in a Burris Compact scope) gives you as big an exit pupil as your eye can use. You'll leave the scope at 3x when you're on the trail, for a wide field should you have to shoot fast. There's time to dial the power up for long, deliberate shots, but you won't have time to dial it down for a buck that jumps at close range.

You may not visit 9x often. About the highest power that gets any use on my big game variables is 6x. In fact, I zero at 6x, test loads at 6x, and practice shooting at 6x. But a coyote on yonder rim, or a 'chuck peering over a rock at 250 yards is easier to see at 9x, and easier to hit.

Because it includes the range of magnification you'll most likely use hunting big game, the 3-9x is among the most versatile variables. The 2-7x, 2 1/2-8x, and trim 3 1/2-10x models also make my short list of good deer scopes. The 3-9x stable is a big one, with scopes listing for as little as $40 to over $1200. The high

Care for your scope. This one bears the rifle's weight; its rear lens is subject to dust and scratches. And the rifle is hard to retreive on the dismount. Wayne prefers a horizontal scabbard, holding the rifle butt to the rear.

volume of 3-9s sold, and the stiff competition among makers for market share in this important arena, make almost any 3-9x a good deal. Pricing, especially near the low end, is very competitive. But to find the right scope, you should know what you're paying for: what's worth a premium and what's not. Here's what I look for:

Fully multi-coated optics. "Fully" means that every lens surface is coated to reduce light-robbing reflection and refraction; "multi" means that several films are applied, to target various wavelengths.

Crisp, repeatable quarter-minute click adjustments for windage and elevation, with knobs you can turn with your fingers, and turrets that are waterproof when caps are off.

An objective lens of modest size–36mm is my favorite–so I can mount the scope low and limit overall rifle weight. A 50mm lens on a 3-9x is useless, bulky, heavy, and costs extra.

Generous eye relief. I like four inches, but a three-and-a-half-inch gap is easier to find and is adequate for most shooters. I don't like scopes with eye relief that changes when you turn the power dial.

A one-inch alloy tube with a matte finish. Bigger (30mm) tubes offer little or no optical advantage, and they add weight. I make sure the "clear tube" is where rings will hold the scope for proper eye relief.

A plex reticle or a modified plex with range-compensating hash-marks per the Swarovski TDS and Burris Ballistic Plex. A heavy plex is worth considering if you hunt often in timber.

A European-style eyepiece on helical threads makes the reticle quick to focus, but you should have to focus it only once (the eyepiece is not for focusing the target). So an ocular housing on traditional fine threads is OK. A rubber ring at the rear protects stock-crawlers like me; but if you mount the scope with a thought to recoil, it shouldn't scar you. By the way, I do appreciate short eyepieces, easy to locate with the ocular lens above the rear guard screw. Lighted reticles don't appeal to me–though I've sometimes wished for lighted deer. Target knobs, like 30mm tubes, have a place in tactical and target shooting, but seldom in hunting. In my view, an adjustable objective isn't necessary on a 3-9x scope.

If you hunt big game with a bolt rifle, odds are you own a 3-9x, a scope that's as common in deer camps as cold coffee and old boots. If you do not own a 3-9x, it's about time you bought one. You might find it's the most versatile sight that you've ever given a squint. ■

12

SHOOTING DEER RIFLES

I t was a tiny patch of pines. At one corner it met the Kanitz sugarbush, an open maple hillside. I'd trudged up the fenceline and stopped just shy of the corner. Russet leaves skittered through the hardwoods. I shivered; Michigan's November wind had bite.

The snap of limbs, and then voices, told me the drivers were close. In minutes they were all but a pebble's toss away, boughs sloughing against canvas farm jackets. I relaxed. No deer in this pocket.

But then a snap and a thud and a whitetail buck popped from pines close enough for conversation. He sunfished and jetted straight-away. A .303 bullet caught him in the back of his neck and slammed him to earth. I couldn't remember lifting my rifle. Truly, sometimes muscle memory beats deliberate aim.

DEER GUNS THAT MAKE YOU LOOK GOOD

Rifles aren't like refrigerators. They don't run by themselves. They're not like televisions that you program with predictable options. Rifles must be carried and shouldered and aimed. How well they perform depends mainly on how well you handle them. In that respect, a deer rifle is a lot like a basketball. Skilled hands can

Any rifle that takes a buck like this is a good rifle. Marksmanship makes it so.

make any basketball do amazing things. But unlike basketballs, all rifles are not the same. Rifles differ in weight, length, balance, operation, and feel. Some are easier to use than others. You're wise to look for one that makes you look good.

A lot of deer hunters think an accurate rifle is the best choice. But a rifle doesn't have to be very accurate to kill deer. A two-inch group at 100 yards means all your bullets will strike well inside deer vitals out to 300 yards–farther than you're likely to shoot. The one-hole groups shooters like to flaunt are evidence of fine intrinsic accuracy, but they say nothing about field accuracy: how the rifle will perform in your hands from field positions.

The Model 94 Winchester became hugely popular with whitetail hunters largely because it pointed so well. In big hands or small, against thin faces and heavy jowls, whether your arms were long or short, a 94 had a wand-like quality. It shot where you looked, almost by itself. The Model 94 and equally lithe 336 Marlin and 99 Savage carbines still make sense for close-cover deer hunting. Now, however, most hunters carry more powerful, more accurate bolt-action rifles. The agenda: longer reach. Big scopes help potent, flat-shooting cartridges nip little groups at long range. At the bench, on targets, and over chronographs, such artillery is impressive. In the field, it often fails. That's because heady ballistic performance comes at the expense of fine handling qualities. Truth is, ordinary deer cartridges in rifles built for easy shooting will give you more success than a high-octane round in a rifle better suited for the bench. Here's what appeals to me in a deer rifle.

A slim profile. Pick up a broomstick and point it as if it were a rifle. Quick, huh? A broomstick is not shaped to help you aim, but it's easy to direct. That's partly because it's slender. Instead of filling your hands like some bulky rifle stocks, a broomstick is free to rotate and pivot in them. Why do you think best-quality English shotguns are so trim? Bulk in a rifle's buttstock puts weight where you must lift it, slowing your shot. Forends contoured for a rest are poorly shaped for your palm.

A long, open grip. A tight, steep grip makes for uncomfortable carry and slow handling. It also forces your trigger finger into a tight curl, preventing a smooth, straight-line pull. The Winchester 94 has a long, straight grip–like British grouse guns. A straight grip prevents the full hand contact that can wed you too tightly to the rifle. Handlebars on racing bicycles could be built thick and shaped to cuddle the fingers. They aren't. Pressure at points of contact is automatically greater, making the bike respond right away to changes in that pressure. A pistol grip can help you steady the rifle and control it during recoil; but you'll shoot better with one very slim up front, opening slightly rearward in a gentle curve that keeps the lower part of your hand well back from the guard.

Modest weight. Light weight gives you an easy carry but makes the rifle hard to "settle" when you aim. It bounces violently with your pulse, yields readily to gusts of wind. Rifles between six-and-a-half and seven pounds appeal to me. Loaded, with sling and scope, they'll scale around eight–light enough to pack all day but with heft enough to control when you're breathing hard. I favor a center of balance on the forward guard screw, or a slight tip to the muzzle.

A comb for the sight. A stock comb should put your eye instantly in line with the sights or on the scope's axis. Some modern combs are too high for iron sights–just as early bolt guns had combs too low for scope use. Cheek support holds your eye still. The weight of your head on the stock steadies the rifle. If you must lift your head off the stock to find the sight, or press hard to get your eye low enough, the comb is impairing your ability to shoot quickly and accurately.

A sight for fast aim. For deer hunting, I use mostly 3x and 4x, sometimes 6x scopes or variables of modest power. They're lightweight with objective lenses of 22 to 36mm. No need for big front glass or more power than 6x, even if you occasionally shoot beyond 300 yards. You'll want a wide, bright field; you won't want to see every blip that your pulse or muscle twitches impart to the rifle, or a sight so high or ponderous that it makes the rifle top-heavy. Where's the weight in a Model 94 or a carriage-class double shotgun? Low between your hands. Compact, lightweight scopes keep it there.

An adjustable trigger. You can't shoot well if you can't control the trigger. Alas, factory rifles these days commonly wear triggers designed by class-action attorneys and stiff enough to hoist a sack of dog food. Insist on a crisp, consistent pull no heavier than four pounds (make mine two). If you can't get that, install an aftermarket trigger by Timney. Don't fret about over-travel–movement of the trigger after let-off. Adjustments for sear engagement and trigger spring tension are what determine the trigger's feel before the shot. After adjusting your trigger, make sure it's safe by slamming the bolt hard a dozen times. If there's even one failure to cock, increase sear engagement or trigger spring tension or both.

A cartridge that won't beat me up. Sure, I appreciate fine accuracy and supercharged bullets that fly chalk-line flat; but they don't help me shoot deer. In fact, a cartridge that makes a lightweight rifle kick hard is on the deer's side. Flinching makes me miss. You too! A .270 that shoots softball-size groups will knock the stuffing out of any deer at any range you're justified shooting from field positions. Maybe you prefer a .243 or 6mm, a .25-06, 7-08 or .280. The .308 and .30-06 have earned their popularity. All are fine deer cartridges–if you load 'em up in a deer rifle you can shoot well.

ZERO

One bitter November long ago, a kid in a hooded sweatshirt took aim at a whitetail buck standing in a stubble field. Shivering in the cold dawn air and shaking from excitement, he couldn't hold the crosswires still, even when he leaned against the snow-capped fence post. "How far?" he wondered. A long shot; the deer looked very small in the Weaver K4. The kid just knew he'd have to hold high. His reticle bobbing above the buck's shoulder, the kid yanked the trigger. The rifle roared, and the buck kept eating. Two more shots drew no reaction from the deer, which, it seemed to the kid, might as well have been cropping wheat on the moon.

Down to his last cartridge, the youngster finally held right on the buck's ribs and forced himself to squeeze. The deer collapsed.

Zero from a padded rest on the forend. Fire three-shot groups, letting the barrel cool periodically.

The kid was elated but as embarrassed with his shooting as with his failure to mark where the buck had stood. He scoured the shin-high stubble for 20 minutes before he found the animal only 160 yards from where he'd shot. The fast spitzer bullet would have hit the buck with a dead-on hold out to 250 yards.

Since then "the kid"–me–has been cautious about holding over. I've found that with a 200-yard zero, there's hardly ever a need to hold high on an animal. If my quarry seems too far for a center hold, I work closer. I seldom shade higher than the backline. A backline hold will kill from 250 to 300 yards. Game farther than 300 looks impossibly small, and is almost always approachable.

The confidence to hold center comes from knowing your rifle is precisely zeroed to give you a long point-blank range. Among the deer hunters I've guided were many men whose rifles were improperly zeroed. Consequently, it became routine to ask: "Why don't we shoot that rifle–to make sure it's still zeroed?" This tactful opener generally prompted one of three responses:

A. "Good idea! It might have been bumped in transit. Besides, I could use a warm-up myself."

B. "Well–OK. Ammo's expensive, and I'm sure it's right on, but I suppose one or two rounds won't hurt."

C. "Naw. This rifle has shot down the middle since Poppa gave it to me in '61. I don't want to mess with it."

All these fellows would shoot, because I gave them no alternative. Usually, the man most reluctant to step to the bench turned in the worst performance. It became an easy call. Any hunter unwilling to test his rifle or himself almost assuredly has something to hide. He may also have a distorted view of shooting: that it is a reflection of his manhood, a measure of competence in a field where every man is supposed to be competent. Such pitiable souls hang their egos with the targets.

Truly, shooting is a skill that must be learned and honed. It cannot be inherited or bought. Hunters who prefer to talk up their prowess without putting holes in paper are, almost without exception, unskilled. A super rifleman can make a poor shot; an accurate rifle can print a loose group. But there are lessons in errant bullets. An accomplished shooter learns from them and loads up for one more string. Whether testing the rifle or yourself, zeroing is the first step. Zeroing connects the bullet path with your sightline at a certain distance. You determine that distance by manipulating the windage and elevation dials. Once you've zeroed, you know where the bullet will hit in relation to your sight.

Here's the procedure. First, check your scope bases to ensure that they are tightly affixed to the receiver. You may have to remove your scope. Taking the bases off lets you check for rust. To remove rust, scrub lightly with a brass brush and solvent. Finish with an oily cloth, then a dry one. You don't want oil between bases and receiver. Use a close-fitting screwdriver to tighten each base down, cinching screws alternately to evenly distribute pressure. Greasing the dovetail cuts on Redfield-style bases eases ring installation.

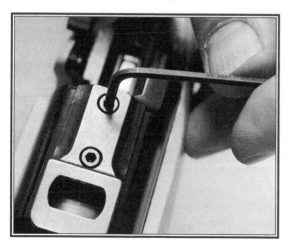

Rings should be spaced to support both ends of the scope well. This is especially important if your scope has a big objective bell or the long, heavy ocular housings of some variables. Extra weight and length on the ends add leverage to any force that might strain your scope tube and affect zero. Accidental bumps and long days in tight scabbards can make your rifle shoot where you're not looking. Most modern scopes tolerate lots

The first step in zeroing a rifle is checking the base screws. Loose mounts are a common problem.

of punishment, but an extension base or ring can be useful for long scopes. The leggy 6X Lymans on two of my rifles needed wide ring spacing, so I used extension bases to add support up front. Conversely, short-coupled variable scopes often require an extension base or ring reversed, so the power-dial clears.

Many hunters mount their scopes too far back, sometimes because the power-dial of a variable won't allow the scope farther forward. This is like placing a television on its side so it better fits between the sofa and rocker! The scope must be mounted so you can easily look through it to aim. If it is too far back (or too far forward), you must consciously move your head to get the full field of view. This not only takes time; it can force you into an awkward shooting stance, straining your muscles and shifting your center of gravity.

Whatever the scope, it should be mounted so you see a full field at first glance.

Even with no ring-spacing problem, it's easy to mount a scope too far back. That's because at home, where you have no target or sense of urgency, you check scope position by bringing the rifle to bear slowly. You're relaxed. You rotate the rifle to square up the reticle while adjusting head position fore and aft. In the field, you focus quickly on your target and lean into the rifle as you pull it home. You've no time for squaring up reticle or refining head position. You jam that butt into place and your eye toward the scope and hold the rifle firmly as you press the trigger. Often, the ocular housing clobbers your brow.

When placing a scope in its rings, mind the eye relief before you twist the scope to adjust the reticle. After checking for manufacturing burrs and filing them out of the rings, wipe them and the scope clean. Then snug the rings lightly around the scope and, using some distant object as your target, quickly cheek the rifle. Pull it hard into your shoulder. Repeat. You'll find you automatically shove your head forward on the stock. Slide the scope in the rings until you see a full field each time you mount the rifle. Now sit, kneel, and drop to prone. An ocular housing that's too close (or too far forward) will give you a reduced field. Prone will place your eye closer to the scope than will an offhand position. In the field, you may have to use both. Once you've established eye relief, pencil lines on the scope fore and aft of a ring, loosen the rings and, holding the rifle out in front of you, rotate the scope so the vertical crosswire is plumb with the buttpad.

Check those pencil lines for position, then tighten the rings.

Cinch ring screws alternately, as you would the lug nuts on an automobile wheel. You don't need goop on the threads to keep them from backing out, but neither should you leave oil on the tube. I wipe most scopes with a tack rag or oily cloth before installing the rings, but a thoroughly dry scope stays in place best.

Scope weight has a lot to do with the load on rings. Big objective lenses and 30mm tubes increase inertia, so when the rifle recoils it has a hard time getting the scope to come along. When rings lose their grip, you lose your zero. A gunsmith friend who has mounted many dozens of scopes met his match when he tried to affix a husky German variable to a four-fifty-something-caliber magnum bolt rifle. The scope kept slipping, even when he tightened the rings so they dented the steel tube and used tape to boost the gripping power! He finally punted, installing a smaller scope.

Once your scope is properly mounted, you'll want to bore-sight the rifle: align the axes of scope and bore without shooting. If you have no straight-line access to the breech, as with auto-loading or pump or lever rifles, you'll need a collimator. This device has a bore-diameter spud that fits in the muzzle, and a screen that appears in front of your scope. You aim at a grid on the screen, adjusting the sight so the crosswire quarters it.

If yours is a bolt rifle or dropping-block single shot, bore-sighting is easier. You remove the bolt or drop the lever, and set the rifle on sandbags so that looking through the bore you can center a target. Without moving the rifle, you adjust your

Adjust the windage dial for still conditions, the elevation dial so you hit point of aim at 200 yards.

reticle so it quarters the target. I bore-sight in my living room by placing the rifle on a soft but flat chair cushion and looking through the bore out the window at a rock on a distant hill.

Bore-sighting is not zeroing; it's simply a preliminary step, a quick way to align bore and scope so you don't waste ammunition trying to get "on paper" at 100 yards.

On the range, I use cardboard boxes as target boards. My targets are notebook-paper sized to give me the sight picture I prefer. Medium crosswires in a fixed 4X scope call for a six-inch-square target at 200 yards, but a fixed 6X scope offers the best picture with a four-inch square. It's important that the white squares be big enough to accommodate the movement of your reticle, small enough to help you discern differences in the size of each quarter. Heavy reticles require bigger targets; post and dot reticles work well with circular targets. For iron sights with a bead in front, big circular targets make sense. The light brown cardboard backer and white target both show bullet holes clearly. My 25X spotting scope picks up .243 holes at 200 yards easily, unless mirage is strong. If you use a black target, or a target with black printing, you'll be walking forward frequently to check for bullet holes you can't find.

Zeroing is a bench project. The object is to make your line of sight intercept the bullet path at a given distance. Tremors and other human interference won't do! Shooting for zero, you'll remove as much of your influence as possible. You have to aim, and you must trip the trigger without disturbing the rifle in its cradle of sandbags. That's all. The fundamentals for getting a dependable zero are the same as those for shooting a tight group: Pick a calm day; take your time; be sure the sandbags support the stock the same for each shot.

For deer rifles, it's a good idea to place targets at 100, 200, and 300 yards. The 100-yard target is to check bore-sighting. Adjust the scope so bullets strike roughly two inches above center, then go to the 200-yard line. At 200, shoot three rounds between sight changes, giving the barrel time to cool between rounds. Hot, sunny days are poor times to zero because the barrel heats fast and cools slowly. I allow at least 30 seconds between shots in a group.

When you've moved point of impact to center at 200 yards, let the rifle cool completely, clean it and fire another group. Mark the first shot from the cold, clean barrel because that's the most important shot you'll fire on a hunt. Keep the target to compare with other targets you'll use later to check your zero. If clean-barrel shots leak out of the group, you might want to try another load, or hunt with a fouled bore.

After you've zeroed, fire from different hunting positions to ensure the change won't affect point of impact.

Where you can shoot 300 yards, by all means do so! The more shooting you do at distance, the more precision you'll bring to your sight adjustments. Shooting only at 100 yards and estimating bullet drop beyond that range is bound to bring you to grief. Refine the zero far away, then check it at short range.

A few cartridges are best zeroed at 100 yards because most of the shooting they're designed for will be at that range, or because they lack sufficient energy to be effective much beyond 150 yards. The .30-30 is a woods cartridge. So is the .35 Remington, the .444 Marlin, the .45-70. Even rifles chambered for 200-yard cartridges can benefit from a shorter zero. The .250 and .300 Savage come to mind. Iron sights don't affect bullet performance; but they can reduce effective range by limiting precision.

The "rule of three" that used to appear in shooting articles from time to time alludes to the idea that if long-range rifle shoots three inches high at 100 yards it will hit about three inches low at 300. This is true only if you have a very flat-shooting rifle. A .30-06 needs a 100-yard lift of three inches to put its pointed 180-grain bullet on the money at 200. It drops three more inches in the next 50 yards or so, and crosses the 300-yard mark about nine inches low. The rule of three, strictly interpreted, applies mostly to 25- to 30-caliber magnums.

Some hunting rifles could well be zeroed for 250 yards. But beyond that you run into mid-range problems. A bullet's arc is parabolic; the highest point above sightline is not in the middle of that arc, but past the middle. For example, the .270

Sitting, with a tight Latigo sling, is the form that will give you lethal hits to 300 yards.

Weatherby zeroed at 300 yards with a 130-grain, pointed bullet will print 3.3 inches high at 100 yards, and 3.8 inches high at 200, where it is nearer its zenith. Four inches is, to my mind, too much lift to ignore–especially if it comes where you can expect a lot of shooting at deer. It is silly to zero for extreme range, where you'll seldom shoot, if by doing so you incur a midrange gap that forces you to adjust your aim.

Not long ago I was sneaking through second-growth Douglas fir. Suddenly, I spotted a whitetail buck 60 yards away. As he turned, I shouldered my Savage 99 and found his forward ribs in the 3X Leupold. The bullet was on its way almost before I realized my finger was applying trigger pressure. The deer ran hard for a short distance and collapsed, both lungs destroyed by the 150-grain Winchester Silvertip. A lot of game is shot like that: right now, right here, with a center hold. A 200-yard zero makes center holds deadly at short and middle ranges so you can forget about shading.

Another time, I found the dot in my 2.5X Lyman Alaskan bobbing around in a tight alley between me and a fine buck that was showing only its ear and eye. Because my zero kept the bullet close to my line of sight at this moderate distance, I was able to hold where I wanted to hit, threading the 165-grain .308 soft-point through the alley to the buck's brain.

Part of the reason many hunters like to zero long is that they overestimate yardage in the field. One fellow told me recently that his .30 magnum could outshoot any rifle between 800 and 900 yards, and that he'd toppled a grand buck at 700 steps by holding a tad over its withers. Now, I'm a country boy, but even a Congressman would have blushed spinning that yarn. The flattest-shooting

Open-country hunting can deliver more venison if you steady your rifle with a bipod.

cartridges around lob their bullets nearly three feet low at 500 yards when zeroed at 200. To keep a .270 Weatherby bullet (muzzle velocity 3,375 feet per second) from sagging more than a foot at 700 yards, you'd have to zero at over 600. That would put the bullet roughly two feet high at 300 and 400. The bullet would be plunging so rapidly at 700 that if you misjudged range by 50 yards, you'd miss the deer's vitals.

A 200-yard zero wrings the most from modern rifle cartridges at the ranges most big game is shot. It lets you aim in the middle for 230 yards or more of your bullet's flight. It complements the 4X scope or low-power variable that's most useful for deer and elk hunting in mixed cover. It enables you to shoot as far as is practical, but also reminds you that to get close is to boost your odds for an accurate shot and a quick kill.

GET REAL ABOUT SHOOTING

Accuracy is a measure of consistency. Anyone can hit a bullseye once; hitting it five times in a row shows consistency that breeds confidence.

But confidence in what? If you shot the rifle from a bench, your job was not to disturb the rifle as you pulled the trigger. You had a bit part. If, on the other hand, you had to support the rifle and hold it still and time the shot, you were the main character.

It's easy to shoot tight groups from the bench. That's why most hunters use it so much, and why most shoot poorly from sitting, kneeling and offhand–positions you'll use in the field. It's always a good idea to rest your rifle, but if a stump isn't handy, you'll wish you'd practiced with that rifle in your hands.

On the hunt, you make the shot. After 35 years of hunting, I can't remember a

rifle that missed. A rifle that shoots into three inches at 100 yards will keep bullets in a deer's chest to 300 and beyond. Chasing minute-of-angle groups is senseless, because from hunting positions you're quite capable of missing targets the size of a small refrigerator. I have.

Once, at a sight-in day on a shooting range, I asked hunters who'd just zeroed their rifles to take one offhand shot at a six-inch circle at 100 yards. Only five hits showed up. The backing

In the woods, steady shooting positions are easy to assume if you've practiced them.

Offhand, keep your left elbow well under the rifle, your right arm horizontal, your head erect.

paper, 22 inches square, had 30 holes. More than a dozen riflemen missed the backer.

As you prepare for hunting season, check your rifle's zero by firing two three-shot groups. Clean the barrel and let it cool between strings. If both groups are centered at 200 yards (figure two-and-a-half inches high at 100) and in each case the first shot is close to the other two, get off the bench.

Use paper targets because they show exactly where bullets strike. Distance isn't important–your goal is to master the fundamentals of marksmanship: position, aiming, trigger control. Before you load up, find the rifle's natural point of aim, and adjust your feet to bring that point of aim onto the target. Don't pivot at the waist or force the rifle over with your arms. You can't hold the rifle still, so your object is to hold the rifle where its constant movement is centered on what you want to hit.

A sling helps you steady the rifle with a shooting loop that adjusts independently of sling length. Give the loop a half-turn out, slip your left arm through it, then run the loop above your triceps, snugging it with a keeper. Flip your hand over the sling so it rests flat against your wrist as you grip the forend. Taut up front, the sling pulls the rifle into your right shoulder as it transfers the weight to your left shoulder. The sling is loose from your arm to the rear swivel.

A strap is not a sling. Without a shooting loop, the strap is pulled tight its entire length, tugging at the rear swivel, twisting the stock and pulling it away from your shoulder. A strap can be used as a "hasty sling" offhand, as you have no anchor for your left elbow and thus cannot keep a loop taut.

In all positions, use bone structure to support the rifle. Muscles tire quickly, then twitch. Sitting and kneeling, keep the flat of your elbow against the flat of your knee. Offhand, your right elbow should be horizontal for a straight pull back on the grip and to open a pocket in your shoulder for the butt. Keep the left elbow well underneath the rifle. Place the butt high enough for a straight-ahead aim.

I typically take a couple of deep breaths before a shot, then let the third leak slowly as I pressure the trigger. My lungs are empty but not collapsed when the shot comes. Trigger control is merely a matter of applying pressure when the sight is on target, and holding it when the sight wanders off. That's easy to explain, hard to do. Resist the urge to squeeze quickly as the sight dives toward the target. Follow through by holding your rifle for a second during recoil, and practice for follow-up shots by cycling the action fast.

I like to fire three-shot groups, one in each of the four positions. Then I rest. Regular practice in small doses helps

Check your zero at camp. It will give you confidence in the rifle. Result: better marksmanship.

you more than a long day at the range every two weeks. Keep your targets; assess your progress. As groups shrink, try to eliminate flyers. Dry firing from field positions at home is a big assist.

You may shoot a deer from a rest this fall. But to count on it is to fantasize. Get real. Now.

SHOOTING STANDING

"Stand up and shoot like a man." Bad advice. You'll shoot much better sitting or kneeling because your center of gravity is lower and you have more ground contact. But if you must shoot quickly or over brush, standing may be your only option. Here's how to practice a position you'll try never to use—but one that could someday put venison on the table:

1 Before you lift the rifle, point your feet properly. Place them shoulder-width apart, with your weight evenly distributed. For starters, a line through your toes should cross your rifle's shadow at roughly a 30-degree angle. That will get you close to a comfortable position; but if the sights are off target, adjust your body by first moving your feet. Find your natural point of aim: the direction in which the rifle naturally points. Do not force the rifle onto the target with your arms!

2 Grasp the grip firmly and pull the rifle's butt into your shoulder. Keep your left elbow nearly under the rifle and your right elbow almost horizontal. Your right shoulder will form a nice pocket for the buttpad. Raise the stock comb to your face; drop your face as little as possible for a firm contact with the comb. Touch the trigger with the first joint of your index finger.

3 Keep your head erect so you can look straight through the sight. Squint if you must. Scopes should be mounted so the rear (ocular) lens extends to the rear guard screw. If you must mount the scope so the lens housing extends more than an inch over the grip, the stock is probably too long for you. Your eye should be about three inches from the ocular lens when your face is as far forward as comfort allows.

4 Take two deep breaths–one as you shoulder the rifle, the other as you let it settle on the target. Relax as you release the second breath; do not forcibly empty your lungs. Now the sight should be on the target, and your trigger finger should be taking up slack.

5 Apply pressure to the trigger when the sight is on target; hold pressure when the sight moves off target. The rifle should fire when the sight is where you want it. When you run out of air or if the rifle starts to shake badly, do not jerk the trigger. Start over. Resist the urge to "time" the shot, yanking the trigger as the sight bounces onto the target. Most often, you will miss.

6 Follow through, maintaining position as the rifle recoils. Call your shot–that is, tell yourself where the bullet hit before you look in the spotting scope or retrieve your target. An accurate call means you had your eyes on the target and knew where the sight was when the bullet left. That is very important! Calling your shots is the first step in correcting problems with position, breathing, and trigger control.

7 Practice offhand more than any other position. Dry firing (empty) enables you to practice more often and without recoil. Get good before you try to get fast. Hurrying a shot teaches bad habits. When a big buck forces you to hurry, you'll be faster and more accurate if you've practiced proper form.

When practicing, cycle your bolt as if you needed a quick second shot. You may, someday.

TUMBLING DEER LIKE GROUSE

Shooting deer quickly is more like shotgunning than sniping. To roll a buck rocketing through the alders, you can't deliberate. But neither is snap-shooting mindless response. It's the practiced coordination of eyes, mind, and hand–right away. You don't need extraordinary reflexes. You do need discipline. Snap-shooting melds position, breathing, and trigger control. Master these fundamentals first. Speed comes later.

Metallic silhouette matches hone your off-hand skills and help you learn to shoot under pressure.

A running deer is like a Sporting Clays target. You have an eye-blink of time to map out a shot path and position your feet as you bring the stock firmly to your cheek, keeping your eye on the target. Already you've shifted your weight to power the swing from your thighs up through your torso. Your arms hold the gun and complete minor corrections to the sight picture, but every shot begins at ground level, where your feet anticipate target direction. Swing "in front of your feet" and you'll miss. Footwork is no more important in boxing or golf.

When a buck breaks for cover, don't delay! On the other hand, your best shot may come a split second after you're ready to press the trigger. Assessing the shot as you mount the rifle is a crucial first step to a hit. Fire as the buck changes direction or ducks a blow-down and you'll have squandered what may be your only chance. Convince yourself that a shot begins as soon as you see the target. Your decisions from that point do affect where the bullet will strike, and when, and whether the deer will be there for it or not.

Calculating lead takes time and often will put your bullet too far forward. For most shots in cover, move the rifle quickly onto the target from behind, and you'll score with no lead at all.

A bullet gets there right away. Deer must throttle back in thickets, and seldom will they cross at 90 degrees to your shot. So forget the arithmetic. Just swing and shoot. Imagine a grapefruit-size bullseye over the buck's vitals. Up close, hold at the front edge of that grapefruit as you swing. If you're swinging from behind, you probably have more than enough built-in lead. Beyond 50 yards, depending on target angle and speed, hold a grapefruit or two in front of the target grapefruit.

Deer look faster than they are, and it's easy to get snookered into aiming too far forward. Remember also that a bullet is not like a charge of birdshot that forgives excessive lead by killing with the tail of a long pellet string. Your bullet must hit with its nose!

Charlie Sisk built the .338/08. Wayne used a 180-grain Nosler Ballistic Tip to down this Missouri buck.

As a youth, I read far too often about shotgunners firing at the first duck and hitting the last, about deer hunters splintering oak limbs a garage-length behind departing bucks. It happens still, because hunters still stop their swing. But if you shoot with a moving rifle and as soon as the sight covers the forward rib, you will kill deer. You'll get them where big whitetails give other hunters a glimpse too brief. And you'll see bucks tumble like grouse. ■